MICHAEL OAKESHOTT AND THE CONVERSATION OF MODERN POLITICAL THOUGHT

MICHAEL OAKESHOTT AND THE CONVERSATION OF MODERN POLITICAL THOUGHT

LUKE PHILIP PLOTICA

State University of New York Press

Published by
STATE UNIVERSITY OF NEW YORK PRESS, ALBANY

Printed in the United States of America

For information, contact
State University of New York Press, Albany, NY
www.sunypress.edu

Production, Laurie D. Searl
Marketing, Anne M. Valentine

Library of Congress Cataloging-in-Publication Data

Plotica, Luke Philip, 1980–
Michael Oakeshott and the conversation of modern political thought / Luke Philip Plotica.
pages cm
Includes bibliographical references and index.
ISBN 978-1-4384-5535-8 (hardcover : alk. paper)
ISBN 978-1-4384-5534-1 (pbk. : alk. paper)
ISBN 978-1-4384-5536-5 (ebook)
1. Oakeshott, Michael, 1901–1990. 2. Political science—Philosophy. I. Title.

JC257.O244P56 2015
320.092—dc23 2014013993

10 9 8 7 6 5 4 3 2 1

CONTENTS

ACKNOWLEDGMENTS vii

INTRODUCTION
Situating Oakeshott 1

CHAPTER ONE
Language, Practice, and Individual Agency 15

CHAPTER TWO
Individuality between Tradition and Contingency 39

CHAPTER THREE
Imagining the Modern State 67

CHAPTER FOUR
Toward a Conversational Democratic Ethos 111

CONCLUSION
Hearing Voices 143

NOTES 147

BIBLIOGRAPHY 181

INDEX 191

ACKNOWLEDGMENTS

I am quite satisfied to recognize that this book—which adopts conversation as a guiding conceptual frame—was shaped through the conduct of many conversations, over many years. Much of my thinking about Michael Oakeshott developed out of my graduate studies and dissertation at The Johns Hopkins University. I should like especially to thank Dick Flathman, who was a tirelessly generous and helpful interlocutor. For everything from encouragement to argument, I also owe thanks to Jeremy Arnold, Shlomit Barnea, Jane Bennett, Mark Blyth, Sam Chambers, Bill Connolly, Jennifer Culbert, Tom Donahue, Paulina Ochoa Espejo, Jake Greear, Joel Grossman, Jairus Grove, Ryan Holston, Dick Katz, Daniel Levine, Jennifer Lin, Terukazu Morikawa, George Oppel, Nobutaka Otobe, Mary Otterbein, J. G. A. Pocock, Mina Suk, Lisa Williams, and Mabel Wong.

Still earlier, my path was shaped by Jeffrey Brand-Ballard, Martha Finnemore, Melissa Schwartzberg, and Bill Winstead. I owe a special thanks and debt of gratitude to Scott Hammond and Howard Lubert, whose political theory courses were decisive influences in my choice of career.

Much of this manuscript was drafted during my time at Virginia Tech, where I have benefited from many excellent colleagues. In particular, I thank François Debrix, Priya Dixit, Jim Klagge, Bettina Koch, Chad Lavin, Tim Luke, Wayne Moore, Scott Nelson, Joe Pitt, Max Stephenson, and Edward Weisband. Portions of this manuscript previously presented and published elsewhere have benefited from the thoughtful comments of Mary G. Dietz, Jonathan Havercroft, Andrew Norris, Cyrus Ernesto Zirakzadeh, and Catherine Zuckert. For his editorial guidance, I also thank Michael Rinella at SUNY Press.

I owe inexpressible debts of gratitude to my family for a lifetime of support and encouragement, especially to my parents who saw the beginning of this work but departed too soon to see its completion. Above all, I thank my wife Stefanie for her love, patience, and inspiration.

An early version of chapter 1 appeared as "'This is simply what I do': Wittgenstein and Oakeshott on the Practices of Individual Agency," *The*

Review of Politics 75, no. 1 (Winter 2013): 45–68; an early version of chapter 4 appeared as "Deliberation or Conversation: Michael Oakeshott on the Ethos and Conduct of Democracy," *Polity* 44, no. 2 (April 2012): 286–307.

INTRODUCTION

Situating Oakeshott

> The way a man manages his own curiosity is always interesting; he is apt to disclose more of himself in the questions he thinks it profitable to ask than in any answers he may happen to provide.
>
> —Michael Oakeshott, *The Vocabulary of a Modern European State*

> Tell me *how* you are searching, and I will tell you *what* you are searching for.
>
> —Ludwig Wittgenstein, *Philosophical Remarks*

Michael Oakeshott (1901–1990) was one of the distinctive intellectual voices of the twentieth century, and his work has left its imprint upon fields ranging from philosophy and political theory to history and education. Oakeshott's influence is due in part to his style of thought, his characteristic way of bringing penetrating yet self-consciously chastening philosophical insight to the remarkably varied themes to which he spoke. The growing interest in his thought is readily evidenced by the wealth of scholarship devoted to Oakeshott in the two decades since his death.[1] Many of the scholarly commentaries fall into two predominant groups. One major strain of scholarship is synoptic in character, devoted to sketching encompassing views of the systematic elements of Oakeshott's thought.[2] Another strain is more narrowly topical, focusing upon specific themes or issues in and around Oakeshott's work.[3] Yet these synoptic and topical strains tend to have several methods or tropes in common. Both approaches often emphasize and chart the continuity (or discontinuity) of Oakeshott's thought, offering a variety of theses about his overall character, development, and significance as a thinker. Synoptic and topical works also tend to classify Oakeshott as a figure of a recognizable philosophical or political brand, whether such classification is incidental to other claims or is a fundamental thesis in itself. We are thus presented with a range of works that explicitly or implicitly draw lines through or around Oakeshott's thought, so as to render it internally coherent and/or unambiguously distinct in its location on the philosophical and political map. While such scholarship has yielded genuine insight into Oakeshott's thought, it has also tended toward the repetition and modification of a rather narrow range of themes, and has thus left much of the richness, scope, and implications of Oakeshott's work unexhausted.[4] Even with the benefit of many volumes devoted to his ideas, there remains meaningful work to be done.

Of the unexplored or underexplored terrain there is much that transcends esoteric themes of interest primarily to Oakeshott scholars. His work speaks profoundly to enduring and contentious philosophical and political debates, often in ways that have yet to be adequately appreciated or investigated. It is to several of these gaps that I hope to speak. My overarching aim in this book is to identify and trace several threads in Oakeshott's work that connect it to philosophical and political debates prominent in the twentieth and twenty-first centuries. The distinctiveness of my approach and results stems not from any radically novel reading of Oakeshott on my part. I do not lay claim to discovery of some hitherto hidden intentions behind his work, I neither fashion nor rely upon a complex conceptual or hermeneutic apparatus, and I would not discount or challenge much of the existing scholarship on Oakeshott. My approach is instead to take seriously and employ one of Oakeshott's own concepts—that of *conversation*—in order to draw his ideas into a series of encounters with major theories and thinkers with whom his work enjoys underappreciated affinities. The result, I believe, is a more perspicuous view of the richness of Oakeshott's thought with regard to several philosophical and political themes that are profoundly interconnected in his work, including individual understanding and agency, individuality and intersubjective practice, the character of the state, and democratic theory. With respect to these themes, I hope to demonstrate and explore the distinctiveness and value of Oakeshott's work—its resistance to capture by reductive philosophical and political categories, the breadth of intellectual traditions, styles, and programs with which it is conversant, and thus its continued relevance to contemporary philosophy and political theory.

CONVERSATION AMIDST PLURALITY, CONVERSATION ACROSS BOUNDARIES

A significant part of Oakeshott's intellectual legacy is conceptual and terminological. Although not given to neologisms, he crafts and employs a number of distinctive concepts (such as modes of experience, enterprise and civil association, contingency, and practice), which he uses with precision and that play substantial roles in his thinking. His texts thus have a distinctive intellectual cadence, due in no small part to the inflections imparted by these terms. One of the most fundamental and fruitful terms in Oakeshott's lexicon is conversation, and I believe that much of his work is best understood as manifesting his understanding of the concept. Indeed, even where the term is not explicitly invoked, it is often implicitly exemplified.

Oakeshott on Conversation

Oakeshott frequently turned to conversation as the conceptual image most appropriate to the understanding of human conduct, thought, and history. Although his extended treatments of conversation are relatively few,[5] the ideas and sensibilities they collect appear again and again throughout his more than six decades of writings. The concept of conversation collects and underscores what Oakeshott consistently viewed as most important and interesting in the world of human affairs: the plurality of agents, of their contingent circumstances, of their understandings and self-understandings, of the traditions and practices they have fashioned for themselves, and of the modes of thought and action in which they struggle to makes sense of and find satisfaction in the world they inhabit.[6] The image of conversation comprehends what Oakeshott believes is the ineluctable character of human thought and conduct, collected processes of intelligent self-development with no ideal end point and only temporary, conditional places of repose.[7]

Plurality manifests in the conduct of conversation, as well as in the conditions that make it possible. Conversation is a fundamentally intersubjective, communicative engagement that "is impossible in the absence of a diversity of voices: in it different universes of discourse meet, acknowledge each other and enjoy an oblique relationship which neither requires nor forecasts their being assimilated to one another."[8] These "voices" signify both individual speakers addressing themselves to one another (which is the image ordinarily conjured by the term) and idioms or languages of human thought and understanding being employed by such speakers. In his turn to conversation Oakeshott explicitly eschews conceptual pictures that present the human conduct reductively as the quest for a single language of understanding, or the manifestation of a fixed list of archetypal personalities, or the recurrence of the same events again and again under nominally different circumstances and descriptions. Viewed through the conceptual lens of conversation, the human world appears as a manifold profusion of persons, ideas, identities, events, and the associations they form circumstantially meeting and addressing one another in a plurality of languages of self-disclosure and self-enactment, some common, some strange, yet none final or exclusive.[9] Thus imagined, humanity is active, diverse, and Protean; individuals are ever making sense of and re-creating themselves and their world through countless unrehearsed adventures of thinking and doing, whose trajectories variously intersect one another, and whose contingent outcomes prompt ever new conversations.[10] Accordingly, conversation signifies not only a particular kind of discursive engagement, but also how understanding, agency, and plurality manifest at diverse levels of analysis. In speaking of the "conversation of mankind," Oakeshott identifies phenomena of human intelligence at both micro- and macrolevels, rendering a particular image of human conduct and history that places plurality and contingency front and center.

Embracing this conception of conversation entails taking a position on how human conduct is best (though certainly not exclusively) understood. Indeed, Oakeshott's turn to conversation should be viewed in the context of his critique of "rationalism," which he understood as the distinctly modern drive to place human thought and practice under the "sovereignty of technique."[11] A core feature of modern rationalism—not only in philosophy and the sciences, but in politics and ethics as well—has been to reduce the plurality of utterances and actions to the terms of a meta-idiom. Whether this takes the form of a historicist reduction of politics to the operation of the universal laws of history, a scientific account of thought in terms of quantifiable physical phenomena, or a philosophical account of knowledge in terms of a method of mechanical inquiry, Oakeshott believed that rationalism has long and relentlessly sought a "a key to open all doors, a 'master science'" which could "impose a single character upon significant human utterance."[12]

Against modern rationalism, Oakeshott presents conversation as

> the appropriate image of human intercourse—appropriate because it recognizes the qualities, the diversities, and the proper relationships of human utterances. As civilized human beings, we are the inheritors, neither of an inquiry about ourselves and the world, nor of an accumulating body of information, but of a conversation.[13]

That is, conversation provides the most apt image of humanity as a plurality of agents, variously the inheritors of the collected, intelligent achievements of those who came before. It best reflects the experiences of persons struggling to make sense of the world and find felicity within it. As initiates into this ongoing conversation, individuals learn and use a multiplicity of "arts of agency," each of which is "an instrument to be played upon, not a tune to be played."[14] Accordingly, conversation neither admits nor requires a "symposiarch or arbiter," a sovereign technique or meta-idiom to direct the contributions of individual participants.[15] Both within and across the boundaries of discrete disciplines or fields, different languages of thought and agency are each allowed their say. Within philosophy, for example, theories and thinkers can be understood as engaging in ongoing discourse, as realists and skeptics, materialists and idealists, epistemologists and ethicists contribute in their distinctive idioms to the play of voices and utterances. Across disciplinary boundaries, philosophical claims enter the greater flow and exchange among other voices—historical, scientific, artistic, political, economic—just as these enter into the realms of philosophy. Recognizing the inevitability and value of such intermingling, Oakeshott defended the freedom and authority of each voice to speak in its own way to its various concerns, insisting only that, as both a practical and a conceptual matter, no voice has a claim to silence or supplant the others.[16] There is, then, a rough and perhaps demanding etiquette required: "the participants are not engaged in an inquiry or a debate . . . a conversation may have passages of argument, and a speaker is not forbidden to be demonstrative; but reasoning is neither sovereign nor alone, and the conversation itself does not compose an argument."[17] Ultimate ideals (e.g., of truth or of justice) may reside in the distance, informing the conversation and urging its course in their respective directions, but they do not dictate its conduct or outcome.[18]

This image of conversation serves as an intellectual *ethos* in Oakeshott's work. Rather than collapsing the plurality of human conduct into a single idiom of understanding (e.g., science, or philosophy), he strives to preserve the phenomena of actual experience.[19] Conversation appears again and again in Oakeshott's work, wherever he counsels against reductionist, rationalist, and dogmatic simplifications of utterance and action. Throughout his long career (from *Experience and Its Modes* to *On Human Conduct* and later essays) and concerning topics ranging from education, to politics, to philosophy, Oakeshott maintained this care and respect for plurality. Thus, the concept of conversation provides a uniquely appropriate frame through which to study his contributions to modern thought.

Oakeshott in Conversation

Although the *ethos* of conversation manifests repeatedly throughout his work, Oakeshott also made strong claims and drew bright lines of exclusion and inclusion, propriety and coherence in matters of thought and conduct. Despite his commitment to the concept of conversation, Oakeshott's treatment of individual voices and concepts is often rigorously or even rigidly schematic. Neither should Oakeshott's abiding attentiveness to seemingly antinomian plurality suggest that his commonest intellectual disposition was blithely or uncritically welcoming of all novelty and unconventionality. It is with good reason that Oakeshott is remembered as a theorist of authority and tradition, in politics and beyond. Even amid plurality, he saw the value of stability and regularity. Nonetheless, I suggest that, suitably qualified and taken as a recurring conceptual picture, conversation provides a key for understanding Oakeshott's work in its own terms, as well as its salience in relation to larger debates and issues in philosophy and politics. Although Oakeshott did not characterize his works as contributions to diverse conversations, it is a small, natural, and largely neglected step to adopt this interpretive standpoint on his work.[20] In doing so, I merely seek to read the coherence and import of his thought by way of a concept to which he repeatedly appealed.

Much like Oakeshott, I turn to the concept of conversation to supply a perspective and minimal framework within which to draw idioms of thought (e.g., philosophical, historical, scientific) and idioms of human conduct (e.g., political, artistic, economic) into mutual engagements, while at the same time recognizing their distinctiveness and irreducibility to one another. However, in the chapters that follow I aim to go a step farther and stage a series of conversations in which central elements of Oakeshott's thought are explored and elaborated in relation to the ideas of other twentieth-century thinkers with whom he shares significant intellectual affinities while maintaining a distinctive (and often critical) voice of his own. My intention is not to establish Oakeshott as a thinker of a certain cleanly delineated category, but to listen for what rises to prominence in his thought when his ideas are placed into exchanges with other important thinkers. Much like the way new ideas tend to emerge when we think and talk beyond our habits, new readings and perspectives on a thinker might emerge when he or she is read in connection with uncommon company. Similarly, I do not aim to deploy Oakeshott's thought to refute other thinkers. This is not to say that I make no arguments and arrive at no conclusions, or that my treatment of Oakeshott is purely dispassionate. Nor do I refrain from argumentative criticism of Oakeshott's own ideas. Rather, in what I hope is an expression of a conversational *ethos*, this book as a whole does not itself compose an argument. I have hoped to write a book that opens new avenues of thinking about Oakeshott, not merely tentatively, only to close them again after proving a point, but as an aid and invitation to understanding his contributions to modern political thought. Nonetheless, I also believe that my approach might illuminate, if not contribute to resolving, tensions and questions surrounding Oakeshott's thought and scholarship devoted to its study.

First, as Bhikhu Parekh has stated, "Since [Oakeshott] did not belong to a single philosophical tradition, he has proved extremely difficult to classify and been subject to much misunderstanding."[21] One might further suggest that much of the misunderstanding regarding Oakeshott has resulted from the persistent tendency in the secondary literature to classify him as a thinker of one or another neat description.[22] Although Oakeshott's own penchant for strong claims and conceptual clarity and rigor has facilitated the frenzy of political and philosophical classifications ascribed to him, a glance at extant scholarship shows a perplexing and often contradictory variety. One finds Oakeshott labeled a liberal, a conservative, a libertarian, an authoritarian, a deliberative democrat, a bourgeois capitalist, a political thinker, an antipolitical thinker, an individualist, a traditionalist, an absolute idealist, a historicist, a foundationalist, an antifoundationalist, a skeptic, and a pluralist. While not all of these descriptions can be true or meaningful at once, there is likely something informative in each, and thus something to be said for the works that have arrived at such classifications. Examining Oakeshott's work with an eye toward eliciting, say, the democratic or conservative dimensions of his thought focuses our attention upon aspects of his thought both within and across individual texts that might otherwise elude us. Such classification has thus undoubtedly rendered intellectual service to students of Oakeshott, yet the practice carries costs. While all textual interpretations bear some imprint of the interpreter, narrow, univocal classifications often craft the very character they purport to discover, muting inconsistent details and thus distorting the materials with which they work. Furthermore, the desire to classify Oakeshott runs notably against the articulation he gave to his thought. Not only does the concept and, more importantly, the *ethos* of conversation that is so central to his work challenge the project of conclusive classification, Oakeshott self-consciously avoided the embrace of simple labels. He claimed to have learned from Hegel and Bradley, but generally avoided proclaiming himself an idealist; he praised Burke and a conservative disposition in politics, but declined invitations to champion postwar British conservatism; he professed a profound admiration for Montaigne and Hume, manifesting and praising a mentality indebted to them, but he did not self-ascribe the title of skeptic. Much as he favored open-ended conversation over closure and monologue, he embraced plurality of disposition and thought rather than exclusive labels and partisan commitments, philosophical or political. Reading Oakeshott as both an advocate of and participant in philosophical and political conversation thus might avoid some prevalent distortions of his ideas without supposing that the solution is to be found in some label (or combination of labels) not yet applied.[23]

Second, reading Oakeshott through his own lens of conversation might help to resolve or make better sense of some of the apparent tensions or inconsistencies in his work (such as between his embrace of plurality and his occasional appeals to unity in thought and experience, or between his valorizations of both tradition and individuality). Grappling with such tensions, numerous interpreters and commentators have advanced theses regarding the developmental trajectory of Oakeshott's work: from early to late, from conservative to liberal, from apolitical to political, from idealist to skeptical, from Hegelian to Hobbesian.[24] Such have been attempts to identify shifts of tone, terminology, and emphasis in Oakeshott's *corpus* and to resolve apparent inconsistencies or contradictions in terms of a supervening intellectual narrative. There is no doubt that elements of Oakeshott's thought visibly changed (e.g., from the language of "modes of experience" in *Experience and Its Modes* [1933] to that of "platforms of conditional understanding" in *On Human Conduct* [1975]), and may contain inconsistencies that must be resolved if one is to construct a comprehensive view. However, much like imposing rigid classifications, tracing unifying trajectories through Oakeshott's work risks generating conceptual and hermeneutical problems and solutions that are artifacts of the interpretive tools employed, and thus accomplishes only a fragile unity that sacrifices or obscures some of Oakeshott's salient insights. Much as the lens of conversation might help us see beyond the appeal and limited utility of rigid categories, it might also free us as readers from the sense that in order for Oakeshott to be saying anything interesting he must really be saying the same thing over and over, only in different terms, or that he moved cleanly and deliberately from one system of commitments to another. As Parekh suggests, Oakeshott was a captive of no single intellectual tradition. It should therefore be unsurprising that his thought about a world of plurality should itself resist reduction to a singular route of intellectual interest or development.

Third, reading Oakeshott through the lens of conversation might better illustrate the resonances between his thought and a multitude of contemporary debates, including some to which he speaks only indirectly. If rigid classifications of Oakeshott as a thinker and restrictive narratives about his intellectual interest and development tend to yield truncated or myopic images of his thought, then such approaches likely also leave us with inadequate understandings of his relevance to ongoing philosophical and political issues. If we take Oakeshott for a political partisan of whatever description, or read his work as a consistent reworking of or retreat from some monolithic philosophical commitment, then his contemporary salience will be typecast, rendered in advance a better or worse representative of some position we already know and over which we have already decided. We may, as it were, miss the trees out of a desire to behold a tidy forest. Yet if we take Oakeshott as a rigorous yet eclectic thinker, engaged in a variety of conversations that bear recognizable affinities and trace common themes but adhere to no single conceptual scheme, then we may find that he speaks to us in ways not previously appreciated. Thus, my purpose is to add to the existing scholarship, rather than to replace or undermine it. Utilizing the conceptual tools afforded by conversation, I offer another way of approaching Oakeshott which has both near- and far-reaching implications. I hope to contribute another voice to the ongoing discussion of Oakeshott's thought, emphasizing and elaborating upon themes in his work that have yet to enjoy the hearing they merit.

Finally, I wish to clarify the relation of my present approach to a somewhat kindred piece of scholarship. As I have suggested, not only is conversation a fundamental concept in Oakeshott's thought, but it can indeed serve as a guiding conceptual picture that helps to situate his thought in a large and varied context of philosophy and political theory. This conversational approach has been approximated in Wendell John Coats's *Oakeshott and His Contemporaries*, which undertakes a survey of Oakeshott's intellectual engagement with and debts to several preeminent thinkers in the Western philosophical tradition.[25] Coats elicits and explores routes of affinity between Oakeshott and some of the thinkers with whom the latter converses, from the ongoing, explicit engagements with the thought of Hegel, Hobbes, Hume, and Montaigne, to the less overt or obvious engagements with Augustine, Constant, and Rousseau. The resulting study identifies in Oakeshott's thought more or less self-conscious traces of his aforementioned "contemporaries," and implicitly situates him within a series of conversations spanning many centuries, and which are far from ended. My own approach resembles Coats's insofar as I also identify routes of affinity between Oakeshott and other significant thinkers, and thus I show them all to be participants in notional conversations regarding philosophical and political topics. However, my approach differs from that of Coats in a few significant ways. First, the thinkers with whom I show Oakeshott to be conversant are not those selected by Coats. Rather than looking to past thinkers in whom Oakeshott's own ideas may have taken root, I look to several of his contemporaries in the more ordinary, historical, and temporal sense. Thus, I show Oakeshott to be engaged in conversations about a world shared and inhabited here and now. Second, while Coats looks to thinkers whom Oakeshott more or less expressly identifies and discusses in his work, I hazard to identify and explore affinities that are generally implicit, unwitting, or unacknowledged. Rather than present Oakeshott as conversing with his acknowledged forebears (a task which Coats and others have fruitfully undertaken), I present him as conversing with significant figures of twentieth-century philosophy and political theory with whose ideas he was almost certainly familiar, but whose work he rarely if ever undertook to discuss.[26] My purpose in doing so is not only to provide a view on Oakeshott that identifies elements of his thought that are interesting for Oakeshott scholars, but also to highlight elements of his thought that speak to broader, less obvious topics and audiences. If, as I suggest, Oakeshott speaks in idioms and to concerns shared with Ludwig Wittgenstein, or Michel Foucault, or

Chantal Mouffe, then he is a relevant voice in those contexts where such thinkers figure prominently. There are, of course, limits to what Oakeshott brings to these conversations, and, as Oakeshott himself recognized, the genius of any thinker is bounded and must be understood within the limits inherent to the form and matter of his or her thought. I acknowledge in the following chapters that Oakeshott's generally admirable penchant for conceptual precision occasionally slides into less salutary forms of conceptual rigidity and fixation, despite evidence that something eludes or exceeds his patterns of thought. His relation to the contemporaries whom I identify is thus attenuated, and requires careful articulation and negotiation if it is to bear fruit. I do not suppose that Oakeshott had any unexpressed intentions to engage with the thinkers with whom I stage conversation. Nor do I suppose that he has something interesting to say about every significant political or philosophical topic, or that saying something interesting is the same as having a systematic view. Yet I do suppose that the substance and relevance of Oakeshott's thought still exceed our current appreciation and that we thus have something to gain by considering his availability in some less familiar contexts.

PLAN OF THE BOOK

The conversations I stage in the chapters of this book neither presuppose nor supply a general overview of Oakeshott's thought and its development. Rather than provide a broad view, as many commentators have already done with a variety of inflections,[27] I focus in each chapter upon more local concerns, providing the background necessary to each. The purpose is to sound further the depths of Oakeshott's thought by drawing him into engagement with other significant thinkers whose ideas continue to influence philosophy and political thought.

In chapter 1, I consider several intellectual affinities between Oakeshott and Ludwig Wittgenstein, some of which have been explored elsewhere and others of which have not. Tracing a degree and depth of commonality of perspective between the two that has not been satisfactorily characterized, I work from conceptual foundations and conditions to their implications, beginning with a characterization of Oakeshott's and Wittgenstein's remarkably kindred views of language. By exploring their understandings of experience, thought, and action as mediated by what Oakeshott called "practices" and Wittgenstein called "language-games," I challenge a long-lived and influential claim about the common ground occupied by Oakeshott and Wittgenstein. Contrary to the interpretation of Oakeshott and Wittgenstein as philosophical and political conservatives who rigidly circumscribe or even deny the possibility of meaningful individual critical agency, I present the two as joined in projects of describing the conditions of individual agency and the extent of its real critical potential. Against the views propagated by David Bloor, J.C. Nyíri, and (in a qualified sense) Richard Rorty, I characterize Oakeshott and Wittgenstein as offering strong accounts of the individuality and critical potential of agency and action, grounded upon social, intersubjective conditions collected in the practices and language-games of a community of speakers. Oakeshott and Wittgenstein therefore strike a needful balance between the individual and her social context, offering the resources with which to defend robust individual agency without neglecting fundamental insights about the situatedness of agents.

In chapter 2, I turn to the related concept of individuality in Oakeshott's thought, and its relation to tradition and contingency. In his reflections upon tradition and its role in structuring understanding and action, Oakeshott describes both a vibrant "flow of sympathy" to be enjoyed and explored, and a set of the limiting, conditioning influences upon choice and action. The emphasis upon tradition may appear to stand in tension with Oakeshott's valorization of individual agency, yet I argue that his treatment of tradition is most fruitfully understood as intertwined with his analysis of contingency as a fundamental, inexorable condition of thought and action. Considering the interaction between these two concepts in Oakeshott's thought brings him into conversation with theorists of tradition and community, such as Alasdair MacIntyre, Edward Shils, and Charles Taylor, each of whom seeks to illustrate how individual agents are deeply embedded in networks of tradition. Read alongside these thinkers, Oakeshott provides a view of individuality and tradition that recognizes the profound effects of intersubjective practices and sentiments without affording tradition an independent normative status.

Building from the broad philosophical themes of chapters 1 and 2, in chapter 3 I take up an expressly political concern and consider Oakeshott's characterization of the "modern European state." In order to elaborate Oakeshott's account of the emergence, conditions, and character of the state, I explore elements of his political thought that resonate with the work of three significant twentieth-century political thinkers who grappled with the concept of the modern state and its attendant philosophical and practical problems: Michel Foucault, Isaiah Berlin, and Hannah Arendt. I begin by examining the affinities between Oakeshott's account of the emergence and character of the modern state and Foucault's analyses of the logic and pragmatics of state power (via his accounts of "governmentality" and "bio-power"). I next consider points of convergence and divergence between Oakeshott and Berlin regarding the condition of plurality in modern political communities and its implications for political freedom. Last, I consider the two different interpretations rendered by Oakeshott and Arendt of the notion that political action properly understood amounts to an activity of caring for a common public condition, which clarifies Oakeshott's understanding of the conditions and limits of politics. The fruits of these three engagements show Oakeshott to be a thinker too rich and complex to be exhausted by the convenient labels of political ideologies, and who speaks across many familiar ideological divides, philosophical as well as political.

In chapter 4, I follow Oakeshott into the political life of the modern democratic state and consider how his thought contributes to the active and diverse field of democratic theory. In respect of his claim that conversation is the "gist and meaning of democracy" he has been labeled a thinker in the deliberative democratic tradition.[28] While there is no doubt that Oakeshott shares and speaks to many of the concerns of deliberative democrats, upon closer consideration his conversational account of democracy does not fit smoothly within any branch of deliberative democratic theory. Turning to Oakeshott's critique of rationalism in politics, his emphasis on plurality, and his chastened conception of politics as such, I argue that Oakeshott speaks as a sometime critic of deliberative democracy as it has thus far been formulated, and in fact shares a number of insights with agonistic democrats such as Chantal Mouffe, as well as with the account of conversation in democratic politics articulated by Stanley Cavell. Exploring these themes and some of their implications I construct a tentative account of Oakeshott's place in the vigorously contested field of democratic theory, and thus of his relevance to one of the most important areas of contemporary political thought.

By showing Oakeshott's engagement with themes shared with other significant twentieth-century thinkers I elicit several of Oakeshott's contributions to conversations in which he is not commonly thought to be a participant, as well as contributions that may be of a surprising character in light of much of the existing scholarship on his thought. I do not, of course, mean to suggest that Oakeshott would have himself drawn all of the implications that I do, nor that contrary conclusions could not perhaps be drawn from his work (however contentiously) regarding some of the themes I address. Yet I believe that the exercises that follow have at least two significant virtues, whatever their exuberances or shortcomings may be. First, I read Oakeshott as a practitioner of one of the activities he praised most highly: conversation. As such, I attempt to find in Oakeshott the richness and dexterity of mind that he advocated, and which (if found) might disclose to us a more varied thinker than we have yet appreciated. Second, if our interest in Oakeshott is to be other than merely historical or ideological, we ought to seek his potential contributions to debates that continue to interest us, even if we must seek his contributions by reasonable implication and inference. This type of exercise is not wholly of my own invention—it is a staple of philosophical and political scholarship. Yet it has been rare and sporadic with respect to Oakeshott, and I believe that this lacuna is worth addressing. As his account of conversation invites such an exercise with respect to his own ideas and their possible projections into other conversations, I consider my approach to be Oakeshottian in a modest yet fundamental sense.

ONE

LANGUAGE, PRACTICE, AND INDIVIDUAL AGENCY

> A culture is built by the piling of individual testimony on individual testimony in a long tradition.
>
> —Stuart Hampshire, *Innocence and Experience*

> We believe, so to speak, that this great building exists, and then we see, now here, now there, one or another small corner of it.
>
> —Ludwig Wittgenstein, *On Certainty*

Throughout the long span of his career, Michael Oakeshott frequently turned to the individual person as the locus of philosophical and political analysis. In his two most expansive and systematic works, *Experience and Its Modes* (1933) and *On Human Conduct* (1975), as well as in the essays collected as *Rationalism in Politics* (1962) and *On History* (1983), the individual is the abiding protagonist. Even when "the totality of experience" is the object of philosophical analysis, this cannot be explained without accounting for the "self, replete with opinion, prejudice, habit, knowledge [that] is implied in every actual experience[, for] to exclude this self from any experience whatever is an absolute impossibility."[1] Likewise, Oakeshott's account of the "modern European state" is inseparable from his account of the individuals therein associated.[2] Yet it is not merely the abstract individual (the individual as philosophical placeholder) that matters to Oakeshott. Rather, it is the individual as a thinking and acting subject, as a concrete historic person who is the (*only*) protagonist of the epic of human conduct.[3] Indeed, human conduct cannot be made intelligible without recognizing and exploring the ineluctable sense in which each individual is an *agent*, an intelligent, self-disclosing and self-enacting doer. Oakeshott's systematic view of agency, developed over many decades, returns again and again to the interrelated roles of concepts and practices in what and how individuals think and do. It is in respect of his rich account of agency as having its own grammars or languages that I believe Oakeshott's work stands to inform and be informed by the later philosophy of Ludwig Wittgenstein. Each thinker develops a view of agency that is essentially a kind of language-use, both literally and metaphorically, and the terms in which they present their respective views of language, practice, and agency complement one another, such that much is to be learned from listening to what they each have to say on a number of common themes. While several of these have been explored, to various conclusions, there is a good deal more to be gathered from a conversation between these two thinkers.

FRAMING THE CONVERSATION

Numerous commentators have identified affinities between Oakeshott and Wittgenstein on a range of philosophical topics, and have most often framed the encounter in one of two ways. First, Oakeshott and Wittgenstein have been addressed to one another in virtue of their general philosophical styles or attitudes. Commentators have repeatedly argued that the two embrace fundamentally similar approaches to understanding and doing philosophy, specifically in opposition to a prevailing philosophical "rationalism" stretching from Descartes to twentieth-century analytic philosophy.[4] Second, Oakeshott and Wittgenstein have been addressed to one another in virtue of their accounts of the conditions of agency and community. Here the two are presented as sharing a concern with the ways in which rules structure and set the bounds of what individuals can say, do, and mean. This approach represents both thinkers as theorists of a situated self, whose identity, capacities, and horizons are drawn largely by the boundaries of the community in which the individual dwells. Some commentators, such as Richard Flathman, have interpreted this affinity in thought between Oakeshott and Wittgenstein fairly liberally, suggesting that the two similarly understand the inner workings and conditions of agency and community but nonetheless understand individual agency as articulated against the shared background of rules and community.[5] Others, such as David Bloor, J. C. Nyíri, and Richard Rorty, have interpreted Oakeshott and Wittgenstein as essentially conservative thinkers, advocates of the community and its customs or rules over and against the individual agent. These two approaches to Oakeshott and Wittgenstein—sketching their critiques of rationalism and their views of situated agency—often converge on the notion that practice underlies theory, and thus that philosophy can at most describe ways of living that are already present in actual human communities. Although there are some who understand Oakeshott and Wittgenstein as describing the conditions of robust individual agency, the majority of interpreters who read the two as addressing a family of overlapping concerns understand them to be essentially conservative thinkers (both philosophically and politically) who privilege practice over philosophy, and the rules and authority of the community over the choices and claims of the individual.[6]

My aim in this chapter is to review and reimagine the conversation between Oakeshott and Wittgenstein, both to identify and clarify their affinities and to challenge a view of individual agency that is common to many readings of the two as kindred, conservative thinkers. From their views of individual agency as ineluctably framed by intersubjective practices of speaking and acting, the claim is often derived that individual agents cannot help but manifest and reproduce robust forms of agreement with the conventions and traditions of their community. This proposition is frequently taken as evidence that critical agency (e.g., in politics) is either illusory or incoherent. J. C. Nyíri and David Bloor are perhaps the clearest and most consistent advocates of such a view.[7] However, something like this view has become common to most conservative interpreters of Oakeshott and Wittgenstein, yet it also continues to capture the imagination of readers who may not be partisans in any interpretive debate, and thus shapes the reception of Oakeshott and Wittgenstein in political and social thought.

I believe that the conversation between Oakeshott and Wittgenstein can be fruitfully restaged, so as to clarify both the depth of affinity between them as well as the implications of their work for political theory and practice. I shall argue that there is adequate textual evidence to reject the conservative reading and thus its political implications. I suggest that if one considers the characterizations of individual agency and its conditions presented in Wittgenstein's and Oakeshott's respective works, then one finds that their discussions of agency intimate and support a deeply individualistic understanding of agency premised upon but not determined by a larger intersubjective background or network of shared concepts and practices. Ultimately, my aim is twofold: first, to construct an account of individual agency that recognizes its intersubjective, social conditions, yet views these conditions from an individualistic perspective, and second, to challenge a common association drawn between Wittgenstein and Oakeshott which suggests that their intellectual affinities are deeply conservative in tenor, and that their respective works present the individual agent as imprisoned within an edifice of convention that is itself beyond the reach of critical reflection and action. I will approach the former by way of the latter.

In order to provide a consistent point of view from which to consider the work of Wittgenstein and Oakeshott, I will employ a useful if simple distinction between *individualistic* and *social* theories of agency.[8] Individualistic theories of agency generally emphasize the individual's capacity to act, a capacity that is not reducible to or fully determinable by an individual's context of action. The most common and familiar individualistic theories of agency that inform the contemporary study of politics (though, as I will show, by no means the only such available) are rational choice theories, social choice theories, and their kin.[9] While such theories do not altogether discount the ways in which individual agency and action are conditioned externally, they treat agency as importantly self-contained, driven by individual rationality, preferences, and calculations, and importantly independent of the hurly-burly of life to which action is a response. What I am calling social theories of agency generally stress the intersubjective conditions and context of individual agency and action. Individual agency is treated as explicable in terms of conditions beyond the agent herself, and thus more or less derivative of some larger social field of traditions, systems, forces, and relations exogenous to the agent.[10]

The tensions between individualistic and social theories of agency, and their applications in political theory, are readily apparent, if not always well documented or explored. While the tensions are genuine, the delineation of one approach from another is often a secondary concern, a trope used to emphasize or amplify other points of contention (such as how best to understand and organize democratic institutions, how best to understand and institutionalize political and legal rights, or how best to defend or undermine particular identities and traditions). Given the secondary status ordinarily afforded to agency as a chip wagered in larger theoretical games, accounts of agency are often assumed and categorized quickly and starkly in reflection on politics, so as to settle the issue of agency at the outset (sometimes by denying the possibility of a middle ground or meaningful debate) and move on to the topics that the respective theorists really intend to discuss. Thus, while theoretical divisions regarding agency are real and, I would add, important, they often receive rather partisan lip service, and often remain among the less developed aspects of any political theory.

With this as my guiding conceptual scheme, I begin, in the next section, by characterizing broadly the affinities I wish to identify between Oakeshott and Wittgenstein, which form the foundation of the view of individual agency I will present. In the subsequent section I consider an influential conservative reading of Oakeshott and Wittgenstein, which presents them as unwavering advocates of a social theory of agency. By way of criticizing this reading I will challenge the conservative claims upon Oakeshott and Wittgenstein and further articulate the theory of agency that I draw from their work. Lastly, in the final section, I consider several of the implications of this theory for our understanding of critical reflection and action in politics.

COMPLEMENTARY VISIONS OF LANGUAGE, PRACTICE, AND CONVENTION

Though there is no direct biographical or textual link between their respective projects,[11] if one looks at the world through the respective conceptual lenses fashioned by Michael Oakeshott (in his work of the 1950s to the 1980s) and Ludwig Wittgenstein (in his work of the 1930s to the 1950s), then one sees strikingly similar pictures. Each viewed the human world not as an inert array of discovered and immutable facts, but rather as an understood world, hard-won through the circumstantial utterances and actions of countless individuals. What is more, the utterances and actions of persons are inexorably structured by the conceptual-practical framework that (following Wittgenstein) one could simply call *language*. That is, for both Oakeshott and Wittgenstein, the human world is a world *in language*—understood, inhabited, and experienced through the inexorable mediating influence of concepts and practices whose use constitutes language-use in the broadest sense.[12] According to this perspective, to look systematically at the world is to scrutinize, more or less explicitly, the conceptual and practical frameworks of language that overlay and organize it in experience. The study of human conduct requires attention to language-use, and parsing human conduct into various domains means investigating various practices of language-use engaged in by individuals in the contingent circumstances they encounter. Thus, for Oakeshott and Wittgenstein, the regularities and systematic structures of the world we understand and act within are (intelligible as) the regularities and systematic structures of language. The later careers of both thinkers comprise projects of applying this general perspective to a variety of intellectual domains, questions, confusions, and problems, on topics ranging from logic, mathematics, and skepticism to history, politics, and theories of action. For present purposes I need only to sketch the contours of the linguistic perspective that I argue these two thinkers share, and which informs and suffuses their respective works.

First, the great diversity and complexity of conduct, different kinds of utterance and action in different kinds of circumstances, can be understood perspicuously in terms of different idioms of language-use. Oakeshott commonly referred to such idioms of speaking and acting as "practices," while Wittgenstein gave them the name "language-games." Practices or language-games are the conceptual-practical structures that frame and ground understanding and agency—they are, so to speak, the air that understanding and agency necessarily breathe. Wittgenstein never offered a systematic definition of a language-game, though much of *Philosophical Investigations* and posthumously edited and published works such as *On Certainty* and *Zettel* consist of demonstrative reflections on language-games. Nevertheless, one could say that for Wittgenstein a language-game is an acquired or learned technique of thinking and acting.[13] Cast in this light, utterances and actions are uses of a technique, an agent following and drawing upon one or another linguistic practice. Somewhat more precisely and systematically, Oakeshott states that a "practice"

> may be identified as a set of considerations, manners, uses, observances, customs, standards, canon's maxims, principles, rules, and offices specifying useful procedures or denoting obligations or duties which relate to human actions and utterances. It is [an] adverbial qualification of choices and performances, more or less complicated, in which conduct is understood in terms of a procedure.[14]

Though their formulations differ in terminology and systematicity, both view the structure of utterance and action in terms of techniques of language-use. As Oakeshott claimed, practices or language-games specify "arts of agency" that individuals employ in conduct as they craft themselves, their actions, and their world.[15] Though these techniques are in some ways constraining, in the sense that they regulate as well as constitute idioms of activity, they are not scripts to be parroted. A competent language-user is the "master of a technique" that constitutes and adverbially conditions a "*capacity*" (*Können*) for intelligent choice and action.[16] Thus viewed, a practice or language-game should be understood as "an instrument to be played upon, not a tune to be played."[17] To speak and act is to make use of the arts of agency afforded by the language-games one has mastered; to understand or make sense of the actions of others is to understand or make sense of the linguistic practices they use, the language-games they play.

Second, Oakeshott and Wittgenstein recognize the intersubjective, social dimension of language-games. As Wittgenstein puts it, our linguistic practices rest upon and illustrate a broadly social, intersubjective substrate, which he calls our "forms of life."[18] That is, our language-games and the arts of agency they constitute and regulate are conventional or customary to a group of language-users. Such arts of agency are in the first and most important instance learned (often ostensively) from others who are already mature users (i.e., "masters") of the respective techniques.[19] Wittgenstein discusses extensively the acquisition of language in the *Philosophical Investigations*, and Oakeshott likewise emphasizes the sense in which individuals are initiated into the practices contained in and conveyed by convention and tradition.[20] An initiate into a language-game (whether a child or an adult) learns from already initiated practitioners, and hence learning language-games has an ineluctably social, intersubjective dimension.[21] The arts of agency are acquired and mastered through life *inter homines*, as conventional techniques are disseminated from adepts to initiates. In addition to how we learn language-games, the uses we make of them have an enduring conventional, social aspect. We speak and act either directly *with* or indirectly *with respect to* others (even the imagined other who "hears" what one "says" to oneself), addressing ourselves through the use of learned conventions of practice to a world of other agents. Even when an agent speaks or acts privately, in physical isolation from others, the practices she uses in some way presuppose and are conditional upon the intersubjective context in which she is situated as a language-user. Though each agent's act is "ineluctably his [or her] own" in respect of authorship, the felicity of any particular utterance or action has a social, conventional dimension, which further means that even the most singular act takes its place within a larger field of custom shared with others.[22]

Third, the practical aspect of language-games as techniques and their conventional aspect as social institutions meet in the rule-character of language-games. Both Oakeshott and Wittgenstein describe the acquisition and use of language-games in terms of rules and conventional techniques, presenting rules and rule following as the conceptual core and paradigm case of language-use.[23] Mastery of a language-game entails mastery of the rules that structure the game, even if one did not learn the game by memorizing rules and does not practice it by self-consciously recalling and interpreting rules. *Philosophical Investigations* deals repeatedly with how rules subtly structure language-games and serve as primary vectors along which convention travels in our linguistic practices.[24] The "private language argument," for example, can be read in part as a refutation of the proposition that some (i.e., "private") language-games float free from intersubjective rules and conventions.[25] "Our talk gets its meaning from the rest of our proceedings," and this larger context is conventional, which means intersubjective and social.[26] Oakeshott likewise identifies a conventional, customary background of our linguistic practices, which he describes as "a capital that has been accumulated" over many years, which agents draw upon, participate in, and contribute to in their utterances and actions.[27] This social background comprises "languages of self-disclosure and self-enactment," which are possessed only in virtue of being learned, and learned only in virtue of being shared with others as customary idioms of conduct that stretch across generations.[28] In an ineluctable yet not exhaustive sense, every manifestation of individual agency—whether playing a game of chess, speaking English, or voting in an election—is describable in terms of rule-following, adherence to and attunement in conventions and institutions shared with others.

The linguistic pictures of Oakeshott and Wittgenstein lend themselves easily to social theories of agency, which stress the external, intersubjective conditions of individual agency. On a cursory review, Oakeshott and Wittgenstein appear to present (or at least to offer the resources to maintain) social theories of agency that reckon convention both the form and the matter of individual action. Accordingly, one might infer that Oakeshott and Wittgenstein understand individual agency as the residue or side effect of social institutions or intersubjective processes. The individual agent, one might say, exists only in a derivative sense—as an evanescent ripple on the surface of the deep water of community, custom, and convention. Such readings have found receptive audiences in philosophy and political theory,[29] yet I will argue that such readings are textually tenuous, conceptually inadequate, and both philosophically and politically misleading. I believe that despite the foregoing sketch, Wittgenstein and Oakeshott share a fourth route of affinity, a fundamentally *individualistic* perspective on agency situated within the context of social practices, and I shall argue that this perspective is not only consistent with the conventionality of language-games but in fact contributes to a more robust and sustainable understanding of the life and force of conventions. Though I do not suppose myself to offer a refutation of the reading that I ultimately reject, my argument against it takes a fresh view of Wittgenstein, Oakeshott, and their complementary insights for political thought.

CONSERVATISM AND INDIVIDUALISM

How one reads Wittgenstein with respect to language and agency inexorably shapes the political availability and valences of his work. As a rule, to read Wittgenstein as offering a social theory of agency carries a range of conservative consequences in application to political theory, whereas reading him as offering an individualistic theory of agency carries individualistic, liberal (though, I shall argue, less than radical) consequences. Although a rough investigation and analysis of a conservative reading of Wittgenstein and its political implications could be undertaken fruitfully without any reference to Oakeshott, considering the two as participants in a common conversation regarding language and agency is warranted for several reasons. First, Oakeshott is often drawn into conversation with Wittgenstein by precisely those thinkers who offer a conservative reading of Wittgenstein, in service of a social theory of agency. Not only do I believe that the conservative reading misrepresents the views of Oakeshott and Wittgenstein, the conservative reading looms large for any attempt to place the two thinkers in conversation. Second, as I argued in the Introduction, the attribution of simple labels to Oakeshott tends to distort his complex ideas. I would add that such labels distort Wittgenstein as well. Hence, reading Oakeshott and Wittgenstein together, against the conservative reading, both challenges one such label and illustrates what is lost when such labels gain currency. Third, as Wittgenstein left us no political theory, the implications of his work for political theory are inevitably extrapolations. Yet Oakeshott's political work is extensive. If, as I have suggested, Oakeshott and Wittgenstein share a number of fundamental perspectives and notions regarding language and agency, then Oakeshott's political thought might be instructive regarding how to understand the implications of Wittgenstein for political theory. I am not suggesting that Wittgenstein's philosophical perspectives on language and agency necessitate the set of theoretical positions on politics that Oakeshott happens to espouse. Rather, I mean only to suggest that Wittgenstein's contributions to political theory (as speculative and wrought as they necessarily must be) shall likely bear a distinct resemblance to Oakeshott's—as if though singing different notes, they nonetheless harmonize.

I will sketch what is perhaps the dominant conservative reading of Wittgenstein and Oakeshott, which is articulated in the work of J. C. Nyíri and David Bloor, and which attributes social theories of agency to both Oakeshott and Wittgenstein. I will then offer an alternative reading that is, I argue, a more faithful rendering of Oakeshott and Wittgenstein, and provides a more coherent sense of how the intersubjective and individual aspects of language and agency are interwoven in their thought. This prepares the ground for a reevaluation of the political implications drawn from the conservative reading.

Convention, Forms of Life and Conservatism

Both Oakeshott and Wittgenstein describe a dimension of conventionality to how language is learned and used that locates the individual agent within a dense network of practices or language-games that she draws upon in her actions. Using these practices, playing these language-games, entails the expression of (almost always implicit) agreement or attunement with other language-users with whom the individual shares forms of life and cultural capital. Any attentive reader of Oakeshott and Wittgenstein must, I think, come to some such conclusions. However, the further specification of the arguments that lead to these conclusions and the implications these conclusions have in political theory can send one off in different directions, despite this initial agreement.

The readings of Oakeshott and Wittgenstein articulated by J. C. Nyíri and David Bloor are similar enough in argumentation, textual interpretation, and political implications that I will treat them as a single view, which for simplicity I will refer to as the conservative reading.[30] The core of the conservative reading and its social theory of agency may be simplified (and occasionally elaborated on its advocates' behalf) into the following form:

1. Individual agency is conceptually and practically framed by language, such that agency and action are inseparable from language-use.
2. Language (in the formal abstract) and language-use (in the concrete) consist of social, that is, intersubjective and conventional, practices.

(As I suggested earlier, these are neither controversial claims about Oakeshott and Wittgenstein, nor do they entail a social theory of agency or conservative implications for political theory.)

3. Beyond the formal sense in which language-use consists in using ineluctably social practices, the conservative reading maintains that individual language-use consists in following the empirically settled and verifiable rules, customs, and conventions of some community; some "we" of which the relevant "I" is a member.
4. Clarifying and amplifying the sense of "following," the conservative reading asserts that meaningful individual utterance and felicitous individual action is the reproduction of custom. For example, adding correctly means to do what others do, or would do, according to a shared rule, such that the real criterion of an individual's doing or saying something correctly is that she does or says what conforms to the form of life of the community.[31] In support of this interpretation, the conservative reading focuses upon Wittgenstein's remarks about following rules and conventions blindly, and Oakeshott's early discussions of tradition, and interprets these as evidence that what an individual says and does is intelligible only insofar as it blindly reproduces custom.[32] Wittgenstein's remarks that "[s]omething must be taught us as a foundation" and that one's "*life* consists in [one's] being content to accept many things" come to mean that an individual's ideas, utter-

ances, and actions are essentially the repetition of what has been inculcated in her by her elders.[33]

5. Individual agency is therefore a rigidly if not exhaustively socially determined capacity to follow the customs and conventions of one's community. Competent, intelligible individual action manifests only and exactly in doing and saying what some community, some "we," does and says. According to Bloor, Wittgenstein "was remorseless in stressing the priority of society over the individual" in just this sense, and in terms that Nyíri purports to draw from both Oakeshott and Wittgenstein, "any human being must, in order to be a human being, be constrained by some form of life, by some network of tradition" immanent to her community, which in word and deed she reproduces.[34]

If one reads Oakeshott and Wittgenstein in this way, then the political implication follows that individual agents are as such incapable of gaining critical purchase by word or deed upon the community to which they belong. The conservative reading pictures the individual constrained by her inherited conventions of thinking and acting in a way analogous to how a person on holiday in a country whose native language she does not speak is constrained to the phrases in her travel phrase book. She must use her inherited conventions whole cloth, for these conventions have been taught to her as a foundation and are for her the horizon beyond which she cannot see. The combinations she composes out of these inherited stock phrases may be novel, but only trivially since what she means, says, and does in her thoughts, utterances, and actions is determined externally and in advance by the conventions she reproduces (and indeed must reproduce) blindly and by rote.

As Nyíri characterizes the political implications of the conservative reading:

> [A]lthough any given form of life, mode of thought and behavior, can be superseded by or have superimposed upon itself other forms of life, it cannot actually be criticized. All criticism presupposes a form of life, a language, that is, a tradition of agreements; every judgment is necessarily embedded in traditions. That is why traditions cannot be judged.[35]

The conservative reading of Oakeshott and Wittgenstein simply "gives the critic no room."[36] In more expressly political terms, criticism of one's own society is vacuous on the conceptual level and fruitless on the practical level. The impossibility of real criticism stems, say Nyíri and Bloor, from the fact that to make an intelligible claim is to play a language-game; to play a language-game is to follow the rules and conventions of one's society (in the sense outlined at 4 above); hence, a genuinely critical stance or act toward one's own society inveighs against its own conditions and undermines itself. The critic either falls into incoherence and imbecility (insofar as she goes off the rails of convention that keep her in agreement with the society she would criticize) or ends up unwittingly justifying the very arrangements she intended to challenge (insofar as making an intelligible claim or coherent argument requires adherence to the body of custom and convention that she meant to criticize). In either case, Nyíri supposes that "'nonconformism' is an anthropological absurdity" because intelligibility to others and robust conformity to the conventions of one's community are both empirically and logically inseparable.[37]

Language Use and Critical Agency

On the conservative reading, one is left with the view that a community's stock of linguistic practices is integral, internally coherent and mutually supporting much like smoothly aligned bricks in a wall. The entirely of a community's language-games are harmoniously arranged such that each conceptually supposes and practically affirms the others. There is no room for critical agency because the harmony latent and manifest within the assemblage of practices is at once necessary, stable, and complete. Although the conservative reading has been challenged,[38] I believe that the full implications of its rejection or refutation have yet to be fully explored and appreciated. This gap leaves underdeveloped the ways in which Oakeshott and Wittgenstein speak to questions of freedom, authority, law, and critique in political theory and practice.

Instead of rehearsing arguments that have been offered against the likes of Nyíri and Bloor, I will offer an alternative view that reverses the method of the conservative reading. In effect, Nyíri and Bloor pose the question "Can one genuinely and intelligibly criticize one's own society?" and draw a negative conclusion based on their interpretations of several of Wittgenstein's remarks on culture, forms of life, conventions, and rules, supplemented by a handful of Oakeshott's arguments against the set of philosophical dispositions and methods he termed "rationalism." Yet the conservative reading starts from a position of feigned ignorance, doubt, or open-mindedness (as if the guiding question were not already adequately and conclusively answered by real practice) and proceeds to derive a denial from an absence. The absence of a robust and explicit theorization of individual critical agency in selections of Oakeshott's and Wittgenstein's work is presented as a conclusive denial or refutation of the intelligibility and even possibility of meaningful criticism of one's own society in word and deed.

Contrary to the conservative reading, I suggest that it would be more faithful to the method and spirit of Oakeshott's and Wittgenstein's thought to abandon the feigned (and, in Wittgenstein's sense, overly "philosophical") ignorance or doubt regarding the *possibility* of critique, and analyze earnestly the facts of the matter. Start neither from the question of whether critical agency is possible, nor from a hypothesis that it is possible, but from the patent fact that individuals engage in a host of "everyday practices of criticism"[39] of the rules, conventions, and forms of life of the community or society of which they are competent members. The relevant question then becomes, "How do Wittgenstein and Oakeshott equip us to give account of this fact?" Proceeding in this fashion, not only does one see that the conservative reading is misleading in its assumptions and nonsensical in its conclusion, but one also sees more perspicuously the individualistic implications of Oakeshott's and Wittgenstein's complementary views of language and agency.

Bernard Williams's essay "Pluralism, Community and Left Wittgensteinianism," furnishes an example of the sort of approach to the issue of critical agency that I have in mind. Williams begins from reasonable characterization of a modern pluralistic society, in which there is fundamental agreement on some practices yet deep and meaningful disagreement on others. He subsequently challenges the alleged necessity of "undiscriminating acceptance of whatever conceptual resources of the society actually exist" that is posited by the conservative reading.[40] Williams argues that Wittgenstein's insights on the conventionality of our linguistic practices would admit the possibility of genuine individual critical agency within the intersubjective network of our language-games and forms of life. Within the network of practices there exist spaces within which one practice may be used to gain critical purchase upon others, to challenge and even to "combat" others.[41] Recognizing the fact that "people have found [within the rules and conventions that they share with others] resources with which to criticize their society," Williams claims that on a Wittgensteinian view (with which I have shown Oakeshott to agree), "[p]ractice is not just the practice of practice, so to speak, but also the practice of criticism."[42] The general attunement in forms of life, in acquired modes and cultivated dispositions of conduct, might shape or constrain the domain of critical agency, but such attunement does not negate critical agency.

As I have discussed, the conservative reading supposes that one must accept the entirety of the practices of one's society in order to use any particular practice contained therein. Wittgenstein no doubt recognized that conventional attunement and stability are necessary in order for our practices to hold good, so to speak. However, the foundations of our practices consist in general patterns of conventional attunement and stability, not total conformity in each and every individual instance. For example,

> [S]ince a language-game is something that consists in recurrent procedures of the game in time, it seems impossible to say in any *individual* case that such-and-such must be beyond doubt if there is to be a language-game—though it is right enough to say that *as a rule* some empirical judgment or other must be beyond doubt.[43]

The individual agent, in order to be a competent language-user, must *generally* manifest attunement with some form of life shared with others. Yet it is not necessary that each and every one of her actions manifest complete attunement or conformity with the entire body of empirical (or normative) judgments of her community. Once we come to some such realization regarding Wittgenstein's view of language and agency, "we shall have less temptation to assume that [the set of practices we share with others] is a satisfactorily functioning whole; and we shall be more likely to recognize that some widely accepted parts of it may stand condemned in the light of perfectly plausible extrapolations of other parts."[44] Oakeshott contributes to the insight that what an individual shares with others who have been initiated into the same network of practices is not a "stock" of phrases, actions, or procedures to mechanically repeat, but a "capital" composed of the various arts of agency whose use individuals have learned and shaped, and which they may creatively and critically use.[45] Neither Wittgenstein nor Oakeshott denies that in order for an individual to be a competent practitioner of any of these arts, she must on the whole be attuned with other practitioners. Yet this attunement on the whole is not and need not be complete or rigidly precise. As William Connolly has argued, the concepts and practices in which we are attuned may be deeply contested, despite being generally shared.[46] An individual may use some of the arts that she has mastered to work upon others, to challenge their current projections, to close some routes of use while opening others, pursuing what Oakeshott called the "intimations" and "flow[s] of sympathy" latent in our shared practices.[47] An individual may engage in genuine criticism without stepping wholly outside the context of shared practice that grounds even the intelligibility of her criticism, and thus falling into unintelligibility or performative contradiction. Rather than dismissing genuine criticism as an "anthropological absurdity," Oakeshott and Wittgenstein give rich accounts of its conditions and potency.

One of Wittgenstein's best-known remarks should, I believe, be read as I have just suggested—as a comment upon the individuality of agency despite the social context in which the individual is situated as a language-user. In section 217 of *Philosophical Investigations*, in the course of remarks the central role that practices of rule following play in language-use, he says:

> If I have exhausted the justifications I have reached bedrock, and my spade is turned. Then I am inclined to say: "This is simply what I do."

One might read this, following Nyíri and Bloor, as the inevitable conclusion that when the justifications we can articulate come to an end, the only explanation for why we individually act as we do is that others in our community also act this way. "This is simply what I do" becomes shorthand for "I learned the ways of my community and cannot see or imagine beyond them; if pressed to justify my words and deeds, their deepest grounds consist in the raw fact that members of my community speak and act in this way; I can and would do no other." As I have suggested, the conservative reading arrives at such exhaustively social interpretations of language-use and agency by mischaracterizing the ways in which language-games and our attunement in how we play them hang together. Contrary to the conservative reading of "This is simply what I do" as total capitulation to the authority of the ways of the community, I suggest an individualistic reading that more coherently presents Oakeshott's and Wittgenstein's respective views, and the insight we have to gain from staging a conversation between them.

Neither thinker suggests that practices or language-games fit smoothly into a singular edifice shared evenly and completely by the members of the linguistic community. Instead, the shared practices or language-games of a notional community are partially and complexly interrelated. Analogously, the instances of individual language-use need not fit smoothly into a singular, organic pattern of utterance and action shared evenly and completely by the members of the linguistic community. (At some level, what I am describing conforms to the Saussurean distinction between individual speech [*parole*] and conventional language [*langue*].[48] The former admits of individuality and variation, while the latter is a body of rule-articulated conventions shared and followed by speakers. Yet, as I am presently suggesting, Wittgenstein's picture admits greater room for individual variation and critical agitation in language-use than the Saussurean structural model of linguistics allows.) It is consistent with Wittgenstein's treatment of rules and conventions of rule following to say that agency is thoroughly conditioned by intersubjective practices and patterns of behavior, yet that agency is still at its core individualistic. An individual can use the language-games of her linguistic community correctly while still making novel uses of the practices she has mastered, and even while using one practice to challenge or disrupt others. A given practice can be the site of critique and contestation even as (and among) individuals (who) use it competently.

The complexity of the individual's relation to the community, and the critical distance it permits, could be further elaborated by picturing how language-games are in fact learned. For example, I did not learn how (and when and why) to make and keep promises by observing and being trained to mimic what "the community" or some notional "we" says and does. Instead, I learned practices of promising from particular individuals, my mother and father, my siblings, my friends, my teachers.[49] In instructing me, these individuals did not themselves reproduce what "we" or "the community" say and do, but what they individually understood to be promising, practices they learned from individuals like themselves, and so on. Instead, language-use is always what particular individuals say and do, who are never mere members of some notional "we" that shares foundational practices, patterns, and dispositions of action.[50] Yes, we must be able (in rare cases, not in ordinary ones) to appeal to what some notional entity beyond ourselves says and does, such as when we are misunderstood, or when we are challenged. However, as Hilary Putnam has it, "[o]ur attunements enable us to understand 'what is going on'; they are not facts that we appeal to in going on."[51] That is, when I engage in a language-game, such as promising, I do not in effect *report* the presence of a verifiable, empirical thing called "our form of life" or "our attunement in practices of promising," nor do I *assume* that such an object would be there if I looked.[52] Instead, I enact a capacity; I make a promise; I express it in the way I learned from other individuals and that has become natural to me; I follow the rules and enact myself according to the technique of the language-game, "blindly," inasmuch as I do not question what is natural to me.[53] My ordinary lack of hesitation in speaking and acting, that I need not and generally do not consult a rule book or empirically verify "our" attunement in practices of promising, illustrates not that I already have such an empirical validation of what "we" say and do, but that only the rarest cases call for such validation. Wittgenstein thus offers a commentary on the naturalness to us of our linguistic practices, rather than a statement of the imperiousness of community and its rules over what and how we do.[54]

Even if we accept this individualistic picture of ordinary, unproblematic language-use, Nyíri and Bloor may still appear to have the edge when an individual's aberrant use of a practice is, as it were, called before the community of speakers for judgment. It may seem that critical agency evaporates precisely when the individual turns a practice against the normal ways of the community. Some have supposed that Oakeshott and Wittgenstein teach that the limits of truth and intelligibility are drawn circumstantially by what the community lets individuals get away with saying.[55] Therefore, an individual's critical agency comes apart when the rest of the community stops listening to her, leaving critical agency fundamentally conditioned and limited by how far others will humor the individual. Despite its appeal, this fallback conservative position likewise rests upon what I believe is a misreading of Wittgenstein and Oakeshott. Even in cases of irregularity or dispute, validation from the community is not necessarily the last word, or the judgment from which we have the most to learn. In the final instance, when dispute over the use of a practice remains and explanations have been exhausted, "This is simply what I do" means something like "This is how I take the world to be." When explanations come to an end there is no deeper or more objective bedrock to which I can refer than how I *take* the world, how I *live* in it.[56] Wittgenstein and Oakeshott each acutely recognized that there is no ground to human community deeper than our attunement in practices, but for each individual practitioner no ground is more fundamental than her own understanding of and ways of enacting the practices she has learned. In another of Wittgenstein's formulations:

> Nothing we do can be defended absolutely and finally. But only by reference to something else that is not questioned. I.e. no reason can be given why you should act (or should have acted) *like this*, except that by doing so you bring about such and such a situation, which again has to be an aim you *accept*.[57]

This position undoubtedly recognizes limits to the free hand individuals have to assail or challenge the practices they share with others—but agents are nonetheless *individual* practitioners, whose individual judgments, intentions, purposes, and performances have genuine weight. Our agreement in forms of life (from adding numbers in the same ways, to finding humor in the same things, to believing in the dignity of sentient beings) is broad and profound, but around the edges we are not in perfect or exact or explicit agreement; we can generally share forms of life and language-games and still encounter confusion, misunderstanding, and genuine, intelligible disagreement.[58]

Rejecting the conservative reading means abandoning one conceptual picture of language-use and agency for another, and here a metaphor may prove useful. Individual language-users may be pictured as akin to swimmers adrift in a boundless, bottomless sea. The conservative reading of Oakeshott and Wittgenstein pictures these individuals staying afloat by clinging to a raft that they all necessarily share; to let go of the raft is to drown. According to this image, individual language-users must obediently reproduce the conventional ways in which the community speaks and acts; to stray from "what *we* say and do" is to fall into infelicity and unintelligibility. The critic is thus pictured as the one who lets go, turns from the ways of the community, and either repents his hubris or sinks into silence. On the alternative reading that I am presenting, individual language-users could be pictured as akin to swimmers adrift in the same boundless and bottomless sea, staying afloat not by clutching to the raft at all costs (i.e., adhering blindly to common patterns of behavior), but instead staying afloat by individually using strokes that they have learned from other individuals. The strokes an individual knows and uses might be shared almost exactly by other individuals, and might have only distant relatives in the practices used by some others. Many different kinds of strokes will serve to keep these individual agents afloat, and all that is required is that the various strokes used by individuals bear degrees of family resemblance.[59] Analogously, individual language-use and agency can be understood as individuals variously using practices in ways that need only share significant family resemblances to the uses made by others. Individual agents may share remarkably significant patterns of conduct without all being locked into blind reproduction of what "the community" says and does. Wittgenstein remarked that even in normal cases "of course, this [e.g., my usage, my action, my claim, my judgment] is also in agreement with other people; but *I* agree with them."[60] As Richard Flathman interprets the affinities between Oakeshott and Wittgenstein on this very point, even rules, which are seemingly the most rigid structures of shared linguistic practices, "take the agent by the elbow, not by the throat . . . the most tightly integrated system of norms and rules leaves scope for variations in conduct."[61] One might conclude with Colin McGinn that "insofar as [Wittgenstein] has a view on the individual/social opposition, he is an individualist."[62] This is not to discount the social conditions and dimensions of language-use and agency, but to take a perspective on them that prioritizes the individual as a linguistic agent.

CONDITIONAL YET CRITICAL AGENCY

My purpose for engaging and subsequently rejecting the conservative reading is twofold. First, somewhat academically, I believe that although it places Oakeshott and Wittgenstein in conversation, the reading spreads an inaccurate picture of these two significant thinkers. Conservative readers of Oakeshott and Wittgenstein correctly suppose that the two view the world in similar ways and that their political significance is rooted in their understandings of language-use and agency. Yet conservative readers take the conditions of individual agency identified by Oakeshott and Wittgenstein to act as simple, rigid boundaries, and thus overplay the constraining effects of intersubjective practices. Second, careful examination and rejection of the conservative reading better illuminates the views that Oakeshott and Wittgenstein properly espouse, as well as some of the political potencies of their reflections on agency and practice. With a more accurate and tenable understanding of their respective works and the affinities between them, we can better appreciate what they intimate about political thought and practice.

Although there have been numerous thoughtful attempts to show the critical voices of Oakeshott and (especially) Wittgenstein,[63] interpreters have not always appreciated the complexity of the balance between the social and individual aspects of language-use, and have tended (in some cases) to arrive at majoritarian or radical interpretations of Wittgenstein's political import.[64] I have attempted to develop a modest, middle position which pictures the agent neither as radically detached from the practices she uses in her self-enactments (a position that both Wittgenstein and Oakeshott clearly reject), nor as strictly determined by these practices (as the conservative view maintains). I need only establish the plausibility of this modest position in order to show that Oakeshott and Wittgenstein hold open space for meaningful critical agency.

Perhaps the most apt analogy that Wittgenstein offers to explain the conditionality of our language-games, and thus of the agency practically structured by them, is the analogy to the hinges of a door. Explaining his notion of the fundamental grounds of our linguistic practices, he says,

> [T]he *questions* that we raise and our *doubts* depend on the fact that some propositions are exempt from doubt, are as it were like hinges on which those turn.
>
> . . .
>
> If I want the door to turn, the hinges must stay put.[65]

This of course does not suggest that some features of our forms of life are forever and with necessity insulated from meaningful critique. It is not, in the example of American politics, that certain political principles such as freedom or equality or popular sovereignty or due process of law are always and everywhere the load-bearing points of the rest of our political system, which therefore cannot be meaningfully criticized or challenged. We can easily imagine and identify situations in which such principles do enjoy this status, but propositions and principles serve as hinges (rendered beyond doubt and meaningful critique) only episodically and in particular contexts. In the context of voting rights, the principle of equality might be a hinge upon which the debate turns—to question or criticize equality in this context is not impossible but self-defeating. The insight that Oakeshott and Wittgenstein offer here is not that some propositions and principles are and must remain simply beyond criticism (as Nyíri and Bloor suggest), but rather that ripping at the hinges is fruitless in just those contexts in which we want the door to turn. Calling an element of our practice into question requires a context in which the question is intelligible, and such a context is framed by concepts, facts, and techniques that are not (and for the moment cannot be) called into question. When Wittgenstein says that "[m]y *life* consists in being content to accept many things" this does not mean that anything must be accepted once and for all, nor does it in any way guide us with regard to what must be accepted in any context, but only reminds us that at every moment, in every contingent context, there shall be some things that one must simply accept if one is to push practice and inquiry onward.[66] Every one of our practices can be subjected to profound criticism, though within contingent limits of occasion, orientation, scope, and depth that cannot be fully mapped in advance.

The point is that, to use our practices critically, we must at the same time affirm their conditionality upon other parts of our conventional practices. These are the hinges that must stay put if the door is to turn. In order to question your calculations, I must (for now) accept our practices of mathematics, let them stay put. I could of course challenge them, but only in a context in which these practices are not a fundamental supposition of the critical inquiry itself. In order to question the meaning of our political rights in a juridical setting I must leave the Constitution in place, so to speak. I must allow it to serve, as it conventionally does, as a foundation of our political rights and a key text in our literature of political practices and institutions. In other contexts I could critically examine and challenge the Constitution in the most fundamental terms, but for now, in this context, it is a hinge for our political and legal practices. Read in this way, Oakeshott and Wittgenstein provide the resources with which to affirm critical agency, while stopping short of radicalisms that suppose that criticism can be freed from its underlying conditions, and can turn upon any practice, in any way, at any time.

Depending upon the standpoint one occupies (e.g., how radical a view one takes of politics), the view I have drawn from a conversation between Oakeshott and Wittgenstein might seem a conservative alternative to an archconservative position. However, the reading I have constructed breaks cleanly from the two main political implications of the conservative reading. As exemplified by Nyíri and Bloor, the conservative reading leads to: (1) the blanket dismissal of criticism as a meaningful activity (and even dismissal of critics as competent language-users), and (2) the blanket affirmation of whatever conventions and practices exist for a given community (simply because these exist).[67] The individualistic reading that I have articulated undermines both of these implications. Criticism is a mode of activity that draws upon the resources of some of our practices to call into question the basis or use of others. As Wittgenstein says, in playing a language-game an individual might invent a new move, giving the language-game itself "a new joint."[68] We can use our practices critically, in order to reflect upon and seek to enact alternatives to other of our practices, all without repudiating basic agreement regarding our shared idioms of speaking and acting. Criticism is not, as Rorty suggests, mere irony or speaking nonsense (i.e., statements that are not candidates to be either true or false) to the community until through luck and repetition it becomes accepted as part of how "we" speak and act.[69] Rather, as Williams observes, criticism is an integral feature of linguistic community as such.

The individualistic view of language-games and agency developed by Oakeshott and Wittgenstein signals, on the one hand, a robust understanding of the conditionality of our practices while at the same time recognizing the availability of meaningful criticism, and, on the other hand, a greater appreciation of the depth to which we must be invested in meaningful practices of criticism. Criticism in word and deed can get traction almost anywhere, in respect of almost any practice. Yet in order to gain genuine purchase on our concepts and practices, we must reorient our relationship to these practices. If criticism is to be more than nonsense at worst and idle talk or posturing at best, then we must change how we live our practices.[70] At a superficial level this is an injunction against hypocrisy—if you would change practice *x*, you should change how you live in relation to it. Genuine contestation of, say, our practices of rights may circumstantially require that we not avail ourselves of the rights whose meaning we contest. (E.g., a critic who claims his or her own freedom of speech in order to argue against the same freedom for others displays both political naiveté and argumentative incompetence. Genuine criticism of such a freedom might call the critic's own standing as a speaker into question.) Yet at another level this is an observation about individual agency in relation to the social world. The individual is inexorably conditioned by the social world in and in respect of which she learns and uses the practices that shape her as an agent. Nonetheless, the actions of individual language-users are the life of these practices. Just as the individual is conditioned by the practices she enacts, her enactments shape the practices themselves.

Perhaps one of Wittgenstein's most profound statements (i.e., so obvious that it cries out for the saying) regarding both language and agency is, "If agreement were universal, we should be quite unacquainted with the concept of it."[71] This, one could say, is the seed from which the larger account of individual agency grows. Wittgenstein's and Oakeshott's accounts of language, practices and agency, premised as they are upon agreement and the manifestations of agreement, hold open spaces for meaningful, unexaggerated critical agency. Though they draw the boundaries more conservatively than some, they better map the "rough ground" on which individual critical agency gets its traction.[72]

CONCLUSION: PHILOSOPHY, AGENCY, AND CRITICISM

Progress in conversation requires the ability and willingness to hear what is being said in new ways, to attend to what is intimated in the familiar phrases and passages, and to explore those intimations beyond their immediate or most comfortable projections. In the conversation between Oakeshott and Wittgenstein there is much to be gained from attending to what have, until now, been recognized only as minor themes. The implications of new experiences of familiar utterances bear upon a wide spectrum of themes, and reshape not only conceptual pictures of agency and criticism, but also of the character of philosophy. Perhaps the most widely recognized point among those who hear a conversation between Oakeshott and Wittgenstein, even those who do not subscribe to the conservative reading, is a notable similarity between the two in respect of their understandings of the character and vocation of philosophy. The common ground is aptly summarized in Wittgenstein's claim that philosophy neither transforms the world nor gives it foundations, but rather describes the world, "leav[ing] everything as it is."[73] Oakeshott adds the insight that philosophy is but one idiom or voice in the conversation of humanity, and it is both a conceptual and practical error to suppose that one idiom or voice in a conversation is capable of guiding or subjugating all others without corrupting something essential to the engagement.[74] While their respective recognitions of the limits of philosophy are essential to their larger pictures of experience, thought, and conduct, this statement of limitation is sometimes mistakenly or exaggeratedly taken to be a fundamentally conservative position even by those who wish to minimize the implications of this conclusion. Oakeshott and Wittgenstein have been taken to claim, in effect, that philosophy *accepts* everything as it is, leaving nothing more to do after philosophical reflection than go back to the patterns of behavior that the community already manifests. Philosophy merely describes customs and conventions, and can gain no critical vantage point on them without falling into some form of nonsense. From such a conservative intellectual position, conservative political implications easily follow. As I have shown above, the step from a conservative reading of language and agency to a conservative stance regarding practice and criticism appears almost automatic.

Yet I have labored to demonstrate that Oakeshott and Wittgenstein in fact hold open the space for significant individual critical agency, as well as for philosophy to inform (if not so much as lead) such criticism. It is perhaps worth adding that, at the level of underlying intellectual disposition and philosophical style identified above, both share a Kantian critical sensibility. Both Oakeshott and Wittgenstein characterize the task of philosophy as the interrogation of the conditions of phenomena. Oakeshott viewed philosophy as a perspective on experience liberated from the fixations of historical, scientific, or practical modes of thought, the activity through which we explore the various "platforms of conditional understanding" that we occupy in thought and action.[75] Thus, philosophy is descriptive in the first instance. However, even though philosophy is not *in itself* a transformative practice of criticism, the understandings that result from philosophical reflection are available to inform critical thought and action. Similarly, Wittgenstein believed that philosophy aims at identifying and representing perspicuously the underlying conditions of phenomena.[76] Yet even though Wittgenstein, like Oakeshott, eschews the instrumentalization of philosophy to practical projects,[77] the insight philosophy provides changes us. The practical aim of philosophy is to "shew the fly the way out of the fly-bottle"—to show us the way out of conceptual pictures in which we become trapped.[78] While such realization is not itself practical transformation, philosophy undoubtedly furnishes individuals with resources that inform practice, even if only by describing more clearly the concepts, practices, and institutions with which we are dissatisfied, and which philosophy itself cannot change.

The characterizations of philosophy that emerge in the conversation between Oakeshott and Wittgenstein dovetail with their characterizations of agency and practices of criticism. To say that philosophy is inquiry into conditions and leaves everything as it is denies to philosophy the unmoored, radical potency to reshape the world by guiding praxis from a sovereign standpoint.[79] Yet taking this position on philosophy entails nothing about the critical potency of individual agents who draw upon philosophical concepts and understanding. The capacities of individual agents to run against the currents of their communities are, one could say, inherent in the very practices that structure the ways of living that are common to any community. Philosophy can describe this situated picture of individual agency, leaving it as it found it, while nonetheless transforming our understanding of what we say and do in our ordinary practices of questioning, disputation, and resistance. As Oakeshott recognized, there need be no inconsistency between seeing clearly the conditions and limits of a phenomenon and dramatic action within that bounded scope.[80]

TWO

INDIVIDUALITY BETWEEN TRADITION AND CONTINGENCY

> But whatever role man undertakes to play, he always plays his own at the same time.
>
> —Michel de Montaigne, *Essays*

> But what about an individual human being? He no doubt has many properties which he shares with every other human being, and some he shares with a particular group of human beings. But . . . what is of supreme interest is just the uniqueness of this very person, the way in which he differs from any that ever came before him or will come after. His individuality, his unpredictability, his uniqueness.
>
> —Maurice O'Connor Drury, *The Danger of Words*

Michael Oakeshott's philosophical and political thought, especially from the 1950s onward, is profoundly individual-centered. Not only is his work formally or methodologically individualistic, as was discussed in the previous chapter in relation to the character of individual agency and action, it is also substantively or normatively individualistic in ways that bear more clearly and directly upon political theory and practice. In his works of the 1960s to the 1980s Oakeshott labors to provide a philosophical sketch of the individual, language-using agent, yet these works go a step farther and consider the cultivated character of such an agent, her individuality. This measured commitment is most readily visible in "The Masses in Representative Democracy" and *On Human Conduct*, where Oakeshott not only describes the self-enacting individual, but valorizes her. The concept of individuality maps descriptively onto the logical form and extension of individual agency—the individual is "what in doing [she] becomes" and in acting the individual enacts herself *as* an individual.[1] Action necessarily individuates; it comprises self-disclosure and self-enactment. Wittingly or not, the exercise of agency situates the individual in her own distinct place in the world. However, the concept of individuality maps normatively onto the pluralistic world of living, breathing agents, actual persons with their own experiences, attachments, aptitudes, thoughts, desires, and purposes. For Oakeshott, individuality is not a generic descriptor, necessarily and thus far equally applicable to all agents. The concept is a term of differentiation and evaluation which may be used to distinguish and evaluate persons. As he stated clearly in his later works, the cultivator and enjoyer of individuality is a virtuoso of agency, she who sounds the instrument of her intelligent embodiment from its lowest to highest registers. What Oakeshott values is neither nonconformity nor eccentricity, but reflective self-possession and pursuits of self-making.[2]

Oakeshott pictures the individual agent situated within sprawling networks of intersubjective practices which supply the languages of her self-enactments. Individuality does not signify the liberation or detachment of the agent from such networks or the conditions they impose, for, as I explored in the previous chapter, Oakeshott understands practices as instruments rather than tunes, arts rather than rituals. Individuality is characteristic of an agent who uses such practices in certain ways, exploring the intimations of natality and self-authorship they contain. In the context of moral and political thought, Oakeshott's treatment of individuality focuses our attention upon the individual agent as she is situated within an intersubjective context that both informs and conditions her actions. The purpose of this chapter is to explore Oakeshott's presentation of the agent, the situation in which she finds herself, and the ways in which she cultivates her individuality. Building upon the discussion of language and agency in the previous chapter, I shall consider Oakeshott's account of individuality and the conditions that both make it possible and provide its boundaries. The two central concepts in Oakeshott's later thought that account for this complex negotiation are *tradition*[3] and *contingency*. Even though Oakeshott has often been read as a champion of tradition, and thus often as an essentially conservative thinker, I wish to show that his understanding of tradition is more complex than it first appears. Though tradition is a central concern throughout his later writings, his treatment of tradition is formal and descriptive rather than normative or vocational. Tradition appears as a conditioning ground of individuality, which is the subject of normative treatment in philosophical as well as political terms.

Gaining a clearer view of Oakeshott's account of individuality as negotiation between tradition and contingency serves several purposes. First, it illuminates the individualistic underpinnings of Oakeshott's philosophical and political work, preparing the ground for the consideration, in the following chapter, of his account of the modern state and the modes of politics distinctive to it. Second, it draws Oakeshott into conversation with thinkers who have struggled to defend or assert tradition (broadly construed) against the alleged disenchantment and social disintegration of the modern age—a concern that Oakeshott, with some qualification, likewise shared. Contrasted with the work of Alasdair MacIntyre, Edward Shils, and Charles Taylor, Oakeshott appears as a committed yet complex individualist. His nuanced account of individuality recognizes the necessary conditioning ground of tradition, yet his wholehearted embrace of contingency in understanding and action casts tradition as a repository of resources to be intelligently used rather than as a collection of scripts or rituals to be followed or reproduced. Oakeshott's understandings of individuality, tradition, and contingency serve as cornerstones of his mature political thought, and are ineluctable themes in his contributions to the conversation of modern political thought.

The first section of this chapter sketches Oakeshott's presentation and analysis of the situation in which the individual necessarily finds herself, and which is thus the scene of agency and individuality. The second section explores the concept of tradition through the lenses of two general views. According to one view, tradition is not only a formal condition of individual agency, it is a substantive vocation to be embraced and pursued, a fixed star by which an individual's actions are guided. According to another view, which Oakeshott theorizes, tradition contains and conveys grammars of understanding and action, which individuals use to contingently enact themselves. The former view presents tradition as something to be preserved and defended against perversion and loss, whereas the latter presents tradition as a resource indispensable to agency and action, but not as a self-standing object of devotion and reverence. The third section explores Oakeshott's understanding of contingency, and thus of the individuality and freedom inherent in individual agency and action.

THE INDIVIDUAL IN HER SITUATION

Oakeshott's account of human conduct is, at bottom, an individualistic account whose fundamental terms revolve around the experience, understanding, and action of individual self-enacting agents. Although the terms in which Oakeshott elaborated his views evolved over the course of his career, there is a fundamental core of claims and insights that appear variously throughout the decades in which he developed his views.

As Oakeshott puts it most directly and vividly in *On Human Conduct*, "To be human and to be aware is to encounter only what is in some manner understood. Thus, it may be said that understanding is an unsought condition; we inexorably inhabit a world of intelligibles."[4] This perspective on the world of experience and human conduct is subsequently given an individualistic inflection. For Oakeshott, the individual encounters the world as a distinct self, a distinct locus of consciousness. It is the individual who is conscious of the world, the individual who makes sense of the world she encounters, and the individual who chooses her actions and utterances in respect of her own thoughts and desires. Yet the world that the individual encounters is not merely given, composed of immediate data, raw facts, or preconceptually intelligible objects. The individual's encounter with the world is active, rather than passive; an individual's understanding, and thus the world she experiences, is an "achievement in . . . reflective consciousness."[5] Everywhere the individual turns, she encounters a world of more or less intelligible objects, patterns, events, and qualities, imbued with meanings, significances, and histories *for her*.

Agency resides and action emerges within this context of individual understanding. In making sense of the world she encounters, the individual frames a situation, within which and with respect to which she chooses to act. Here Oakeshott's indebtedness to both Hobbes and Hegel manifests in a rich account of the contours of intelligent agency. The conscious agent is enmeshed in personal experience. The world, for her, is the world she understands and understands herself to encounter in her experience. The individual strives to make sense of this world, continuously constructing, inhabiting, and moving amongst "[t]emporary platforms of conditional understanding"[6] from which she gains her personal, contingent vantage points on an intelligible, significant world "composed not of 'things' but of 'meanings.'"[7] The conditionality of these points of repose in the activity of understanding consists partly in their tentativeness, imperfection, and openness to revision, and also partly in their personal quality, the fact that they are always the understandings of some individual, achieved by and for her, as the person she is, standing where and when she does.[8] In fashioning and inhabiting temporary platforms of conditional understanding, the individual cannot help but frame the world in terms related and responsive to her desires, purposes, and projects. As she arrives at judgments about the factual character and contents of the world, her attentions regularly shift to deliberations about what she desires and values and subsequently about how the world she encounters approximates or deviates from wished-for conditions she would see made actual.[9] By her present lights, she imagines conditions the world might contain in terms of their possibility and likelihood, their desirability, and the means by which they could be brought about. These engagements of practical reasoning culminate in an action chosen and intended to bring the actual world somewhat closer to some wished-for condition. Thus, from the engagements to understand the world, to the actions intelligently chosen to enact some change in it, Oakeshott emphasizes the individual. Thoughts and actions are always and everywhere those of some particular person in her particular circumstances. Oakeshott's emphasis upon individual agency and action follows from his most basic philosophical views regarding the human world and how we come to be aware of and inhabit it.

Despite this fundamental focus upon the individual, conscious agent, Oakeshott nonetheless thoughtfully acknowledges and explores the features of the individual's situation that are not merely reducible to the contents of her own mind. Every action must be understood in terms of the individual who performs it, and the situation within which she came to conceive of, choose, and enact it.[10] Yet the features of an individual's situation that are relevant to understanding and action are never merely or exhaustively of her own creation, nor are they merely subjectively her own. Oakeshott views the individual as situated within the frame of a personal understanding, but this standpoint is itself inseparable from intersubjective networks of concepts, artifacts, conventions, and the utterances and actions of other persons. In making sense of the world and choosing her self-enactment, an individual actively engages with a situation whose essential components include aggregations of utterances and actions of individuals like herself, which come to her as tangible echoes of human intelligence. The individual agent makes use of concepts and conventions that she has learned to use, and that are for her the "arts of agency" that make her self-disclosure and self-enactment possible in itself and intelligible to others.[11] Agents and their actions always inhabit an intersubjective context, stretching through past, present, and future.[12]

The situation that is an individual's context of action comprises many relevant features, some evanescent and shifting, others enduring and stable. Natal, emergent features might include the immediate events or utterances and actions of others that prompt the individual to action, or that shape her ongoing activities of making sense of the world and enacting herself within it. An earthquake shakes the building, prompting panic and endeavors to respond; an unknown individual cries for help, inviting a choice; another's gestures invite interpretation of the intentions they convey or obscure. Though such features may have profound and enduring consequences in the life of an individual, in themselves they are fleeting, and quickly become casualties of the march of time. However, many (and perhaps most) features of an individual's understood situation are enduring remnants of the past, however implicit these may be. Some remnants are merely private memories of previous experiences; the individual interprets the present in light of her recollections of past understandings and actions. Yet others are essentially intersubjective, possible only in virtue of the collected words and deeds of a plurality of persons. The concepts that an individual employs in making sense of the goings-on in her experience are almost always the bequest of those who went before, even if she uses these concepts in hitherto unprecedented circumstances, in response to dramatically new circumstances. Likewise, the practices that an individual draws upon as the arts and instruments of her intelligent self-enactment are enduring reifications of past expedients invented by individuals to cope with their circumstances. In much the way that "practice" is the Oakeshottian concept that best and most broadly captures the intersubjective conventions and artifacts that individuals make use of in deliberation and action, "tradition" is the concept that perhaps best identifies the dimension of temporality of these same things.[13] Oakeshott's concept of a practice, like Wittgenstein's concept of a language-game, identifies something that persists and recurs. Even though practices and language-games change over time, as individuals make various and often creative uses of them, there is no practice or language-game without some substantial measure of stability across time and circumstance. Individual agency presupposes intersubjective observance.

Stated summarily, Oakeshott characterizes the individual as a reflective, intelligent agent whose context of action is what she understands it to be. Yet this individualistic account is by no means solipsistic or atomistic (if this latter term implies that the individual may be detached from her context and entirely remain who and what she is). Agency is inseparable from practices that human beings have invented for themselves, and that endure over long periods of time as they are used and transmitted within and across human communities. Even in his most individualistic moments, in his highest praises of individuality and most rigorous theorization and defense of individual agency, Oakeshott recognizes the necessary grounds collected and transmitted in traditions. However, this necessity may be variously interpreted, and it is the burden of the next section to differentiate Oakeshott's interpretation from another that has its lively advocates, and with which his own has sometimes (incorrectly, to my mind) been associated.

TRADITION, ITS STATUS AND FUNCTION

Tradition is an elevated concept in moral and political thought. Like the concepts of freedom or virtue, tradition enjoys a distinctive gravity and is recognized in most of its employments as denoting a fundamental feature of the human condition. Blaise Pascal described tradition as "a second nature which destroys the first,"[14] thereby capturing a notion that Michel de Montaigne had explored extensively in his *Essays,* that Jean-Jacques Rousseau would use to depict the depravity and possible redemption of modern humanity, and that David Hume would make a central doctrine of his empiricist philosophy of mind. Whether in laudatory or critical idioms, Western moral and political thought acknowledges the profound ways in which tradition acts upon human beings. As Hannah Arendt observed, it is the peculiar fate of human beings that whatever touches their lives for a prolonged period is apt to become a condition of human life.[15] Tradition fits this claim by definition—tradition is that which repeatedly touches human life. From "Political Education" to *On Human Conduct,* Oakeshott echoes this sensibility in his own distinctive way. Yet caution is warranted in discerning the way in which he takes up this theme. I shall suggest that Oakeshott's embrace of tradition as a condition of agency is idiosyncratic, and does not match the modern doctrines more often associated with the label *traditionalism.* I shall especially strive to distinguish Oakeshott's view of tradition (as a generic term for the repository of intersubjective practices) from views that treat tradition as a robust way of life, a fabric of communal existence with a presumptive or ultimate existential or moral standing of its own. It will thus become clear that Oakeshott views tradition as an indispensable yet imperfect and porous foundation for individual agency and individuality.

Tradition as the Present Past

Both views of tradition—Oakeshott's and the stronger view from which I shall distinguish it—purport to describe roughly the same features of life *inter homines.* Edward Shils provides a robust and inclusive statement of what the term tradition captures:

> Tradition . . . in its barest, most elementary sense . . . means simply a *traditum*; it is anything which is transmitted or handed down from the past to the present. . . . The decisive criterion is that, having been created through human actions, through thought and imagination, it is handed down from one generation to the next. . . . Tradition . . . includes material objects, beliefs about all sorts of things, images of person and events, practices and institutions. . . . It is the past in the present but it is as much part of the present as any very recent innovation. . . . [It is] that which has exemplars or custodians.[16]

Although the components of tradition may be clearly and rigidly specified and fixed, there is an essential indeterminacy and open-texture to what may constitute tradition and how it may be transmitted. Norms of social etiquette, the recitation of certain words or performance of certain songs, physical structures, paintings, books, routes of travel, ways of seeing and thinking—all of these may acquire the character of tradition. The modes of transmission may vary as widely as the components transmitted. Yet, in all their variety, traditions share several common features.

The foremost is that every tradition is a human artifact. Raw features of the natural world are not traditions until and unless human intelligence and agency are somehow addressed to them. All instances of tradition are therefore echoes and imprints of past words and deeds carried into the present. Furthermore, artifacts become traditions if and when they endure through explicit or implicit observance. That is, tradition is a persistent object of habit and attention for some number of human beings, a recognized part of their way of life. Finally, insofar as tradition is a bequest from the past preserved in the present, tradition has a social, intersubjective dimension. An individual may have a personal disposition or a habit, but a tradition (properly understood) is a disposition or habit that obtains among a group of individuals, and that is observed and transmitted by them. Thus, the traditions of an association or community are habits of sociability and points of reference for collected identity. In all of its facets and functions, tradition is the present past, and its observance is both an individual performance and an intersubjective practice.

Yet this is a simple sketch of a robust concept. Defined in these terms, tradition is little more than a pattern or a vessel. Both trivial and salient customs fit this description, which leaves the normative dimension of tradition unspecified. Many traditionalists (both practical adherents and ideological crusaders) ascribe great normative weight to tradition and present shared customs as the essential bond that connects them as a community and orients the lives of individual practitioners toward a horizon of meaning and purpose.[17] Tradition thus appears as a way of life in itself, or as the foundation upon which any intelligible and coherent way of life must ultimately rest. While Oakeshott emphasizes and theorizes the importance of tradition, he nonetheless stops short of this strong, normative view and instead articulates a view of tradition that is individualistic yet takes the intersubjective dimension of custom and convention seriously.

Tradition as Vocation

The fact that the past persists into the present can be interpreted in many ways. Traditions can appear profoundly important. To members of religious congregations, for instance, or fraternal organizations, or ethnic communities, or social and political movements, traditions can be of fundamental cognitive, affective, and practical significance. They knit together a community of individuals according to shared beliefs, objects, and actions, which constellation orients the purpose and identity of the group. Tradition grounds not only a sense of history, of having predecessors from whom one has inherited *tradita*. Individual as well as collected observance of traditions can serve to shape and anchor present identity. Here, individual identity is wed to group identity; a way of life is oriented by a sense of participating in a larger pattern that is imbued with its own standing and value; that not only *is* observed, but *should* be. Tradition, taken in this way, is something like a vocation or calling, something to be embraced and pursued. In contemporary moral and political philosophy, tradition has been carefully elaborated in such terms by Alasdair MacIntyre and Charles Taylor. Notwithstanding the differences between them, they are among the most thoughtful theorists and advocates of a family of views that many more embrace unreflectively and inarticulately.

In this robust sense, tradition constitutes the essential social fabric of a community. The customs that a group of individuals share are intersubjective patterns of thought and conduct that give their assemblages of ideas, utterances, and actions the coherence of a way of life. The individual agent finds herself situated within a way of life, shared with others in meaningful and ineluctable ways. Her rootedness is deep and constitutive; the community, framed by its traditions, is the background against which she appears (even to herself) as an intelligent moral agent. According to MacIntyre,

> [W]e all approach our own circumstances as bearers of a particular social identity. I am someone's son or daughter, someone else's cousin or uncle; I am a citizen of this or that city, a member of this or that guild or profession; I belong to this clan, that tribe, this nation. Hence, what is good for me has to be the good of one who inhabits these roles. As such, I inherit from the past of my family, my city, my tribe, my nation a variety of debts, inheritances, rightful expectations, and obligations. These constitute the given of my life, my moral starting point. . . . I find myself part of a history and that is generally to say, whether I like it or not, whether I recognize it or not, one of the bearers of a tradition.[18]

The traditions in which individuals are necessarily situated are various and complex, rather than monolithic. Each individual is rooted in a variety of overlapping and cross-cutting traditions (e.g., of a family, a church, an ethnic group), some of which may reinforce one another, others of which may stand in tension with one another, or which may even harbor tension within themselves.[19] Yet these traditions are the given context in which the individual appears, to herself and to others, as an agent in the proper sense. She articulates her identity and her agency through coming to embrace or reject, understand or misunderstand, the traditions into which she is thrown. In respect of the traditions in which agency is situated, "acting well is not a matter of making choices as an individual, but of recognizing the virtues internal" to the customs and conventions of one's community.[20] As MacIntyre presents the individual's relation to tradition, and thus her relation to other participants in these traditions, she is born already chosen and claimed as a bearer of certain traditions. Although he criticizes Edmund Burke's presentation of tradition, there is a significant patch of common ground.[21] Both characterize the individual as indebted to the traditions into which one is placed at birth. Traditions are not just past expedients the individual fortuitously inherits and may shake off without loss when she has the opportunity and inclination; rather, the customs into which she is thrown enjoy a normative standing of their own, beyond the claims of any individual who shares in them. Traditions not merely request observance and defense, they deserve it; traditions make claims upon individuals for which and to which the addressees are responsible.

Understood in this way, as the given (sentimental, practical, and intellectual) context in which the individual finds herself, and to which she is in some significant way obligated, tradition bears upon the substantive content and purpose of selfhood. An individual's self-awareness and agency necessarily take shape within and with respect to the context of her inherited customs. The resources furnished by traditions profoundly influence the individual as a thinking, judging, and acting being. In Charles Taylor's formulation,

> [L]iving within such strongly qualified horizons is constitutive of human agency. . . . To know who I am is a species of knowing where I stand. My identity is defined by the commitments and identifications which provide the frame or horizon within which I can try to determine from case to case what is good, or valuable, or what ought to be done, or what I endorse or oppose. In other words, it is the horizon within which I am capable of taking a stand.[22]

Although both MacIntyre and Taylor recognize agents (in the healthy, fully formed sense they respectively characterize here) as capable of arriving at novel interpretations and enacting themselves in ways that may challenge or destabilize the intersubjective context into which they have been thrown, they nonetheless emphasize the temporal, conceptual, and normative priority of traditions to the selves they variously shape. An individual may come to embrace and incorporate the features of her context, but she cannot choose it. Tradition is always first on the scene, both temporally and causally, and the individual is a creature of these traditions before she has either the capacity or the opportunity to call them into question. Not only did the traditions that claim the individual exist prior to her emergence on the human scene, the active identification with and understanding of one's traditions is a matter of self-awareness and agentic competency. Failure to recognize and subscribe to one's native traditions signifies that something has gone wrong, both empirically and normatively, something that ought to have been learned has gone unlearned or has been learned incorrectly.

Taylor understands traditions as among the chief features that give form and content to the moral horizons of the individual, which map and orient her within moral space. It is within this space that the individual comes to understand herself and what is of importance to her, drawing sense and purpose from her inheritance.[23] An individual who lacks this orientation is deprived of something fundamental and without substitute. MacIntyre likewise portrays the self and her constitutive relation to tradition in terms of being born into a preexisting and unfolding narrative of meaning, relation, purpose, and place: "[T]he story of my life is always embedded in the story of those communities from which I derive my identity. I am born with a past; and to try to cut myself off from that past . . . is to deform my present relationships."[24] According to this view, tradition calls to or claims the individual, announces both substantive features of identity and practical directions in which it must find its expression and fulfillment. The elements of tradition that bear upon individual identity

> are not characteristics that belong to human beings accidentally, to be stripped away in order to discover "the real me." They are part of my substance, defining partially at least and sometimes wholly my obligations and my duties. Individuals inherit a particular space within an interlocking set of social relationships; lacking this space, they are nobody, or at best a stranger or an outcast. To know oneself as such a social person is . . . to find oneself placed at a certain point on a journey with set goals; to move through life is to make progress—or to fail to make progress—toward a given end.[25]

The self-constituting dimensions of tradition, the ways in which they frame moral space and orient the individual within it, are naturally linked to normative, prescriptive dimensions. The inheritance of a way of life is, according to both MacIntyre and Taylor, inseparable from the inheritance of ways of reasoning, of understanding and evaluating possible courses of action, of inquiring into the right kind of life and how to achieve it. The *tradita* that claim the individual not only inform and condition her understanding of herself as a creature of wants and abilities (situating her, as it were, subjectively in moral space), they inform and condition her understanding of what is worthy of desire and pursuit (situating her objectively in moral space).

The constitutive view of tradition as a calling or vocation ties past to future through the present nexus of an individual agent's life: "To be an adherent of a tradition is always to enact some further stage in the development of one's tradition."[26] Understanding a tradition is a lived, enacted engagement. One does not "know" the "principles" intimated by one's inherited traditions prior to or apart from participating in the way of life in which these principles are manifest.[27] There can be, in other words, no Cartesian detachment from the moral points of reference contained in tradition (a stance that both MacIntyre and Taylor take political liberalism to have reified into an overarching project).[28] This is not to say that an individual cannot take a critical stance against one's tradition; it is, rather, to insist that arriving at a critical rejection of or detachment from one's traditions means the loss of the orienting and supporting foundation upon which meaningful selfhood and agency rest. Proponents of tradition in this robust, constitutive sense have argued that modern societies overflow with dispossessed individuals, adrift in an atomistic culture that trades upon the notion that authenticity and purpose can be achieved only through rejection of inherited norms and identities, and the creation of a new self through explicit and self-chosen attachments.[29] Such a stance is, of course, possible, but its achievement is lamentable and its persistence is catastrophic.

The political valences of this constitutive view of tradition are familiar by now. In the famous articulation given it by Burke, tradition is presented as the prescriptive substance of individual and social identity. The true rights and obligations of individuals, their proper places in society, are codified in and communicated by the edifice of tradition, which links the living to the dead and the yet unborn.[30] Hegel and his Anglophone disciples gave the constitutive view of tradition a metaphysical and teleological orientation, interpreting individual identity and conduct as contributions to a larger process. In *Ethical Studies*, Bradley pictures the individual agent as a being whose personal frontiers are drawn negatively by the texture of the social organism of which she is a member. Individual identity is formed within this inherited context, and the horizons of intelligent agency are set by one's location and function within a social context of which one does not choose and from which one cannot coherently detach oneself. The concrete structures of this context that bear upon agents and their actions are the duties of their respective stations (be they high or low), which are expressed through the maxims, customs, and usages of a community's traditions. As Bradley quotes Hegel (twice, actually): "The wisest men of antiquity have therefore declared that wisdom and virtue consist in living in accordance with the customs of one's nation."[31] Some have interpreted Oakeshott as a synthesis of the Burkean and idealist strands of the constitutive view of tradition. More recently, a constitutive vision of tradition circulated in the so-called culture wars and the liberal-communitarian debates that occupied political theorists for nearly three decades, many of whose controversies continue to simmer under different descriptions.[32]

I should not like this schematic, simplified presentation of tradition understood and embraced as a vocation to obscure the breadth or plausibility of its appeal. What MacIntyre and Taylor discuss systematically and in the language of academic philosophy is intuitive and fundamental to multitudes of ordinary individuals. Persons who draw their senses of substantive identity, meaning, and purpose from the religious or ethnic traditions in which they participate are intimately familiar with what these philosophers describe. Political movements of conservative, sectarian, nationalist, and separatist varieties draw insensibly or explicitly upon the sense of necessary rootedness and vocational engagement that this constitutive view of tradition explores. There is much to be said in favor of such a view, regardless of the individual, social, and political expressions it may be given. Not the least of which is the perspicacity of its purchase on political and philosophical orthodoxy in the modern West, and its sensitivity to the experiential dimension of meaning and belonging. Yet its most articulate proponents have tended to present a simple dichotomy: either we embrace some constitutive view of tradition, or we surrender to atomism, disconnection, and disenchantment. This conclusion follows not from the recognition that traditions and what they contain supply invaluable resources that condition identity and agency, but from a particular way of characterizing these resources and their use. It is one thing to view the individual as situated in semantic and moral space that is significantly structured by traditions; it is quite another to view an intelligible, meaningful life as necessarily committed to the enjoyment and further development of an inherited way of life (as MacIntyre, for instance, suggests).

Oakeshott's view of tradition has often been misunderstood precisely because it has been associated (by both his defenders and his critics) with a constitutive view. J. C. Nyíri, for instance, attributes to Oakeshott (and Wittgenstein) the view that since "every judgment is necessarily embedded in traditions," it follows that "traditions cannot be judged," for there is no footing on which the immanent critic might stand.[33] Tradition becomes a sort of logical straightjacket, a tool that cannot be used to disassemble itself. Others, such as, J. G. A. Pocock have cast Oakeshott as a quasi-Burkean traditionalist without the cosmic pretensions,[34] while Paul Franco, Andrew

Gamble, and Hanna Pitkin have variously characterized Oakeshott's critique of rationalism as leaving room for little but uncritical "endorsement of whatever has emerged from traditions of behavior."[35] In short, many have regarded Oakeshott as a conservative defender of society's past and present arrangements against both change and rational criticism. In the previous chapter, I provided an argument against this view (be it held uncritically or not) drawn from Oakeshott's formal account of practices and agency. Here, I wish to advance the same cause along a different front, by way of elaborating his view of tradition. What I hope to show is that Oakeshott takes tradition seriously and shares common ground with MacIntyre and Taylor, but that he nonetheless offers a coherent alternative to the constitutive view they articulate.

Tradition as Language of Self-Enactment

Oakeshott's explicit treatment of tradition spans his work from the 1940s to his final mature works of the 1970s and 1980s. Much like his account of the individual in her situation more generally, his account of tradition developed in meaningful ways while retaining the same core claims and insights. In a number of postwar writings, his treatment of tradition is part of his response to the looming tendencies of rationalism in political and social thought which he perceived were subjugating "every department of intellectual activity [to] the sovereignty of technique."[36] Against the arid and reductionist character of rationalism, he turned to tradition as a descriptive and explanatory concept in the study of the politics and history of a society. Yet even in its earlier iterations, his characterization of tradition differs fundamentally from the sort of constitutive view just discussed.[37] Rather, it puts flesh on the bones of the account of individual agency explored in the previous chapter, and sketches the more robust network of intersubjective practices within which the individual, self-enacting agent is ineluctably situated.

The individual is, according to Oakeshott, always mired in the activity of understanding, of coming to make sense of her situation and of choosing how to act within it. Her life exhibits a Hobbesian restlessness and relentlessness, continuously encountering the world in experience, which is to say, in the engagements of understanding, deliberation, and action. Yet this exhibition and application of intelligence is not a given, and its form and content are neither matters of course nor unconditional. The agent is a historic being, furnished with particular arts of agency which are for her the grammars through which she addresses herself to an understood world in her thoughts, utterances, and deeds. Oakeshott's most developed and precise discussion of these arts comes in his account of practices in *On Human Conduct*, where he describes them as "languages of self-disclosure and self-enactment" that condition thought and action, but which are ultimately "instrument[s] to be played upon, not [tunes] to be played."[38] In choosing and doing, agents employ the practices they have learned and mastered, expressing themselves through the adverbial medium of a language of agency. With respect to this account of agency and its conditions, the concept of tradition describes perhaps the primary mode in which such arts or languages are transmitted and learned. As Oakeshott suggests,

> A human life is composed of performances, and each performance is a disclosure of a man's beliefs about himself and about the world and an exploit in self-enactment. He is what he becomes; he has a history but no "nature". . . . Being human is recognizing oneself to be related to others, not as parts of an organism are related, nor as members of a single, all-inclusive "society," but in virtue of participation in multiple understood relationships and in the enjoyment of understood, historic languages of feeling, sentiments, imaginings, fancies, desires, recognitions, moral and religious beliefs, intellectual and practical enterprises, customs, conventions, procedures, and practices.[39]

So conceived, the individual is the inheritor of and initiate into a conversation rather than a ritual or enterprise. Her intellectual and agentic maturation consists in joining an ongoing engagement of intersubjective address in which what is communicated is not simply a record of what has been thought and said and done, but the very languages in which human conduct has unfolded. Traditions are salient insofar as they are, as it were, repositories of such languages and the literatures of utterances and actions articulated in them.

In learning various arts of agency, an individual is not trained in the use of a "stock" of routines and rituals, but is rather initiated into the enjoyment of a "capital" that "has been accumulated over hundreds of years," that is, is never "fixed and finished," but grows and transforms through its creative use by individuals.[40] In this characterization, Oakeshott aims to offer an alternative to the image of tradition (or culture or civilization) as "a groove within which we are destined to grind out our helpless and unsatisfying lives," a rigid pattern to follow, or a static list of performances to reproduce.[41] Although the practices collected and conveyed in traditions serve to condition agency, to set circumstantial adverbial limits, they

> do not provide a single unambiguous norm. Perhaps, then, it is not too fanciful to say that what we receive from our "tradition" is a number of "intimations." Certainly, what we receive does

> not point in a single direction: there may be many messages, but no categorical injunction.[42]

This is a fluid, open-textured, creative characterization of tradition. The inheritances into which an individual agent is initiated are "flow[s] of sympathy" that she explores (perhaps unwittingly) in her various self-enactments.[43] Here Oakeshott's account of tradition resonates with that of Edward Shils, who claimed that "[t]radition is not the dead hand of the past but rather the hand of the gardener, which nourishes and elicits tendencies of judgment which would otherwise not be strong enough to emerge on their own. In this respect tradition is an encouragement to incipient individuality rather than its enemy."[44] An individual is, for instance, initiated into the traditional ways in which a certain historic group of persons makes and keeps promises, or expresses consent. In her inheritance of these traditions she learns contextual practices, and *how* and *when* she learns them undoubtedly shapes and conditions the range in which she can go on using them for herself.[45] Yet whereas Shils (like MacIntyre and Taylor) rests the realization of such individuality upon the "givenness" and "sacredness" of the principles, practices, and order of tradition, thus reintroducing a robustly vocational or constitutive dimension, Oakeshott's account of agency and of the realization of individuality in intelligent self-enactment embraces tradition as one ineluctable condition among many, which is neither given nor sacred and need not "elici[t] reverence and awe."[46] In learning how her elders make promises or express consent, the individual is not learning rituals to be observed, let alone revered. Though she may come to find value in tradition, she is not being drawn insensibly into the promises that her elders have already made, or to consent to what they have consented to merely by employing the resources she has inherited. Rather, she is learning a language in which she can and must and shall make her own promises, and decide and express her own consent. Whereas the constitutive view pictures the individual initiate as fenced in by an organic whole comprising traditions, Oakeshott pictures her as a learner who acquires capacities that point in novel directions, which lead away from the scene of initiation and toward horizons that are ineluctably her own.

This can all be understood as a finer description of the engagements of constructing and occupying temporary platforms of conditional understanding. Inherited traditions inevitably condition the individual's engagements to make sense of herself and her situation, and to enact herself in this context of understanding. At every moment, her identity and agency are bounded by the practices she has mastered, the language-games she has learned to play. She understands and acts in the idioms of particular practices, which are never merely her subjective creation, but have come to her by way of inherited traditions and her intercourse with other persons. This characterization of conditioned agency "does not reduce conduct to a process or impose upon it the character of a *mere* habit. Customs, principles, rules, etc. have no meaning except in relation to the choices and performances of agents; they are *used* in conduct" and do not produce or demand any particular performances.[47] In other words, individual agents stand in a hermeneutical relation to the traditions and practices they inherit and learn. Here, Oakeshott's thought bears an affinity to Friedrich Nietzsche's account of the willful, creative individual, an account that MacIntyre explicitly repudiates in his defense of tradition.

> Ultimately, the individual derives the values of his acts from himself; because he has to interpret in a quite individual way even the words he has inherited. His interpretation of a formula at least is personal, even if he does not create a formula: as an interpreter he is still creative.[48]

As Oakeshott variously claimed, from *Rationalism in Politics* to *On Human Conduct,* even the most robust, internally complete tradition must be understood by an individual agent in her understood situation; in availing herself of the practices she has learned, the individual interprets their contents in light of her own experiences, intellectual and agentic resources, and current circumstances. The true adept of a tradition draws upon its resources as one draws upon the grammatical structures of a natural language—the inheritance gives more or less determinate form to expressions and actions whose content, direction, and purpose they do not and cannot specify. What is more, this interpretive process is creative, with individual speakers and doers minutely and gradually transforming the very traditions and practices they "preserve" through continuing their use.[49]

At least two significant implications follow from this view of tradition, which present more starkly its contrast with the constitutive view. First, although Oakeshott recognizes individuals as the beneficiaries of an intersubjective bequest, he rejects characterizations of individuals as indebted to traditions. As he puts the point, comprehensively:

> [I]n order to recognize this various inheritance of practices in its proper character as a human achievement and as a condition of all human self-disclosure and self-enactment, we do not need to follow those who tell us that its author is Man and that its current repository is Society, who are tireless in inviting us to understand ourselves as debtors. . . . This so-called "social inheritance" is an accumulation of human understandings and is composed of the

> moral and prudential achievements of numberless individuals expressed in terms of rules and conditions which specify a multiplicity of particular practices. It is a collected, not a "collective" achievement. It can be enjoyed only in being understood and understood only in virtue of having been learned. . . . In short, the arts of agency are nowhere and never to be found save in the understandings of adepts[.][50]

Oakeshott acknowledges that traditions and the practices they collect "may differ in their dimensions, their complexity, and their density; they may range from a protocol to what may be called a 'way of life,'" but he nonetheless stops short of the constitutive view and articulates a fundamentally individualistic perspective on traditions and practices.[51] Even at its most profound, complex, and dense, a tradition "is neither fixed nor finished; it has no changeless centre to which understanding can anchor itself: there is no sovereign purpose to be perceived or invariable direction to be detected."[52] This is the fullest expression of the sense that a tradition is a capital to be understood, interpreted, and used individually rather than a stock of habits, rituals, and purposes to observe and pursue.

Second, although Oakeshott's view of tradition centers upon the individual and the uses she makes of the resources of the traditions and practices she has inherited, his perspective differs substantially from that of rational choice theories and their political expressions. Advocates of the constitutive view often characterize and criticize dominant varieties of political liberalism as relying upon "the ideal of the disengaged self, capable of objectifying not only the surrounding world but also his own emotions and inclinations, fears and compulsions," an "unencumbered self" whose identity and agency is prior to and wholly separable from the attachments into which he is born and the ends he pursues.[53] Whatever can be said about the felicity of this as a characterization of the work of John Rawls and other self-avowed political liberals, Oakeshott's view of agency, practices, and tradition clearly does not fit this description. Indeed, Oakeshott is if anything critical of the ways in which liberal political thought has tended to approach some of the most fundamental questions of political thought, not to mention political practice.[54] On his view, the individual agent is always situated within a context, many features of which are beyond her choice, but none of which are merely given. In thinking, deliberating, and acting, the agent draws upon inherited resources that condition but do not determine what she thinks, chooses, and does. Oakeshott thus presents an individualistic account that treads middle ground between a constitutive view of tradition and the alleged liberal view of the disengaged, atomistic, unencumbered self. The former he regards as smothering, while the latter he would agree is too arid to satisfy. Oakeshott's alternative is a genuinely distinctive voice in an ongoing conversation about the conditions that bear upon agency, and how they appear historically, socially, and politically.

The Many Aspects of Tradition?

Despite the appeal of Oakeshott's view of tradition, I feel neither justified nor inclined to claim that it mirrors what tradition "really is" in some independent, categorical sense. It is both more plausible and more consistent with his philosophical style to picture tradition, which is an artifact of human intelligence and agency, as itself responsive to human intelligence and agency. In language offered by Hilary Putnam, but with which I believe Oakeshott would concur in spirit:

> [A]ny choice of a conceptual scheme presupposes values, and the choice of a scheme for describing interpersonal relations and social facts . . . involves, among other things, one's *moral* values. One cannot choose a [conceptual] scheme which simply "copies" the facts, because *no* conceptual scheme is a mere "copy" of the world. The notion of truth itself depends for its content on our standards of rational acceptability, and these in turn rest upon and presuppose our values.[55]

We cannot identify the facts of the matter about tradition independently of the values we bring to this search for facts, and to the interpretation of them in their respective contexts. Hence, it is possible that MacIntyre, Taylor, and Oakeshott all have something insightful to say about tradition, although their accounts describe different aspects and their emphases respond to different values, and although these views are self-standing and are not merely partial glimpses of some totality or raw truth of tradition. MacIntyre's and Taylor's respective accounts reflect substantial valuations of tradition *in itself*, as an intersubjective, intergenerational artifact to be observed and preserved. Each recognizes to some extent the standing or worth of the individual, but they arrive at it by way of the traditions in which one participates. Oakeshott's account, however, reflects a greater valuation of agency. Traditions are meaningful and salient insofar as they provide conditioning ground against which intelligent self-enactment gains some of its traction. Both approaches to tradition are in their own ways coherent and compelling, and they need not be deeply or unrelentingly antagonistic. Yet while the constitutive view pictures tradition as something that must be lived, Oakeshott's account shows how tradition can, in nontrivial instances, be taken seriously without being taken constitutively.

CONTINGENCY, ITS STATUS AND FUNCTION

Though the imagery of practices and traditions as arts or languages of self-enactment renders the individual agent and her context in rich terms, Oakeshott's understanding of contingency completes his account of agents and their individuality. Where tradition signifies stable, regulative, and routinized features of human conduct and its conditions, contingency signifies chance and choice, the rupture of stability and fixity, and the emergence of the new and the singular. Accounts of Oakeshott as a traditionalist and a conservative correctly identify (though sometimes mischaracterize) his emphasis of tradition, yet these same accounts often electively neglect or underestimate the place of contingency in his philosophical and political thought. Many such readings have consequently neglected or underestimated Oakeshott's account of individuality, and its centrality to his view of agency and politics. I suggest that finding his place in the conversation of modern political thought requires that we consider the linkages and tensions between tradition and contingency, and the enactments of individuality that are possible where these two concepts meet.

Agency, Understanding, and Action

Oakeshott uses the concept of contingency to articulate and synthesize two fundamental features of agency and its conditions. First, the context of agency is always an individual's understood situation. Oakeshott explains that "[t]he starting-place of doing is a state of reflective consciousness, namely, the agent's own understanding of his situation, what it means to him."[56] Every instance or exercise of agency thus begins with an individual who has "an understanding of himself in terms of his wants and his powers and an understanding of the components of the world he inhabits" in respect of how he relates or stands to it.[57] This starting place of action is contingent in that it is not merely found or received; rather the individual must *make sense* of it and render an intelligible situation out of an "unrecognizable confusion of all that may be going on."[58] Throughout all stages of his career, Oakeshott was stringently critical of what Wilfrid Sellars termed the Myth of the Given—the belief in an immediate, raw, noninferential, pre-thought, or un-thought register of experience that penetrates individual consciousness and authoritatively commands or determines it.[59] Oakeshott argues that in making sense of the situation he encounters, the individual unavoidably adopts a fundamentally active, creative stance. The individual must think, judge, deliberate, and decide in order for there to be, for him, an understood situation within which and in response to which he enacts himself. An individual's context is thus contingent in the sense that it is, for him, constituted in the exercise of individual intelligence rather than delivered to him intuitively or immediately.

Traditions and practices are essential to the activities of understanding, insofar as they collect and communicate the languages in which individuals think, judge, deliberate, and act. There is a productive, yet undeniable tension at work. Traditions and practices provide measures of regularity and boundary against which understanding and agency get their traction. Concepts, theories, techniques, and languages are learned resources that somewhat abate the contingency of an individual's situation, giving him a tentative and conditional footing to stand upon moment to moment.[60] However, traditions and practices are not scripts to follow or rituals to reenact; they condition agency, understanding, and action without so much as determining them. The traditions and practices upon which an individual agent stands are themselves contingent artifacts that had to be fashioned, that are mortal, have their histories, are susceptible to change, and that exist only in the uses made of them by individuals by their own lights and in their own circumstances. Oakeshott insists that even practices "which have been expressly designed are not merely current 'patterns of conduct' of acknowledged utility or propriety; they are footprints left behind by agents responding to their emergent situations, footprints which are only somewhat less evanescent than then transactions in which they emerged."[61] In his emphasis upon contingency, Oakeshott not only denies "the Given" in the form of immediate intuitions, he likewise denies it in the form of immemorial or prescriptive traditions and practices. The languages in which individuals conduct the activities of understanding and self-enactment are themselves a contingent human bequest, the products of understandings and choices, subsequently inherited, learned, and used. Thus, viewed from any angle, agents and agency appear as paradigms of contingency even as they inhabit traditions and practices.

The second fundamental aspect of contingency is a philosophical elaboration upon the ordinary sense of the term: the goings-on that an individual encounters (be they impersonal objects and events, or the actions of other individuals) are contingent insofar as they could have been otherwise.[62] There are, of course, languages of description in which any object, event, or action could be characterized as *necessary* in the strong sense of the term, as a rigidly determined and inevitable step or culmination. Such necessity is familiar to many scientific and historical modes of thought, yet Oakeshott maintains a skeptical perspective on such intellectual dispositions, emphasizing instead the intellectual, explanatory stances of chance and choice. From his early theorization of the modalities of experience (according to which science and history are perspectives on experience, not its entirety) to that of platforms of conditional understanding (according to which historical and scientific propositions are conditional, and stand in a co-constitutive relationship to their objects), Oakeshott suggests that doctrines of necessity spring from a narrowness of mind, specifically the inability or unwillingness to recognize the conditionality of experience and understanding.

Thus far, there is an apparent affinity between this account of contingency and that developed by Richard Rorty, whose own account is influenced by his reception of Oakeshott. Nonetheless, Oakeshott's account is distinct and, I would suggest, richer. Rorty treats contingency as a feature of the human condition that is essentially mute (if not quite brute), the "sheer" anti-Given of "time and chance" to be iconoclastically recognized and tepidly embraced that we may lose our affection for the other Givens that have for so long bewitched us.[63] Oakeshott makes more of contingency than this. He embraces the concept of contingency as "instrument of understanding" that identifies continuity and relation while destabilizing the notions of necessity and teleology of which he is skeptical. The concept intimates and invites a general way of seeing, thinking, and understanding which both problematizes necessity and teleology, as well as a positive, constructive perspective on what is left in the wake of their departure from the human scene.

> [C]ontingency purports to be distinguished from all other kinds of significant relationship: from the sort of interdependence which the components of a teleological, an evolutionary, a mechanical, an organic, or other such process or system enjoy in virtue of the regularities which constitute the process or the structure which constitutes the system; from a relation of necessity; from a relation of cause and consequence; from functional dependence; from a relation of implication or entailment (like, "ought" implies "can").[64]

As Oakeshott tacitly acknowledges, contingency is one among many lenses through which one may view any particular state of affairs, and the others to which it may have something to be said in their favor. Yet only by viewing a state of affairs *inter homines* through the lens of contingency do we render it intelligible as *human conduct*, rather than as the continuation of some determined sequence or pattern. Notions of necessity mitigate and obscure the active dimensions of the human condition that Oakeshott seeks to valorize: that human beings are agents, that they are themselves complex, historic assemblages of understandings and actions, irreducible to the play of mechanistic, organic, genetic, or teleological causal forces.[65] The concept of contingency shifts the focal point of reflection upon the human condition from the allegedly given, necessary, and determined to the intelligent, the adventitious, and the chosen—or, one might say, from a world of objects to a world of meanings. Nonetheless, this world of meanings is itself a world of connections.

> A contingent relationship . . . is a sequential relationship of intelligent individual occurrences where what comes after is recognized to be conditional upon what went before, not merely because before and after cannot here be reversed, nor (of course) because what went before is recognized as a causal condition or because they are recognized to be functionally related, but because they "touch" and in touching identify themselves as belonging together and as composing an intelligible continuity of conditionally dependent occurrences.[66]

Every agent makes sense of the world she encounters, and in so doing constructs narratives of meanings and relations. Contingency identifies a style of such narrative, as it were, one that emphasizes the "contextual" relations of objects, event, agents, and actions such that their content, meaning, and significance are mutually constitutive.[67] Whereas a teleological narrative of an individual making a promise might describe agent and action in terms of the unfolding of a moral principle in history, and a mechanical, causal narrative of the same might describe agent and action in terms of a sequence of conditioning culminating in a trigger event, a contingent narrative would describe agent and action in terms of the ways in which the identity of the agent is related to her understood situation and a practice she has learned. In this narrative, her self-enactment is not the vessel through which something beyond herself moves. It is, rather, her intelligent, deliberate, meaningful response to a world that she understands in a certain way, a world in which she is conditioned by practices into which she has been initiated, and within whose languages she thinks and acts, but which never merely cause or determine what she thinks and does. Hence, Oakeshott's emphasis upon *contingency* is part and parcel of his emphasis upon agency and individuality. His account of tradition and practices reminds us of the ways in which agents, their understandings, and their actions are conditioned—rooted in an intersubjective world. Yet his account of contingency attenuates this conditioning relationship, reminding us of the sense in which human conduct (and thus the human condition) comprises enactments of intelligence, of which only genuine, actively thinking, self-authoring agents are capable.[68] As Oakeshott has it, "A sequence of contingently related occurrences is not a process in which there is room to manœuvre; it is wholly composed of manœuvrings in touch with one another."[69] The human condition is an ongoing conversation, comprising utterances and actions responding (in whole or in part) to other utterances and actions, and in such conversation the idioms of teleology, mechanism, and organism are out of place. Such instruments of understanding focus our attention upon a world intelligible to humans, but not a genuinely human world.

Freedom, Natality, and Individuality

Oakeshott situates his valorization of the individual agent within the conceptual frame of contingency, and central to the image of agency he celebrates is his rather unconventional account of freedom understood "not [as] 'free will' but [as] intelligence."[70] With respect to human agency and action, freedom "denotes a formal condition of all conduct recognized to be human," recognized to be "an expression or exhibition of intelligence."[71] Freedom is thus co-extensive with agency itself, signifying "the formal detachment of certain conditions that is intrinsic to agency" rather than some faculty of autonomy or some condition sporadically achieved in the circumstantial exercise of agency.[72] On Oakeshott's view, the agent is "free" insofar as she enacts herself in response to a world about which she has fashioned an understanding, employing practices that had to be learned and can only be used in virtue of being understood. Such freedom is only conceivable and consequential in a world of contingency, and it is implicitly disparaged or denied by theories that reduce action to behavior that is determined, whether organically, mechanically, or teleologically. Emphasizing the connection between freedom and contingency, Efraim Podoksik has characterized Oakeshott's theory of freedom as a theory of "recognized contingency" that "highlight[s] the significance of choice and deliberation in human action."[73] Considered prima facie in respect of its emphasis upon the inner life and intelligent choice of the individual, this view bears little resemblance to theories of so-called negative freedom, which define freedom in terms of the absence of certain external conditions (e.g., locked doors or restrictive laws backed by sanctions).[74] Rather, Oakeshott's view appears to resemble theories of so-called positive freedom, which emphasize the presence of certain internal conditions (e.g., self-mastery, autonomy) and their realization through action.

Yet Oakeshott self-consciously cultivates and maintains a middle ground, especially in his account of what he generally calls *civil* freedom.[75] He distances himself explicitly from the positive theories of freedom found in the works of Rousseau, Hegel, and Bosanquet, at least insofar as these thinkers cast freedom in teleological terms, and thus connect an agent's freedom with the realization of some normatively authoritative, independently describable ground, something that can be spoken of coherently in terms external and even opposed to the individual and her intelligent self-enactment. His account likewise differs from those that internalize this teleological dimension, and recast the same basic theory of positive freedom in terms of an agent's deepest motivations or truest purposes.[76] By treating freedom as a formal condition of human conduct, intrinsic to agency, Oakeshott avoids resting an account of freedom upon some empirically verifiable convergence between a passion, purpose, or principle and its circumstantial yet objectively correct expression. Instead, freedom is essential to action as such. The genuine agent is distinguished not by the possession or achievement of a "free will" or by the satisfaction of a "true self," but by her intelligence in deliberation and doing. Thus, freedom, in this sense, permits and even demands us to distinguish agency from mechanism or behavior, regardless of the complexity or simplicity of the historical or metaphysical framework in which these reductive concepts are placed.

However, when extended to human conduct within what Oakeshott calls civil association, his account of freedom takes on a more recognizable flavor. As he treats freedom as a formal feature of agency that manifests in the self-enactments of individuals, Oakeshott characterizes civil or political freedom in terms that comport generally (though eccentrically) with theories of negative freedom. Where he discusses civil or political freedom, it is in terms of conspicuous absences. First, while indeed civil freedom involves the availability of certain institutions and procedures (e.g., individual rights, equal protection under the law),[77] these are themselves so many instances or examples of the absence of "overwhelming concentrations of power, [which is] the most general condition of [civil] freedom, so general that all the other conditions may be seen to be comprised within it."[78] Thus, although civil freedom is not strictly identified with the absence of obstacles or of domination, it can only exist where agents enjoy social spaces not overly impeded or obstructed. Second, Oakeshott scrupulously maintains the distinction between any particular constitution of government (e.g., representative democracy), or any particular social purpose or project (e.g., self-government, or economic prosperity) and the condition of civil freedom. Civil freedom flows not from some identifiable common good, shared purpose or mode of collective action, but instead denotes the absence of any such overarching, collective good, purpose, or mode of action to which agency is subordinated, or in respect of which individual actions are organized and evaluated.[79]

In both its philosophical and civil inflections, freedom identifies a feature of intelligent agency that Oakeshott believes is both fundamental and valuable. Recognized and understood as an agent in the sense that Oakeshott describes, the individual appears as "not Adam, not Prometheus, but Proteus—a character distinguished from all others on account of his multiplicity and of his endless power of self-transformation."[80] Thrown into a world composed in the main of other agents, and the words and deeds collected in traditions and practices, agents are nonetheless perpetual beginners whose self-enactments are the articulation of a self whose identity and conduct is never reducible to what came before. Oakeshott elevates this image of the individual as a self-fashioning, yet conditioned agent, making it the centerpiece of his philosophical and political thought. Agency is, on this view, inseparable from both freedom and from virtuosity. Intelligent self-enactment consists in individual performances in the language of practices, and every such performance consists in casting off a mooring, and beginning an endeavor whose end is yet to be fashioned. Thus characterized, the individual is always in the middle of things, engaged in natal performances of understanding, self-reflection, and self-creation. Yet Oakeshott maintains a careful balance between commitment to individual agency and the dispositions to enjoy and explore it in self-enactment, on the one hand, and recognition of the conditioning grounds supplied by practices and tradition, on the other. In his rich description,

> The self here is a substantive personality, the outcome of an education, whose resources are collected in a self-understanding; and conduct is recognized as the adventure in which this cultivated self deploys its resources, discloses and enacts itself in response to its contingent situations and both acquires and confirms its autonomy. [Yet] the experience of this disposition [does not] imply the worship of nonconformity, a devotion to arbitrary so-called "self-expression," or a resolution to be different at all costs. The conduct it prompts is not composed of unconditional choices, and it does not require indifference to moral or prudential practices or aversion from any but self-made rules. It is composed of actions and utterances which reflect the contingent sentiments, affections, and beliefs this particular self has made its own, performed in its own subscriptions to practices whose resources it has made its own. The autonomy of such a self and the independence or originality of such conduct lies not at all in an unconcern for the conditions which specify the arts of agency.[81]

In his characterization of agency, Oakeshott maintains a distinction between the Protean individual and both the antinomian nonconformist and the Romantic worshipper of spontaneity and self-expression. The Protean individual is a conditioned, contextual being, whose understanding of her own conditions strike her as invitations to fashion herself, rather than as burdens to be lamented or evaded. This is Oakeshott's melding of tradition and contingency—what the former stabilizes is for the latter a point of departure.

What, then, is the individuality that Oakeshott valorizes? As the above passage indicates, it cannot be pure autonomy—unconditional self-determination, rational or otherwise. It likewise cannot be sovereign self-artistry—play beyond all rules or practices. The brand of individuality Oakeshott characterizes and praises is, rather, virtuosity in self-enactment. The agent attains individuality in coming to understand and explore the intimations of her present self, taken not as a radically self-produced identity nor as a blank canvas to be limitlessly embellished, but as a person with an intelligible history, yet without a nature. Her individuality consists in her self-aware exploration of the proposition that she is what in doing she becomes. It is this character whom Oakeshott praises both in itself, and in distinction to the characters he terms the individual *manqué* and the anti-individual.[82] Whereas the Protean individual manifests an abiding "disposition to cultivate the 'freedom' inherent in agency (and not to regret it),"[83] the individual *manqué* distrusts and despairs over her own agency, and the anti-individual seeks the displacement of this freedom (in herself and in others) through enterprises that elevate collective purposes and projects over those of mere individuals. The virtuoso of self-enactment understands herself pressed by tradition and circumstance, facing out into the abyss of contingency, promising a future and a self yet to be fashioned. Her virtuosity, her individuality, is inseparable from the manner in which she acknowledges and even embraces this situation. Where individuals *manqué* shrink and shudder, and anti-individuals cry with rage, Oakeshott imagines the Protean individual contented despite her lack of final repose.

There is, however, another dimension of individuality inherent in Oakeshott's account, but which is not given explicit formulation. In choosing the figure of Proteus as the emblem for the virtuoso of self-enactment, Oakeshott places self-making and unmaking at the heart of agency. The Protean image of agency and individuality, in the words of George Kateb, "cultivates a sense of individual infinitude; that is, a sense of one's inner ocean, of [every individual's] inexhaustible internal turbulent richness and unused powers."[84] There need be no conflict between such a description and Oakeshott's account of individuality situated between tradition and contingency. To call an individual's potential for self-enactment inexhaustible is not to suppose it to be unconditioned. Similarly, to speak of an agent's inner infinitude identifies a sense of as-yet-uncompleted self-understanding and self-enactment, rather than an affirmation of boundless and insuperable creative power. Individuality is, for Oakeshott, inseparable from exploring the intimations of a self that is conditioned but never determined, set upon and constrained by circumstance but intelligently and reflectively self-directed. An agent capable of such exploration and self-making may rightly be called "a world, an infinity, a being who is irreplaceable"[85] without supposing her to be only what she has independently and intentionally fashioned, an atom in a sea of other atoms. It is here, in this picture of individuality, that the importance to Oakeshott of both tradition and contingency is most starkly apparent. He offers a view of agency that, like his view of freedom, navigates a middle course between familiar extremes. To one side lie accounts of the individual as the emanation of super-individual networks of tradition, discourse, or power-relations, to the other lie accounts of the individual as radically autonomous or sovereignly self-generating. The latter Oakeshott regards as superhuman, and both conceptually and practically impossible; the former he regards as subhuman, inhuman, yet possible and often all too real. Only the agent who is what she understands herself to be and is what in doing she becomes, wrought in languages of agency she has inherited, mastered, and made her own, only she bears a fully human face. It is this individual whom Oakeshott praises and celebrates. In valorizing her, Oakeshott makes his most profound and enduring contributions to thought about agency and the individuals who live it.

THREE

IMAGINING THE MODERN STATE

> For by art is created that great Leviathan called a Commonwealth, or State (in Latin Civitas), which is but an artificial man, though of greater stature and strength than the natural, for whose protection and defence it was intended . . .
>
> —Thomas Hobbes, *Leviathan*

> [M]en are apt to make gods whose characters reflect what they believe to be their own.
>
> —Michael Oakeshott, *On Human Conduct*

Few of the thinkers to whom Oakeshott's works are indebted are identified by name, and fewer still earn explicit admiration or deference. Thomas Hobbes is a notable exception, who enjoys a degree of favorable distinction shared perhaps only with Michel de Montaigne. Oakeshott praises *Leviathan* as "the greatest, perhaps the sole, masterpiece of political philosophy written in the English language,"[1] and the culmination of his political thought in *On Human Conduct* is substantively shaped by his engagement with Hobbes (more so, I would suggest, than by Hegel or Burke or Hume).[2] Beyond satisfying an interest in intellectual lineage, reflection on this lasting impression provides a frame through which to approach Oakeshott's project of eliciting the character of the modern state, as well as several of the conclusions he reaches about this character.

The genius of *Leviathan*, Oakeshott suggests, is its "transposition of an abstract argument into the world of imagination."[3] It presents a theory of the state that conveys at one and the same time an account of its supposedly necessary logical structure and a rhetorically potent image of its genesis and instantiation. Yet imagination serves an explanatory as well as descriptive role in Hobbes's theory. In his emphasis on human will and artifice, Hobbes traces the origin of the state not only to the deliberate decisions of individuals, but to an imaginative outlook that stands behind these actions. The acts of will through which human beings create the state are the consequents of trains of mental discourse and deliberation, fueled and informed not only by the data of the senses but by the work of understanding and conceptualization that Hobbes calls imagination. Although the images in which imagination and understanding trade are first "begotten upon the organs of sense," the broad strokes of his account present the individual qua willful artificer as always already the individual qua imaginer.[4] Though the Leviathan is born of will, it is conceived in imagination.

Oakeshott learned from Hobbes a style of political thought, which profoundly informs the account of the "modern European state" that is the centerpiece of *On Human Conduct*.[5] The state is at once the artifact of deliberate human choices and the reflection or projection of an image.[6] In creating the modern state, individuals wrought an institutional embodiment of their understandings of themselves and their world, their hopes and their fears. A theory of the modern state is thus inextricably joined to an account of modern humanity's self-understandings, and accounts of actual states necessarily explore the circumstantial imaginations and strivings of particular collections of persons who sought their own reflections in their institutions. *On Human Conduct* could be read profitably as an analysis of how two very different ways of imagining the state took shape in the West. Oakeshott treats the history of the modern state as the history of a species of human artifact, wrought by human will. Though the actual forms that the state has taken since the Middle Ages have never been the mere institution of a blueprint—"Each was the outcome of human choices, but none was the product of a design"[7]—actual states are nonetheless artifacts whose character is ineluctably responsive to the philosophical, political, and moral imaginations from which they have in various ways sprung. His method, particularly in the third essay of *On Human Conduct*, is to treat conceptions of the state as "imaginative interpretation[s] of human existence," albeit within variously circumscribed ranges of concern, and with very palpable and significant consequences.[8] Thus, theories of the state are inseparable from (though not simple products of) understandings of the human condition. How individuals understand their own identities, predicaments, aspirations, and their relations to one another in respect of these features cannot but influence the form and matter of their political thought.[9] As Oakeshott laboriously argues in the first essay of *On Human Conduct*, understanding is the conscious (if not precisely causal) root of human conduct. The notion that the state is a creature of imagination, wrought by will, carries the sense that actual states are contingent, worldly approximations of imagined societies—that is, some group of individuals "whom chance or choice have brought together" striving to inhabit more or less completely some "common dream."[10] The character of the actual state is more or less responsive to the character of the dream that animates it, insofar as the imaginary through which the state is viewed continually shapes the practices through which it is maintained and modified. Imaginative interpretations of human existence condition the horizons of understanding which are the circumstantial horizons of conduct as well.

The forgoing is intended to provide an interpretive frame for Oakeshott's characterization of the modern state and to circumscribe our expectations of what we might find therein. The characterization crafted in *On Human Conduct* is among the most widely circulated elements of Oakeshott's political thought, though its circulation has not always been accompanied by perspicuous understanding. Reception of his reflections on the state has most often been mediated by ideological readings and commitments. Some readers have cast the fruits of *On Human Conduct* as a methodologically rarefied continuation of his allegedly conservative political thought (in respect of the work's theorization of authority and obligation), while others have received it as a rigorous statement of liberal political theory (in respect of its theorization of the rule of law, individuality, and freedom).[11] Both casts of mind bring into sharp relief salient features of Oakeshott's account of the state, such as its central concepts or conceptual limits, and thus render intellectual service. Yet with their insight comes significant myopia. Ideological or ideologically framed readings of Oakeshott's political thought tend to simplify or elide the more complex ways in which his account of the modern state is conversant with a wide range of political and philosophical perspectives. It is precisely this broader conversance that I wish to explore, and that I believe is facilitated by approaching Oakeshott's characterization of the state as a reflection on the imaginations that have expressly or insensibly shaped the worldly forms and fortunes of the modern state.

Representing Oakeshott's substantial work on the state, especially in *On Human Conduct*, as a careful study of complexly interwoven, imaginative views of individual agents, the nature of society, and the institution of the state opens it to a wider world of thought. When read as a reflection on the ways in which our images of the individual, society, and the state have been variously accommodated to one another, Oakeshott's theoretical narrative participates in larger conversations in twentieth-century political, social, and moral thought, beyond the strictures of "conservatism" and "liberalism." Rather than an ideological statement, his work appears (as I believe it was intended to appear) as a self-conscious contribution to an ongoing, critically reflective enterprise, which Hannah Arendt described as "think[ing] what we are doing."[12] Though Oakeshott's place in this endeavor is beyond the scope of any single work to map, and though other works have made overtures in such a direction, this chapter is a reading of Oakeshott's characterization of the modern state as it is conversant with the related reflections of three significant twentieth-century thinkers. In the first section that follows, I provide a sketch of Oakeshott's characterization of the individual, society, and the state. In the second, I consider the affinities between Oakeshott's characterization of the apparatus and projects of the modern state and Michel Foucault's analysis of the logic of modern state power. Section three considers Oakeshott's pluralistic vision of modern society in conversation with the related vision of Isaiah Berlin. Lastly, section four elicits the convergences and divergences between Oakeshott and Arendt regarding the nature of political life and the conditions and limits of political action.

THE STATE, BETWEEN PURPOSE AND PROCEDURE

The central task of Oakeshott's later political thought is to render the character of the modern state intelligible.[13] In *On Human Conduct*, this character study (which is by turns descriptive, normative, and even polemical) is framed in terms of two opposed animating ideals that have historically competed for the soul of the state, which he terms "enterprise association" and "civil association." His analysis is therefore conceptual, about the possible forms the modern state might take, though his conceptual treatment often appeals to or follows historical accounts of the partial realizations of the two opposing ideals in actual societies. Yet it is also informed by Oakeshott's reception of Hobbes. Ways of imagining the modern state are recognized as part and parcel of ways of imagining human conduct itself, and their force derives at least in part from how they comport with deeper convictions regarding individual identity and agency, and regarding the nature of the good that persons might or should enjoy either individually or together. The ideals of enterprise and civil association rest upon two different styles of imagining both transitory and enduring interactions between individual agents, suitably generalized to the level of society as a notional whole. However, tempered by his skeptical and pluralistic commitments, Oakeshott eschews the notion that any actual state could manifest either ideal purely and without exception. Actual states are as various and diverse as their artificers, and thus every actual state will exist somewhere between the ideal poles of civil and enterprise association, existing as an assemblage of dispositions composing a recognizable but never altogether unambiguous character.

Enterprise Association and the Teleocratic State

The ideals of enterprise association and civil association express distinct images of human conduct, and picture the state in terms drawn from these respective understandings of how a plurality of individual agents interact with one another. From the perspective of enterprise association, conduct *inter homines* is

> relationship in terms of the pursuit of some common purpose, some substantive condition of things to be jointly procured, or some common interest to be continuously satisfied. It is association not merely concerned with satisfying substantive wants, but in terms of substantive actions and utterances.[14]

Though enterprise associations may vary widely in terms of scale, the substantive conditions sought, the substantive actions required, the degree of completeness of the association, and the duration of the associative engagement, all such share a common character. It is a "'managerial' engagement" instrumental to the accomplishment of some *telos* shared (notionally or tangibly) by a community of agents.[15] Familiar examples of such associations are economic corporations, religious congregations, sports teams, charitable organizations, political parties, and professional guilds, and the variety of ready examples show this idiom of association to frequently be valuable and advantageous in practice.

Insofar as it models conduct between individual associates, the ideal of enterprise association entails a general view of those persons. When a group of individuals is imagined as a "community of wills" with a given *telos* as their common object, or as a "community of choices" instrumental to its realization, the identities of agents *as* associates are defined primarily in terms of the degrees to which their endowments, choices, and actions further the ends of the association. As the ends to be furthered are substantive conditions (such as the material prosperity of the corporation or the spiritual purity of the congregation), individual associates are recognized as persons whose choices serve or hinder the realization of these conditions, contributing to their provision and enjoyment, or detracting from them. When associated in these terms, individuals are subjected to a double feedback effect. Individual character and identity come to be defined, more or less deeply and exclusively, by one's participation in the enterprise. The individual takes onto herself, and has impressed upon her, the substantive identity of an enterpriser of a certain sort—a member of this team, or this church—and even if her identity comprises other dimensions as well, some significant portion of who and what she is becomes mediated by her identification with her place in a shared enterprise to pursue a common *telos*.[16] What is more, the demands of the enterprise tend to influence the associates' understandings of their own agency and its potential, desirable, and permissible uses. In a religious congregation whose *telos* is the purification of the will and redemption of the soul through subjection to the law of God, associates become accommodated to a view of their own agency and subjectivity that fits this end and the problematic from which it is deliverance.[17] Oakeshott sometimes refers to these effects in his discussions of the *personae* that individuals adopt as associates—yet, despite his keen appreciation of the centrality of self-understanding in the experience and conduct of the individual, he sometimes fails to appreciate the degree to which the person becomes assimilated to the *persona* in a more profound sense.[18] Nonetheless, all the elements are ready at hand in his account of understanding, agency, and association in *On Human Conduct*.

Oakeshott devotes considerable discussion to how the modern state has been imagined on analogy to an enterprise association, and thus as "a many united in respect of a common purpose."[19] At different times, under different circumstances, and with different ends in view, the modern state has been envisioned as a community of wills directed, more or less perfectly, toward the pursuit of substantive conditions to be enjoyed as a common good. In some incarnations, the state has been viewed as an essentially spiritual enterprise (e.g., Calvinist Geneva or the Massachusetts Bay Colony); in others, as an all-encompassing corporate endeavor to produce and enjoy material prosperity (which, on Oakeshott's reckoning, has taken both individualist [e.g., capitalist] and collectivist [e.g., socialist] forms). However, these are artifacts patterned from a common image of human association. Viewed on analogy to a common enterprise,

> [the] modern European state [is] understood as a corporate association[,] the office of its government [concerned with] the direction (and perhaps imposition) of a common substantive purpose or system of substantive purposes upon the association, [its] "law" [understood] as the rule-book of corporate association and therefore as rules related to the pursuit of the common purpose concerned, and [its] associates [recognized] as integral members of an association devoted to a common purpose, understood and understanding themselves as comrades in an undertaking.[20]

Oakeshott refers to a state fashioned after this pattern as "teleocratic, the management of a purposive concern" through the institutions and powers of the state.[21] The specific shapes that a state so conceived may take are as diverse as the enterprises that can capture human imagination and motivation, and most enterprises have sought their reflections in the state.

Civil Association and the Nomocratic State

Though Oakeshott treats the two images of the state fairly equally in his historical narrative of their geneses and fortunes, he devotes a far greater share of his theorizing to civil association than to enterprise association. There are, I believe, two complementary explanations for this fact, which provide a fuller sense of the scope and import of Oakeshott's theory. First, Oakeshott does not merely strive to "make clear the categorical distinction between [enterprise association and] civil association,"[22] but goes farther and actively advocates the superiority of civil association as an animating image for the state.[23] Though Oakeshott takes care to identify the poles between which the soul of the modern state is stretched, he is clearly not impartial regarding the choice between the two. One need only read a handful of pages from *On Human Conduct* or "The Masses in Representative Democracy" to surmise that Oakeshott believes that there are a variety of human goods that can only be achieved or sustained under the conditions of civil association.[24] Second, Oakeshott takes greater conceptual pains to theorize civil association because there are few analogs that might facilitate our understanding of this idiom of association apart from theories of the state itself. Thus, it seems that the burden of proving plausibility weighs more heavily upon civil association than enterprise association because its instances in human experience are fewer and its intuitive appeal is subsequently weaker.

Like the ideal of enterprise association, the ideal of civil association expresses a theory of agency and action, and is explored in terms of Oakeshott's account of intersubjective practices (discussed at length in the previous two chapters). A practice, he maintains, is "an instrument to be played upon, not a tune to be played," a set of adverbial considerations to be subscribed to in choosing and doing, rather than a list of substantive actions to perform or goods to achieve.[25] Whereas enterprise association is modeled on a robustly teleological image of action (undertaken for the sake of securing a certain end), civil association is modeled on a minimally teleological, "non-instrumental" or "moral" image of action (undertaken in a certain *manner*, irrespective of the substance of the action or the ends toward which it strives).[26] It is "association in terms of a practice" comprising adverbial rules that together constitute "a language of self-enactment" to which an individual can subscribe in any number of actions.[27] Agents so associated share a framework of rules that announce conditions to which they can all subscribe in their various chosen actions, yet which do not direct their substantive conduct. That is, civil associates stand related in terms of rule-articulated *manners* of acting (e.g., "justly," "civilly") but not in terms of the actions they perform (e.g., donating to a religious organization, or voting in an election) or the ends toward which these actions tend (e.g., the salvation of souls, or the victory of a certain set of policies). This is the image of a plurality of individuals associated in their subscription to a common set of rules, even though they might differ with respect to the enterprises they pursue as they subscribe to the rules.

The fundamental distinction at work here—between instrumental and noninstrumental rules and actions, from which the distinction between purposive and nonpurposive association is drawn—is one of the most difficult and contested aspects of Oakeshott's political thought. His claims that rules can be noninstrumental and that associations can subsequently be nonpurposive are simply beyond the credulity of many of his readers, and are often passed over quickly or flagged as a chief (and perhaps crippling) flaw in his theory.[28] Critics have suggested that Oakeshott rigidly reduces human association to the bare and impoverished terms of rule-abidingness or legality, or that he makes an unsustainable leap from the fact that every action is performed in some manner to the claim that individuals could stand associated purely in respect of the manners in which they perform widely divergent actions. It is not my purpose to adjudicate this dispute about Oakeshott's theory, in part because it will likely be unconvincing to partisans of enterprise association (particularly at the level of the state), and in part because I believe the dispute itself distracts from the deeper purpose of Oakeshott's account of civil association. His deeper purpose, I suggest, is to vindicate the possibility and desirability of a pluralistic society in relation to which the state stands as an apparatus of ruling and adjudication, rather than of purposive management.

Oakeshott's conviction that such an arrangement is possible, if only in partial and imperfect form, is rooted in his account of the individual agent as an intelligent, self-enacting practitioner. Building upon one of Oakeshott's own examples, one could say that the fact that a group of individuals may all speak the same natural language while pursuing widely different lifestyles and purposes in their utterances suggests the plausibility of a state that, as it were, is the keeper and enforcer of a social grammar, but that dictates few if any substantive expressions, let alone the purposes to be furthered by individual utterances.[29] For instance, just as individuals may deliver given utterances honestly or dishonestly, offer assistance respectfully or condescendingly, individuals may stand associated in their commitment to speak to one another honestly or act toward one another generously without thereby being united in the pursuit of "truth" or "the common good." Whereas Oakeshott presents enterprise associations as theoretically grounded, first and foremost, in an account of the ends of the enterprise (against which the contours of agency appear), he presents civil association as grounded upon the account of the individual agent that underlies it. As suggested above, enterprise associations tend to cut the image of the agent to fit the measure of the purposes to be pursued. The account of civil association, on the other hand, is grounded in a view of the intelligent, self-enacting agent whose paradigm image is "not Adam, not Prometheus, but Proteus—a character distinguished from all others on account of his multiplicity and of his endless power of self-transformation."[30] Indeed, it appears that Oakeshott's commitment to this view of agency is more profound and precious to him than the ideal of civil association itself. As David Mapel aptly suggests, the "defining aim of civil association is to express and protect the realization *by* 'agents' that they *are* 'agents,'" in precisely this Protean sense.[31] The exercise of agency by individuals is so fundamental and so valuable that "the state . . . ought to be conceived and conducted so as to protect and to foster individuality."[32] Oakeshott thus recommends civil association as the form that large-scale human association ought ideally to take in order for agents to be unobstructed and uncompromised by purposes not their own, and policies requiring them to cultivate some character not of their own choosing.

Imagined as civil association, the state is a chastened entity, though an indispensable one in respect of the framework of rules it maintains. Oakeshott recommends a *modus vivendi,* though not of the sort attributed (correctly or not) to Locke, Mill, or Rawls.[33] Civil association is not a framework for protecting natural rights, or for promoting utility or justice or any other alleged "first virtue of social institutions."[34] Oakeshott pictures a society of individual agents

> who are joined in no common purpose or engagement, who may be strangers to one another, the objects of whose loves are as various as themselves, and who may lack any . . . allegiance to one another . . . [but] that somewhat "watery" fidelity called civility.[35]

Beyond the wink toward an Aristotelian phrase, this description most clearly echoes Hobbes. Much like Hobbes, Oakeshott regards human plurality as a condition too fundamental and recalcitrant to be reduced via the state to a condition of unity focused upon one or several common enterprises. For both, though in suitably different terms, only a state that imposes rules but not ends comports with the fundamental character of the diverse agents out of whom or by whom it is composed. Giving comprehensive expression to what such a state excludes from its own interest and competence, Oakeshott says,

> Civil association is a moral [i.e., noninstrumental] condition; it is not concerned with the satisfaction of wants and with substantive outcomes but with the terms upon which the satisfaction of wants may be sought. . . . The terms of a practice of civility, then, are not conclusions inferred from the postulates of civil association, from theorems about the so-called natural conditions of human life, from theorems about the dispositions of human character, from theorems about contingent human wants, purposes, and imagined satisfactions, or from theorems about "social ideals" or so-called "real social conditions"; nor are they inferences from the norms of a current morality . . . or from those of a pretended *summum bonum civile* or "ideal justice."[36]

Such a state is neither the locus of the good life, nor the organizing or managing apparatus for its pursuit—instead, it is an authoritative institution which secures conditions that make any number of individually chosen good lives possible and generally compatible with one another, circumstantially affecting how individuals may seek them without claiming or directing the energies of agents for the purposes of "society," "the common good," or "the state" itself.[37]

Such a quasi-Hobbesian image of the state has been pejoratively described as a "zookeeper," whose function is to hold society and its members captive for the sake of the (thin and often unsatisfying or even dehumanizing) good that they crave but cannot see.[38] Indeed, this is a criticism often leveled at liberalism by those who desire richer notions of participatory citizenship and robust civic identity. If this criticism is meant as a reminder that a strictly imagined civil association fails to square with a number of other commonly held political and moral values, then it is well placed, and Oakeshott appears to agree even if he draws from it a somewhat different lesson. He never, in fact, claims that a state purely adhering to the description of civil association could altogether tame or displace the perennial human desires for robust community (whether these be good or bad in themselves), and he does not suggest that sustaining a state that approximates this image would be easy. Put mildly, the creation and maintenance of any such demands "a disciplined imagination" and the willingness to set aside from politics many of the most inspiring and demanding projects of which the human mind perennially dreams.[39] Such a state undoubtedly imposes a form of bondage to civil law, and demands that individuals build their respective towers of Babel for themselves, at a human scale, rather than make such obsessions the official policy and common end of an irreducibly pluralistic society.[40] Yet according to Oakeshott's vision it is the enterprise state that is the zookeeper, which manages the lives and substantive pursuits of captives to a project.[41] Civil association, at its best, forbids a certain class of (often incomparably appealing) pursuits at the macrolevel, whereas various iterations of the enterprise state resemble one another in that they tend to subordinate, discourage, or even forbid pursuits that do not contribute to the common enterprise.

Any assessment of these characterizations and their respective claims upon our imaginations would do well to recall how Oakeshott himself understood this opposition between two images of the state. The dueling images, in their various empirical instantiations or approximations, have rarely if ever won a conclusive or lasting victory. Instead, modern states are always stuck somewhere in the middle, and thus each actual state "may perhaps be understood as an unresolved tension between the two irreconcilable dispositions represented by" civil association and enterprise association.[42] The modern state, he suggests, walks a rope stretched between two poles. At different times and places, under the sway of the pressing contingencies of the day, actual states have found it more desirable, or perhaps irresistible, or simply more plausible to stumble toward one or the other. The tension between the two has, through historical development and intellectual fancy, become irreconcilable, with the two ideals meeting as antagonists.[43] Despite his occasional rhetorical excesses, which are liable to present civil association as realizable without admixture, his more considered analyses soberly counsel against such expectations. The fortunes of the modern state shall unfold (as they always have) *in medias res*, at the intersections of competing images, ideals, and practices. It is Oakeshott's recognition of this ineluctable feature of modern political theory and practice that situates him as a participant in many conversations, prepared and disposed to think across boundaries within which his interpreters have often fenced his ideas.

THE MODERN STATE IN HISTORY: GOVERNMENTALITY, BIOPOWER, AND ENTERPRISE

> The state is a practice. The state is inseparable from the set of practices by which the state actually became a way of governing, a way of doing things, and a way too of relating to government.
>
> —Michel Foucault, *Security, Territory, Population: Lectures at the Collège de France, 1977–1978*

> Each [image of the modern state] is an idiom of contingent human character known only in actions and utterances . . . each is a historic character and a character on the wing continuously exposed to modification in intercourse with the other.
>
> —Michael Oakeshott, *On Human Conduct*

Michael Oakeshott and Michel Foucault are not often read as thinkers with much in common. Certainly, when read through strongly ideological lenses, they could appear as little more than caricatures of one another: the former, for instance, valorizing Protean self-possession, the latter treating the individual as a "fictitious atom of an 'ideological' representation of society" "carefully fabricated" by techniques and discourses of power.[44] When the two are read as sharing intellectual ground, the commonalities are drawn quite narrowly, often highlighting just enough incidental affinity (whether meaningful or superficial) to make the gulf between them all the more apparent and its insurmountability all the more certain.[45] While their styles of thought indeed diverge in many ways, as often do the objects of their intellectual interest, their respective analyses of the modern state, its history and its character, bear far greater (and more consequential) affinities than Oakeshott's (and Foucault's) commentators have recognized.

In a series of related works from the 1950s to the 1980s, Oakeshott crafts his historical and conceptual narrative of the modern state, and the battle for its soul, reaching its ultimate formulation in the language of enterprise and civil association.[46] He describes the modern state as emerging from the collapse of medieval political and social institutions, and developing along two distinct but ultimately parallel trajectories. The newly emergent state became increasingly institutionally complex, developing an apparatus of government whose scope and power was without precedent. Coeval with the expansion of the state's administrative apparatus were struggles to harness the state to various and competing imaginative understandings of the human condition. Some envisioned the state as the custodian of a common enterprise, and called upon its apparatus of government to arrange society according to plans and techniques meant to optimize certain substantive conditions (though these varied widely from state to state, and from age to age). Oakeshott thus describes not only the emergence of the modern state as a new kind of institutional assemblage, operating at an unprecedented scale, he describes a "new political experience [of] 'State-life,'" and with it the emergence of new understandings of the logic and vocation of government, which have shaped the fortunes of actual states.[47]

In his writings and lectures of the 1970s, Michel Foucault traces similar (and at times the very same) historical developments, and his analyses of the modern state in terms of the institutional logics and practices of "discipline," "governmentality," and "bio-power" theorize concepts and practices that are at the heart of Oakeshott's account of the modern state. From the late Middle Ages to the twentieth century, the state has come to control a far more complex and effective apparatus of power than previously existed, and this apparatus has been joined to a variety of equally novel projects and enterprises.[48] Identifying and exploring the unrecognized affinities between Oakeshott's and Foucault's respective accounts of the modern state facilitates a better understanding of each, individually as well as in the conversation of modern political thought. Both analyze the modern state as a contingent constellation of ideas, practices, and concrete objects that has emerged in particular historical contexts. Both recognize the "apparatus" of the state to be more than a simple, transparent, self-announcing institutional edifice. Foucault's complex sense of the term as identifying an "ensemble consisting of discourses, institutions, architectural forms, regulatory decisions, laws, administrative measures, scientific statements, philosophical, moral, and philanthropic propositions" finds a fruitful interlocutor in Oakeshott's characterization of the state as a complex set of practices, comprising a heterogeneous ensemble of cultural, political, scientific, and (broadly) philosophical languages and literatures.[49] Both agree that the state is an ensemble of practices, and thus also are the dimensions and functions of its apparatus. Against this background understanding of the state, each engages in a form of "historical ontology," recognizing that even (or perhaps *especially*) the most foundational features of the human world are conditioned by and inextricable from our modes of conceptualization and practice.[50] Oakeshott (in his attempt to "understand [the state] in terms of its postulates") and Foucault (in his attempt to view the state as it appears deprived of, or at least distanced from, the discourses which naturalize it) adopt perspectives on the state (and thus on a focal point of modern political thought and practice) that are both critical and constructive, problematizing and pragmatic.[51] Eliciting points of methodological and substantial agreement between these unlikely interlocutors does not elide or mitigate the ways in which each might meaningfully critique and correct the other, yet approaching them as participants in a common conversation yields a more articulate understanding of the modern state than either offers in isolation.

The Modern State Apparatus

The modern state, as both Oakeshott and Foucault understand it, is a contingent phenomenon whose character took shape gradually through countless yet recognizable modifications of medieval social and political conditions. Though each offers a distinctive description of these conditions and their subsequent modifications, their accounts overlap substantially and informatively. Oakeshott describes the medieval state as a kind of "corporation aggregate," a community of persons whose relations to one another reflect a sense of natural or even divine order, "united in respect of a common substantive purpose."[52] Ruled by traditional authority wed to religious practices and the law of custom, the medieval state was most frequently understood as "a community with a teleology of its own into which that of the individual soul had been assimilated" and the activity of ruling was exercise of "custody [over] the material, moral, and spiritual welfare" of this community and its members.[53] Though it bore the impress of purposiveness, the medieval state had not yet become an enterprise association in the modern idiom. The discontinuity between the medieval and modern teleocratic state is partly a matter of the horizons of medieval political imagination and partly a matter of institutional capacity. On the one hand, "there was little in the appearance of a late medieval realm and the conduct of its ruler to evoke an interpretation of its character in either of the two most plausible idioms of corporate association, military or economic: it was too late for the one and too early for the other."[54] Though the welfare of the realm, variously understood, was the chief concern of ruling, the public pursuits of that welfare were imagined narrowly by modern standards. On the other hand, and perhaps more importantly, the medieval state was logistically incapable of exercising a more complete form of custody over the realm, its inhabitants, and its resources. Structured as a network of hereditary estates held together by a variety of loyalties and antagonisms, it was too loosely interconnected, and too poorly furnished both technically and technologically, to construct an expansive administrative apparatus.

According to Oakeshott, the emergence of the modern state from the constellation of medieval conditions came about by a variety of expedients enacted in response to local conditions (even if they were interpreted through cosmological lenses), and thus the exact path of development by which any particular modern state emerged may vary dramatically from that taken by others. However, the common theme that ushered in the age of modern states was the consolidation and innovation of powers in the hands of a sovereign administrative state.[55] While Oakeshott identifies this transformation in broad terms as the dusk of one epoch and the dawn of another, and Foucault theorizes some of its most subtle and consequential details, both grapple with the same developmental moment. The emergence of the modern state was coextensive with the articulation of an institutional apparatus, yet the apparatus itself grew along two intersecting and complementary axes. As the once traditional and scattered institutions of rule in the medieval state were consolidated into the framework of modern government, increasing its powers by way of addition and concentration, the institutional nodes and conduits through which its powers circulated multiplied, forming a sprawling yet increasingly dense and interconnected network through which the state operates.[56] Foucault most famously describes the simultaneous intensification and diffusion of state power, the centralization of its control and multiplication of its sites and modes of application, in his account of the modern disciplinary society in *Discipline and Punish*. With the crystallization of the modern state, the administration of justice through the legal code and its enforcement through punishment "shifted from the vengeance of the sovereign to the defence of society."[57] Accordingly, the uses of state power multiplied, dividing the overwhelming punitive force of sovereign violence upon subjects (focused spectacularly on the body of the condemned) into countless transactions between state and subject that secure the docility of the governed. The terrifying apotheosis of sovereign power in the figure of the monarch and the punishment meted out by his executioner was tamed, displaced (though not altogether eliminated) by the scientific and paternalistic figures of the prison warden, the school superintendent, the political economist, the physician, the psychiatrist, and the professional military officer. Whereas the medieval subject felt the heavy touch of the state infrequently yet unmistakably through the tax collector and the bailiff, the modern citizen (through what Foucault calls "the infinitely small of political power")[58] feels the lighter touch of the state with such frequency and ubiquity that it often goes either unnoticed or misunderstood.[59]

Foucault, like Oakeshott, finds the origins of these institutions comprising the outer reaches of the modern state apparatus in local expedients addressed to immediate, if perennial, problems—war, poverty, disease, famine, crime, madness. Yet the institutions themselves did not evolve entirely independently of one another. The rise of systematic, rationalistic social science and its various instruments of measurement, calculation, classification, and organization attended the development of modern disciplinary institutions. The fields of criminology, public health, psychiatry, political economy, pedagogy, and statistics were siblings insofar as they borrowed from and lent to one another intellectually as well as practically. Thus, their manifold resemblances in terms of both theoretical moorings and social applications come as no surprise to Foucault, who with rhetorical flourish asks: "Is it surprising that prisons resemble factories, schools, barracks, hospitals, which all resemble prisons?"[60] As components of the modern state apparatus, these institutions are distinct yet inseparable, ever more completely partitioning society into categories and individual cases yet at the same time totalizing society into a unified field to be known and managed.

Thus, both Oakeshott and Foucault identify the emergence of the modern state from the medieval state as a process of institutional transformations: from a ruler personified in the body of the sovereign to an increasingly impersonal apparatus of government; from a visible, yet impossibly distant focal point of sovereignty to a subtle dissolution of the spectacle of sovereignty, which replaces the majesty of the state with the omnipresence of its institutions, rules, and officials.[61] The growth of the modern state apparatus, and thus its possible uses, was inseparable from the broadening of the horizons of its imaginable, plausible uses.

Projects and Tactics of the Modern Enterprise State

As the modern state apparatus became more fully articulated and its growing capacities became better understood and more widely employed, political imagination apace grew. Though neither Oakeshott nor Foucault suppose that understandings and uses of the state are deterministic products of its institutional expansion and thickening, both recognize that medieval political thought and practice were meaningfully circumscribed by the limited capacities of the state itself. New capacities made thinkable and desirable new aspirations and projects. Yet Oakeshott and Foucault both reject simple, linear pictures of causation. The capacities of the state and the understandings of its possible and desirable uses developed together, as emergent, co-conditioning phenomena, with neither getting far ahead of the other. Thought and practice worked hand in hand, with new institutions both embodying and prompting new rationales for government. In their accounts of the imbricated and increasingly complex institutions and logics of government, Oakeshott and Foucault demonstrate the greatest degree of intellectual affinity, as they render bare the soul of the modern enterprise state, partly in service of description and partly in service of a normative critique.

Oakeshott describes the modern state as pulled between the conceptual poles of enterprise and civil association, and though he recommends the virtues of the latter over the former, he provides a detailed account of how the enterprise state has perennially tended to eclipse its antagonist in practice. As medieval conditions perished and individuals struggled (with more or less felicitous results) to make sense of and find satisfaction within a world in which communal orders and traditional certainties had been shaken or demolished, many looked to the ascendant state to secure the conditions conducive to such satisfaction.[62] Those who embraced the challenges and promises of Protean agency desired a government that would hold open the social spaces in which individuality could be cultivated and enjoyed, a state that would provide a (noninstrumental) framework of law addressing agents who are obliged to subscribe to its requirements in their chosen self-enactments. The modern state, imagined as civil association, could fruitfully avail itself of greater institutional complexity and administrative capacities, but the understandings of human agency and individuality from which it springs set conceptual limits to its employment as a managerial apparatus to shape society. A society of Protean individuals needs an authority to administer law, but has no use (and understandable distrust and even disdain) for a leader or manager.[63] Actual states have variously approximated such "civil" ideals, but since the Middle Ages the prevailing winds of Western political and social history have blown steadily at the back enterprise association.

As the modern state apparatus grew in complexity and reach, so too have the imagined projects that it was called upon to manage and promote.[64]

Though the ends to which the state might direct society vary as widely as human imagination can conceive, there are two broad classes of ends that have come to dominate in the history of the modern enterprise state. In one of its variations, arguably the first to emerge from the ashes of medieval feudalism and most directly indebted to those departed conditions, the enterprise state was essentially pastoral, its ends to promote the spiritual welfare and "*post mortem* salvation" of individuals and the worldly rectitude of communities bound together under divine order.[65] At a practical level the evolving modern state apparatus meshed well with pastoral enterprises. As Foucault notes, "[P]astoral power is an individualizing power. That is to say, it is true that the shepherd directs the whole flock, but he can really only direct it insofar as not a single sheep escapes him."[66] Even apart from the extremities of Calvinist Geneva or Puritan Massachusetts, history furnishes countless examples of the modern state serving pastoral enterprises to greater or lesser extents. Indeed, the pastoral ideal has never vanished altogether, and it continues to be the object of significant political mobilization throughout the world. However, according to both Oakeshott and Foucault, the most prevalent and characteristic end to which the modern enterprise state has been practically joined is not spiritual welfare, but economic productivity and prosperity. Rather than tend to society understood as the flock, the state has more and more come to manage society understood as the household, workshop, or market.[67]

Though the modern state apparatus emerged along with the distinctly modern enterprises to which it was joined, there are several turns of mind that trace the path the state has followed. Foucault argues that a decisive step was the conceptualization of society in terms of "territory" and "population," framing society as a composite of resources and a site of state intervention for their exploitation and management.[68] Although Foucault looks to the eighteenth century as the era in which territory and population displaced earlier notions of the realm and its subjects, Oakeshott traces its origin to the earlier, proto-scientific vision of Francis Bacon. As the earliest arrival of its kind, the Baconian ideal of the modern enterprise state mixed religious and scientific-economic idioms (though the latter were rudimentary by comparison to those that would emerge in the eighteenth century, from St. Simon[69] and the physiocrats). In the world viewed through Bacon's eyes "an immense vista of human improvement is opened up before us, and government (using and promoting the extension of every intimation of power to control and master men and things) is the chief agent in a pursuit of perfection" understood as the subjugation of a God-given reserve of resources.[70] Such perfection requires systematic, technical knowledge of the natural world and a state apparatus commensurate to the task of managing the productive forces of society for the sake of securing earthly prosperity. Viewed through the Baconian lens, the subjects of the state appear as themselves a kind of resource to be managed productively and efficiently—as a population about which knowledge can and must be continually acquired for the sake of optimally arranging its forces and outputs.[71]

With time, as earlier pastoral aspirations retreated into the sects and congregations of increasingly pluralistic societies, and the administrative apparatus of the state grew (often as the result of modern wars and the economic mobilization and centralization that attends them),[72] the scientific and economic dimensions of the Baconian vision were refined and their practical applications multiplied. Society, viewed as population, and thus as both a body of resources and a production/consumption engine, became the site of expansive intervention by the state. The increasingly rationalized, bureaucratized, technocratic state apparatus provided the tools with which to impose managerial measures in the name of prosperity and the conditions necessary to secure and enjoy it. With regard to the enterprise state, Oakeshott identifies the roots of what Foucault later describes as its outer limbs: the sociopolitical imaginary that envisions society as being, rather than merely having, an economy and envisions the state as the managerial apparatus to secure its optimal productivity, distribution, and consumption.[73]

Foucault's analysis puts a finer institutional point on the general drift Oakeshott discusses. The rise of the modern enterprise state in its numerous productivist idioms was coeval with the innovation of new disciplinary institutions, variously imbricated with the state but extending beyond it. In addition to their self-ascribed goals, institutions such as the school, the prison, and undoubtedly the factory—supported and regulated by the state, if not established and managed by it—multiplied the interventions to which the individual was subject, and which subtly shape, multiply, and direct her aptitudes and capacities.[74] Yet neither Oakeshott nor Foucault attributes this to the unfolding of a diabolical conspiracy. In response to perceived problems in society, the modern state gradually developed and maintained an institutional apparatus that partook of the logics and "knowledges" of the new human sciences.[75] Much as the hospital and the factory looked to statistics and social science to guide internal reforms aimed at dealing with immediate exigencies, the state drew upon the same intellectual fields to inform and direct its interventions into public health and political economy. Without any overarching plan to adopt a disciplinary model, the state and its institutions borrowed, pioneered, and disseminated techniques for intervening into society, defending it from itself as well as from external threat, steering it by myriad pressures and adjustments toward a newly imagined catalog of social necessities and desirabilities.

Although each of the human sciences left its imprint upon the nascent enterprise state, Foucault and Oakeshott variously suggest that political economy proved to be its indispensable master science, and it is because of the central role of political economy in the modern enterprise state that Foucault identifies its full dawn in the eighteenth century.[76] In respect of its concern with the capture, intensification, and management of the productive as well as destructive forces of society understood as a population, political economy generated a set of rationales and techniques to orient and guide the state apparatus. What Foucault calls "governmentality"—an ensemble of rationalized techniques of state intervention into society "which essentially bears on the population and calls upon and employs economic knowledge as an instrument"[77]—marks a developmental threshold for the modern state, the sign of its flowering into a distinctly modern, managerial, and custodial enterprise. In addition to the disciplinary practices and institutions that serve governmentality and its rationalization of society and economy, the conceptual locus of state power slowly shifted from the juridical power of prohibition and death toward what Foucault calls "biopower," power over biological life itself, its functions, maintenance, production, and reproduction.[78] Like disciplinary interventions into society, biopower affects the circulation of agents, actions, and concepts in society, arranging persons and things so as to maximize the ends of the population and the economy. Biopower, then, furnishes a distinctive idiom in which the enterprise state may be imagined and the realization of its ends may be sought. These Foucauldian themes are ultimately aspects (though tremendously consequential aspects) of what Oakeshott recognizes and criticizes as "rationalism." As a style of thought and guide to practice, rationalism "seeks to judge everything at the bar of human reason," understood in the disengaged, instrumentalizing sense that one finds in the work of Bacon, Descartes, Comte, and the natural and human sciences that are deeply indebted to them, and which have themselves supplied the logics of the disciplinary institutions so essential to the modern enterprise state.[79] The concern with managing life that increasingly underlies modern politics dovetails with the tendencies, in both science and philosophy, to reduce agency to terms of biology, genetics, or neuropsychology and thus reduce the individual to a composite of forces to be systematically studied, rationally understood, and practically optimized.[80]

Despite differences of emphasis and terminology, Oakeshott and Foucault arrive at strikingly similar conclusions in their analyses and diagnoses of the modern enterprise state. Under the sway of rationalism and governmentality the authority of the juridical sovereign is replaced with the "sovereignty of technique" managed and directed by technocrats; the image of the state as a noninstrumental apparatus of rule and adjudication gives way to the image of the state as a purposive apparatus for "arranging things so that this or that end may be achieved."[81] Here a fundamental antagonism between the enterprise state and civil association is readily apparent. Whereas civil association comprises individuals associated in respect of a framework of noninstrumental laws (whose authority is entirely independent of their circumstantial utility or approval), the economic idiom of the enterprise state pictures individuals as contributors to and consumers of a common stock of resources, and replaces civil authority with instrumental legitimacy inseparable from success in the pursuit of enterprises.[82] That is, the laws of the enterprise state are, at bottom, instrumental to a schedule of ends, which constitute the *telos* of state and society. In both its capitalist/individualist and socialist/collectivist idioms, the state became in ever greater measure the manager of an economy, whose laws must be fine-tuned to some authoritative, prudentially appealing understanding of what serves the economy, and thus the population.[83]

A Critical Conversation

While it would be naive to deny significant affinities between Oakeshott and Foucault, it would be careless to neglect truly their fundamental and formidable divergences. (However, viewed through the lens of conversation, this diversity of views is an asset rather than an obstacle.) Their diagnoses of the modern state and its problems intersect and overlap in striking and meaningful ways, even as the potential remedies they envision diverge sharply—though they are not, I suggest, unintelligible to one another. Starting from some points of affinity, charting several divergences will serve to articulate common ground as well as fruitful tensions, which might help us to appreciate better the insights of both Oakeshott and Foucault, and what they have to say to one another.

Oakeshott's mature political thought hinges upon his considered conviction that something has gone amiss in our understanding of the state, our imagination regarding its appropriate employment, and our subsequent political practices. In works of the 1940s and 1950s, Oakeshott diagnoses modern politics as given over to the hopes and follies of rationalism, abandoning the requisite (nondogmatic) skepticism on which politics thrive in favor of a Pelagian, perfectionist faith in the rationalized state and its transformative capacities.[84] In his later works, Oakeshott's diagnosis and criticism shifts toward a perceived conflation in modern politics of authority and power. *On Human Conduct* presents, among other things, a distinction between two images of the state cast in terms of two different understandings (or misunderstandings) of the concept of authority in politics: one which views authority as a quality of the state and law independent of the desirability of what these require of individuals, and another that views the authority of the state and law as derivative of the ends toward which they aim.[85] Many of the fundamental tensions between the civil and enterprise images of the state can be rendered in terms of understandings of authority, and Oakeshott believes that the civil image better respects the fundamental character of individual agents.

Foucault likewise presents a critical view of modern politics, one that shares a good deal with Oakeshott's, especially regarding the growth and mobilization of the state apparatus. However, Foucault theorizes a course of remedy radically different from Oakeshott's. Whereas the latter recommends the image of civil association and its attendant formal-procedural conception of political authority, the former believes that we have yet to liberate our political imagination from the figure of sovereignty. "We need to cut off the King's head" and abandon the juridical image of the state.[86] These divergent courses of remedy nevertheless spring from a common assessment: the modern state is, in its logic and its practices, an enterprise state. Neither thinker is nostalgic for the medieval state, but their visions look toward starkly different horizons. Oakeshott wishes to keep the juridical state, in a chastened, civil form. He thus embraces something resembling what Foucault calls a "liberal" state, a state stricken with and guided by a fear of too much government—or, more correctly for Oakeshott, fear of government of a certain character or ambition.[87] Foucault, quite to the contrary, wishes to abandon the modern state, as the seat of sovereignty and juridical authority.

Though there are deep differences between the normative horizons to which Oakeshott and Foucault would strive, we impoverish our understandings of each if we suppose that they merely contradict or talk past one another. While it is true that Oakeshott's political theory (in respect of its reliance upon a theory of the state) shares elements with the liberal view that Foucault criticizes, it should not be forgotten that Oakeshott was himself robustly critical of liberalism in terms that Foucault understood and shared. Both find deeply problematic the enterprise state which joins a legal framework to tasks of economic management in both their laissez-faire and centrally planned varieties (though only Oakeshott approaches both with the same measure of criticism). They likewise criticize common liberal assumptions about the character of the individual agent and the notional society ("naturally") comprising the aggregate of these individuals. Foucault goes to the length of claiming that the individual is a product of networks of discourses and practices such that the individual is little more than "a particular way of dividing up the multiplicity [of society] for a discipline [rather] than the raw material from which it is constructed."[88] This perspective on the conditions (indeed, the *production*) of agency assails the archetypal image of the individual that liberal thinkers developed from the seventeenth to the twentieth centuries. However, as I have argued in the previous chapters,

Oakeshott's characterization of agency complicates the very same atomistic liberal tradition—not by denying the primacy of the individual as an experiential and agentic node (if that is indeed what Foucault does), but by rendering a systematic account of the agent as a historic, embodied consciousness, ineluctably situated in intersubjective networks of practices. Within this network, the agent is still capable of freedom and individuality in a way that Foucault challenges and underestimates (though never exactly denies), but she is by no means the "unencumbered" or "disengaged" self that liberalism has allegedly theorized.[89] Hence, in both their characterizations of agency and their accounts of the governmentality of the modern (enterprise) state that bulks so large in lives of individuals, Oakeshott and Foucault articulate critical alternatives to dominant political imaginaries (liberal or otherwise).

Moreover, Foucault's thought supplies a corrective to one of the major deficiencies of Oakeshott's. In theorizing the modern state, the latter elides the functions of nonstate and infra-state institutions within and alongside the state apparatus. This lacuna appears to result, at least in part, from Oakeshott's analysis of enterprise association as an ideal more appropriate to nonstate and infra-state institutions (such as churches and business firms) than to the modern state. He attributes the ills and missteps of the modern state to its adoption of the wrong guiding ideal, perhaps borrowed from other institutions, rather than to a more complex interplay between the state apparatus and other institutions that simultaneously imitate and inform it. While Oakeshott may be forgiven for concentrating his attention upon competing visions of the state, his often myopic exclusion of external factors places serious limits upon his insight into modern political life. On this score Foucault appears to have the more robust view, at least of the relevant institutional terrain. While both thinkers explore the development of the modern state within a larger context of the genesis of modern institutions, Foucault constructs a more complex narrative of causal interconnection and institutional isomorphism.

> I don't want to say that the State isn't important; what I want to say is that relations of power, and hence the analysis that must be made of them, necessarily extend beyond the limits of the State. In two senses: first of all because the State, for all the omnipotence of its apparatuses, is far from being able to occupy the whole field of actual power relations, and further because the state can only operate on the basis of other, already existing power relations.[90]

Although he inveighs against the juridical state, and frequently looks beyond the state apparatus in his analyses of power, any account of modern social and political life must attend to the state and its complex interactions with other institutions. Thus, rather than portraying a stark choice between a civil ideal and an enterprise ideal, Foucault's account of the state depicts countless choices between institutional models that often blur into one another, mimic one another, and ultimately empower and constrain one another. Oakeshott's thought regarding the state can accommodate this richer descriptive, explanatory, and normative language, but not without loosening somewhat its grip upon the civil/enterprise binary. Such an accommodation might draw upon the treatment of the mutually constitutive antagonism between distinct modes of political imagination and practice in *The Politics of Faith & the Politics of Scepticism*, where two opposed visions of politics and the state are understood in terms of continual relationships of borrowing, tempting, competing, and rejecting. Civil association could be affirmed as the appropriate guiding ethos for the modern state without giving short shrift to the admixture of civil and enterprise ideals in actual states.

At the same time, Foucault's thought stands to benefit from conversation with Oakeshott's. Foucault's account of modern institutions is so encompassing that his appeals, in his later works, to individual practices of freedom and resistance tend to read as fleeting afterthoughts.[91] In treating the individual as an effect of discursive and institutional power relations, he portrays a subject who is too permeable and malleable to meaningfully assert herself against the context that has produced her.[92] His work unmasks so insurmountable an institutional edifice that there appears neither a plausible course of liberation from it, nor an agent capable of such a monumental task.[93] Alternatively, Oakeshott's account of agency theorizes an individual who is profoundly situated within intersubjective networks of practices (and their attendant relations of power), yet whose capacity for self-articulation and self-enactment is sufficiently (though never completely) independent of such networks to enable genuine resistance. The Protean individual is not a sovereign individual; her subjectivity and its transformations are not solely of her own devising. Yet she is no mere byproduct of classification and control. While Foucault perhaps offers the more compelling institutional analysis, Oakeshott offers the more compelling phenomenology of agency. As political thinkers, the two may still part company starkly, over issues highly salient to each, but there is much to be gained from appreciating the remarkable expanses of complementary ground they share.

Oakeshott ultimately believes in both the adequacy and the prudence of state-centric political theory and practice. For all the nuance of Oakeshott's characterization of the modern state, in both its main idioms, Foucault provides needful reminders and correctives to those who wish to keep the state at the heart of political theory. His analyses of discipline and governmentality blur lines that Oakeshott perhaps believes can be kept improbably clear between enterprise and civil association, and thus insist that we deepen further the analysis that *On Human Conduct* fruitfully begins. Yet Oakeshott's broader account of the emergence and horizons of the modern state reminds us that Foucault's analyses respond to a fairly narrow set of intellectual concerns, and should not be supposed to exhaust the historical, conceptual, or practical character of the modern state (or how the individual is situated within this evolving context). I mean to suggest that reading the two together should serve to enrich our appreciation of both, and thus our political imagination as well, whether we wish to retain the state or decapitate the sovereign.

E PLURIBUS PLURUM: BERLIN, OAKESHOTT, AND THE PLURALITY OF SOCIETY

> In the sum of the parts, there are only the parts . . .
>
> —Wallace Stevens, "On the Road Home"

That images of the state are inexorably animated by images of society is a fact lost on neither Oakeshott nor Foucault. The institutional apparatus of the modern state is addressed to society, its power is exerted upon and throughout society, and thus imagining the state and imagining society are unavoidably kindred activities. A view of the one finds a referent in a view of the other. Oakeshott's account of the modern state and his critique of enterprise association are inseparable from his image of modern societies as pluralistic collections (not collectives) of agents, capable of intelligently forming and pursuing their own diversely understood projects. Hence, a perspicuous understanding of his political thought cannot be had without a perspicuous understanding of his notion of human plurality and the character of its manifestations in modern societies. Many of Oakeshott's interpreters have recognized the importance of plurality, not only to his political thought, but to his philosophical and metaphilosophical vision.[94] Yet the dominant view has tended to be that Oakeshott's characterization of plurality and its implications for his political thought are to be found in his underlying or lingering philosophical idealism. Paul Franco, for instance, claims that Oakeshott's political thought is rooted in "an effort to grasp the nature of the wholeness or unity of experience more profoundly," while Richard Flathman sees Oakeshott's lingering idealist commitments as guiding "the most valuable parts of all his later thinking," including his understanding of plurality.[95]

Despite the undeniable traces of Oakeshott's early, strict idealism in his later political thought, I believe that giving too much weight to his early philosophical vocabulary and style distorts a significant feature of his later thought about society, and thus about the state and politics. Built upon his characterization of individual agents, Oakeshott's understanding of society (as articulated in *On Human Conduct*) again bears more substantial, consequential, and underappreciated affinities to Hobbes than to late-nineteenth and early-twentieth-century idealism. Society appears as a notional aggregate of individual agents drawn together contingently by dense networks of practices through which individuals (cannot but) enact (only) themselves. Subsequently, the impress of his early idealism on his later political thought is less profound than is often supposed. What is more, in virtue of this pluralistic view of society and his essentially agency-centered image of individual persons, I suggest that Oakeshott articulates (however tacitly) a variety of value pluralism meaningfully akin to that theorized by his contemporary Isaiah Berlin. Contrary to Franco's analysis—which distinguishes Oakeshott from and favors him over Berlin, largely through recourse to Oakeshott's earliest style of idealism—I mean to show that their pluralistic images of society bear substantial and consequential affinities. By sketching the expanse of ground they share, I hope to show that Oakeshott's late political thought pictures the plurality of society in terms that abandon the latent idealist impulse to treat plurality, in both the first and last instance, as a contingent quality of some more fundamental unity. Coming to better understand Oakeshott's pluralistic image of society also serves to elaborate the depth of and rationale for his preference for civil association, as well as his characterization of political activity within such a mode of association.

Berlin: The Plurality of Agents and of Ends

Given the nature of the affinity I wish to elicit between Berlin and Oakeshott, it would be apt to begin with Berlin's now famous view of plurality.

> [T]here are many different ends that men may seek and still be fully rational, fully men, capable of understanding each other and sympathizing and deriving light from each other. . . . Forms of life differ. Ends, moral principles, are many. . . . Values may easily clash within the breast of a single individual; and it does not follow that, if they do, some must be true and others false. . . . The notion of the perfect whole, the ultimate solution, in which all good things coexist, seems to me to be not merely unattainable—that is a truism—but conceptually incoherent. . . . Some among the Great Goods cannot live together. That is a conceptual truth. We are doomed to choose, and every choice may entail an irreparable loss.[96]

Stated differently, human beings and their cultures are inexorably individual. Their views of the higher and lower, the permitted and forbidden, the virtuous and vicious, the obligatory and the supererogatory, are not merely numerous and frequently divergent, they are fundamentally plural. Thus, whether across cultures or within the circumstantial deliberations of a single person, not all values are commensurable, they are neither reducible to a single currency that may be weighed and balanced on a single scale, nor are they susceptible to hierarchical ranking. Likewise, within the conceptual expanse of each value, such as liberty or equality, there exist a plurality of competing inflections and aspects, which are likewise often in tension and ultimately incommensurable.[97] Yet such values, and the tensions between them, are nonetheless genuine. Moral dilemmas and conflicts between goods are, in theory and in practice, ineluctable components of the human condition, of having and striving for ends, and of the use of practical reason as such.

Berlin's cognizance of value pluralism develops from his readings of the history of ideas, punctuated by the works of Niccolò Machiavelli, Giambattista Vico, and Johann Gottfried Herder.[98] In their distinctive ways, each posits a plurality of ends, which clamor to orient the dreams and conduct of persons and peoples, yet which reduce to no transcendent, a priori schedule applicable in all times and places. Whether by accident (e.g., Machiavelli) or by design (e.g., Herder), each presents a view of human conduct as continually framed and reframed by evolving, situated moral, religious and political practices, and imaginaries between (and within) which there can be no final or incontestable settlement. Berlin finds such accounts to be both conceptually compelling and validated by reflection on the history of moral and political thought and practice, and he finds the various monistic views which seek to unify this plurality (from pseudo-scientific consequentialism to doctrines of divine revelation) as prisoners of unattainable and incoherent ideals (however worthy or desirable their component values may be). Few views of the human condition could be more starkly opposed to the ethical spirit of the absolute idealism that the young Oakeshott described as his greatest influence.[99] One need only recall F. H. Bradley's holistic, organic characterization of the relation between the individual, the community, and the good to see the integrating, unifying treatment that British idealism often gave to the apparent plurality of human values and the agents to embrace them.[100] In both moral and political thought, late-nineteenth and early-twentieth-century idealism described as a single fabric what Berlin and his inspirations described as an intricate and irreducible patchwork.

This apparent tension between Berlin's image of plurality and the idealism that shaped Oakeshott's early work, as well as the tense and distant relations between the two in their professional and personal lives, has prompted interpreters to emphasize the points of divergence between the them. Though both were clearly opposed to prominent reductive trends in modern political and moral thought (which Berlin termed monism and Oakeshott termed rationalism), Franco's assessment is representative of the common view that Oakeshott's pluralism is rooted in his early philosophical idealism, which divides experience into modes, and strives to comprehend the unified totality of experience without arrest or modification. Though Oakeshott counsels the philosopher to be aware that no such unity will ever be achieved in thought or practice, the idea of such a unity ought to guide the philosophical enterprise and thus whatever such an enterprise has to say about morality and politics. If this is an accurate assessment of Oakeshott's mature views (and not simply the metaphilosophical framework of *Experience and Its Modes* [1933]), then Oakeshott would indeed appear opposed to Berlin at a fundamental level. The premises at the core of their moral and political visions ostensibly contradict one another—for the latter, plurality is the real and unity the illusory dream; for the former, plurality is the apparent and unity the reality that makes its appearance possible. If this be correct, then Berlin and Oakeshott could only find shared ground in moral and political thought in spite of their deepest commitments.

Yet I believe this interpretation of Oakeshott is incorrect, and would offer an alternative. I submit that the apparent wedge between Oakeshott and Berlin regarding the nature and depth of plurality is the product of a commonly adopted interpretive frame stipulating that Oakeshott's early idealism is the dispositive element in his later thought and thus reads his relationship to Berlin's account of plurality through the restrictive lens of his early idealist commitments. More is to be gained, and less unnecessarily discarded, by taking the final statements of Oakeshott's views in *On Human Conduct* as dispositive, and reading his lingering idealism through the lens of his final considered view. If one takes *On Human Conduct* as the primary evidence of Oakeshott's views, then Berlin and Oakeshott appear to espouse fundamentally similar understandings of the nature and depth of human plurality, and thus may be far more interesting and fruitful interlocutors than has thus far been appreciated.

Oakeshott: Individuality, Plurality, Society

Though its initial articulations may have been prompted or shaped by British conservative attitudes toward the postwar Labour Party, Oakeshott's theoretical account of "society" stands on its own feet. In his later works, his characterization of society, like his political theory, rests upon his theorization of individual agents and the intersubjective practices through which they conditionally associate. As both an embodied locus of agency and a substantive personality, an individual agent is conditioned (in both the limiting and enabling sense) by the myriad practices she has learned in her intercourse with other individuals, and which together form an agent's intersubjective grammar of understanding and action. In respect of sharing, using, and caring for assemblages of practices, individuals stand related in recognizable modes of association—from belonging to team or church, to working for the same business enterprise, to being citizens of the same state. Yet there is no mysticism in this process of aggregation, no point at which the collect*ed* practices or purposes of individuals become a genuinely collect*ive* entity.[101] Thus, for Oakeshott, society is properly a collection of individual agents and the practices and modes of association that contingently and conditionally articulate more or less dense networks of relations among them.

Starting from his view of agency, practices, and association, one can derive three significant conclusions about plurality and society in Oakeshott's later works.

First, plurality is the fundamental characteristic of human society. This conclusion follows from Oakeshott's account of agency and association as inexorably conditioned and mediated by practices, which serve as the lineaments that draw a collection of individuals together. Any notional collection of intelligent, self-enacting agents in respect of the understandings, imaginaries, and arts of agency that they (always imperfectly) share is fundamentally plural. There is and there "can be no unconditional human association such as the current use of the words 'social' and 'society' suggest" when they are used to identify an entity drawn together and associated comprehensively, naturally, or in terms of an organic substantive condition such as an alleged common good.[102] Every actual society is a complex tangle of practices and modes of association, which frequently pull in competing or opposed directions. Individuals are conditionally drawn together "in recognizing the conditions of some specific practice," some shared idiom of action that is for them a temporary island on a permanently unsettled sea of contingency.[103]

Second, there is no organic social whole, no entity comprising the "alleged totality of human relationships" that answers to the name "society."[104] Every society is a conditional collection of diverse individuals and the agentic capital they have inherited, preserved, and created in their endeavors of self-enactment. As I explored in the previous two chapters, the arts or languages of self-enactment that individuals have mastered and the countless uses they make of such resources compose intersubjective patterns in respect of which individuals stand related to and associated with one another—but there neither is nor can be perfect or complete attunement between any two individuals. This view of agents and association underlies

Oakeshott's rejection of organic or holistic images of society and humanity. Nevertheless, some of Oakeshott's interpreters have cast this late view in essentially idealist terms. Franco reads the later works as attempts to understand more richly the unity underlying the experience of plurality. Similarly, Efraim Podoksik attributes to Oakeshott's later works the view that "[m]odern society . . . is not and cannot be a whole. It is *perceived* as consisting of plurality of independent agents."[105] Like Franco, Podoksik finds in *On Human Conduct* variations on a persistent idealism tracing back to Oakeshott's early reception of Hegel and Bradley. Modern society *appears* pluralistic on account of our perhaps unavoidable abstractions in thought and experience, and an adequate philosophical understanding of society requires the surrender of all such abstractions.[106] Yet Oakeshott's characterization of society in *On Human Conduct* and contemporary works appears quite different, all but abandoning the style of organic or holistic idealism found in his early works. By 1975, and perhaps much earlier, Hobbes had mostly displaced Hegel and Bradley. Though Franco, Podoksik and even Flathman present Oakeshott's recognition of plurality as a legacy of his early idealist compartmentalization of experience into modes, I believe that he abandons the lingering traces of social holism, and with it go the views that the state is the social whole viewed from a partial perspective, and that the plurality of society finds its worth and coherence in underlying unity.[107] Oakeshott's admiration for Hobbes and his growing distaste for the enterprise state won out, leaving an individualistic understanding of plurality according to which "Man" and "Society" are at most shorthand expressions for the profusion of individual agents and their contingent practices and modes of association.

Third, Oakeshott's compound view of agency, practices, and society generates (perhaps unintentionally) a variety of value pluralism fundamentally akin to Berlin's. Beginning with his work of the 1940s, Oakeshott maintained that practices are the fluid medium in which human values are suspended, and thus that values are inseparable from the actions and forms of life in which they are imagined, expressed, contested, and pursued.[108] Berlin likewise came to such a conclusion, informed by his readings of Vico and Herder. Values find their life in the actions and understandings of individuals who are profoundly situated within intersubjective historical contexts. As society is a plurality of individuals conditionally and variously associated through complexes of practices, never shared totally and by all, value pluralism is an inherent feature of modern society. The "Great Goods" are not reconcilable within a single practice or way of life. The conceptual and practical media in which values live are inexorably plural, and thus our values themselves cannot but be plural as well. Although arrived at by a different path, and perhaps only incidentally, Oakeshott's value pluralism is far more like Berlin's than has been appreciated. Plurality of persons, practices, and values is a feature of the human condition, rather than a partial, arrested experience of it. As Hobbes argued in his characteristic idiom, Oakeshott and Berlin argued in their own: humanity comprises an ever-shifting plurality of persons, whose values are inseparable from their individual and collected ways of thinking and acting, and thus shall remain "as various as themselves."[109] By the publication of *On Human Conduct*, the earlier notion of a meaningful totality behind or above this plurality had faded.

Oakeshott's pluralistic account of society dovetails with his images of enterprise and civil association. Like Berlin, though perhaps more deliberately and systematically, Oakeshott argues that the different substantive ends sought by individuals represent different systems of value, often incommensurable to one another, and thus not susceptible to unification in a common enterprise. Thus, his endorsement of civil association as an image of the state is built, not upon an ideological commitment to a certain set of values (e.g., "life, liberty, and property") and policies or programs instrumental to them (e.g., a "free market"), but upon a theoretical commitment to the individuality and plurality of agents in whose thoughts and actions values take concrete form. This is, I believe, precisely why he does not seek to formulate a theory of justice, a scheme of indispensable rights, or a robust account of political life. In place of comprehensive normative ideals he offers a perspicuous account of agency in whose terms such visions might be articulated and judged.[110]

POLITICAL ACTIVITY AND CARE FOR PUBLIC THINGS

> One of the main tasks of philosophy is to show the limits of what at first sight seems limitless.
>
> —Maurice O'Connor Drury, *The Danger of Words*

Oakeshott situates a carefully circumscribed account of political activity within the contours of civil association and pluralistic society, and his understanding of political activity bears significant and illuminating affinities to Hannah Arendt.[111] In broadest terms, the two share avenues of intellectual concern and characteristics of intellectual disposition. Both are at times nostalgic and describe the condition of modern humanity as "marked by loss"[112] of conditions that were once enjoyed to a greater and more appropriate degree. Oakeshott regards the emergence of the modern enterprise state (especially in its economic inflections) as the displacement of the civil ideal,[113] while Arendt, as shall be illustrated below, narrates modernity in terms of the abandonment of political action in favor of material abundance. In analyzing and evaluating such loss, their respective projects are marked by nonideological conservatism that aims to sustain and conserve something valuable yet endangered in Western culture. Yet despite these dispositions, both valorize human creativity. What Arendt terms "natality" and Oakeshott terms "self-enactment" signify the fundamental character of human agency and action. Their respective accounts of political activity and its proper ends are to be found where these dispositions of thought converge, and their struggles to reconcile conservation and innovation often express a common sensibility.

Oakeshott and Arendt—to whom one could, with qualification, add Berlin and Foucault—are intently critical of the drift of modern political thought and practice. Each identifies a painful irony at the heart of the modern human condition: we experience "an alienation of ourselves from this world which we have made for ourselves."[114] Even as our scientific knowledge and technological capacities have transformed the material conditions of human society, often in distinctly salutary ways, our politics, and thus our capacities to shape and inhabit a shared world, have become comparatively impoverished. Oakeshott and Arendt both regard political activity, properly understood, as an intersubjective practice of caring for or tending to the conditions of a shared world, and juxtapose politics to the ever more prevalent and potent pseudopolitical activities of managing society understood as a substantive enterprise. Their attitudes of nostalgia, conservation, and creativity converge in their respective accounts of a reimagined, disciplined understanding of political activity which could liberate politics from the seductive but impoverishing and imperious idioms of economic management, moral perfection, spiritual salvation, or worldly conquest. Each writes as "a critic who works within a tradition while attempting to renegotiate its fundamental assumptions,"[115] appealing to intellectual resources that have fallen into neglect, disfavor, or misunderstanding, but suitably reimagining them for contemporary conditions.

In what follows, I place these two constructive critics of modern politics into conversation on two related themes. First, I consider the view that each articulates of politics as a self-consciously limited, yet indispensable, sphere of activity which cares for a public condition in respect of which individual agents are related as citizens. Second, I consider the critiques they offer of modern politics that have become ever more fixated on the management of (often economic) enterprises. Along the way I will have occasion to identify some of the substantial distinctions between their respective views, which render in stark relief the terms in which fruitful conversation between Oakeshott and Arendt can be sustained.

Politics and the Public Condition

The political theories of Oakeshott and Arendt are animated by a common, pluralistic sensibility. In Arendt's phrase, "men [*sic*], not Man, live on earth and inhabit the world. While all aspects of the human condition are somehow related to politics, this plurality is specifically *the* condition—not only the *conditio sine qua non*, but the *conditio per quam*—of all political life."[116] The human world comprises individual persons, irreducible to the species, to organic collectives or historical epochs, or to other natural or necessary orders, immanent or transcendent, each of whom is thrown into a world of others in which she must make sense of her surroundings and of herself, and must enact herself in light of her understanding and judgments.

Political activity is premised upon this fundamental, irreducible plurality. It is, in Oakeshott's phrase, "the activity of tending to the general arrangements of a set of people whom change or choice have brought together."[117] By way of their politics a plurality of persons deliberately, self-consciously gets on together, constructing and maintaining a mode of relationship. Yet not all activities that fashion or sustain a condition *inter homines* are properly, genuinely political. Rather, the activities of politics build and care for a common, public condition, understood narrowly, characterized so as to exclude some of the vastest tracts of human interest, which, though they stir our dreams and motivations, belong to something other than politics.[118] Oakeshott and Arendt both insist upon discipline of imagination and aspiration in the realm of politics. Individuals act politically when in word and deed they address themselves to one another in projects of fashioning and preserving a shared world that serves to both connect and separate them, drawing them into association as individuals, while systematically preserving their distinctiveness and plurality.[119] Although the precise character of this public condition differs for Oakeshott and Arendt, each sees politics as categorically distinguished from activities aimed at unifying plural individuals in the enjoyment of substantive moral, religious, or economic conditions. So imagined, politics denotes a public idiom of human relation and conduct that is at once chastened and of fundamental importance, and that, suitably practiced, is "as rare as it is excellent."[120]

Oakeshott situates his account of politics within his theory of civil association—an idiom of nonpurposive association that secures for individual agents conditions favorable to their chosen courses of self-enactment, but which does not endorse or impose any particular substantive condition or pattern upon them. Indeed, Oakeshott's so clearly favors this characterization of the modern state that he presents politics as activities almost exclusively peculiar to this mode of association. Individual agents stand as civil associates in respect of sharing practices of civility comprising adverbial rules articulated and condensed in an authoritative framework of law. This idiom of association relates individuals as practitioners of a noninstrumental practice, a grammar of agency consisting not of commands to follow, but of "prevailing winds which agents should take account of in sailing their several courses."[121] Individuals related as civil associates share a common, public condition—which Oakeshott terms *respublica*—but this condition is narrowly defined, amounting only to the assemblage of noninstrumental practices that are the terms of association. The legal system and its component rules are the central index or repository of these practices, but Oakeshott maintains that rules are never more than "abridgments" of the complete practices that are the languages in which agents intelligently enact themselves.[122] Thus, the *respublica* common to civil associates takes a determinate shape (like any system of law, convention, or language, it contains identifiable elements susceptible not only to understanding and use, but also to contestation and criticism), but neither defines, nor is itself,

> a common substantive purpose, interest, or 'good.'" . . . It is not a suppositious sum of all approved purposes, a purpose which remains when all competing purposes have cancelled one another, or one which represents a consensus or harmony of purposes from which discordant purposes have been excluded, or one upon which all of a majority of associates are agreed. . . . Nor is it a "policy" composed of "managerial" decisions and constituting a strategy or a tactic in terms of which a common purpose might be contingently pursued. . . . On the contrary, it is a manifold of rules and rule-like prescriptions to be subscribed to in all the enterprises and adventures in which the self-chosen satisfactions of agents may be sought.[123]

This is the image of the modern state as a *modus vivendi*, framed by a legal system that formalizes and adjudicates the noninstrumental practices that are the vernacular language common to a plurality of associates who need share only this authoritative framework.[124]

Oakeshott's noninstrumental vision of civil association sets the horizons for his chastened vision of politics:

> Politics is the activity of attending to the general arrangements of a collection of people who, in respect of their common recognition of a manner of attending to its arrangements, compose a single community. . . . [T]he form it takes . . . is the amendment of existing arrangements by exploring and pursuing what is intimated in them. The arrangements which constitute a society capable of political activity, whether they are customs or institutions or laws or diplomatic decisions, are at once coherent and incoherent; they compose a pattern and at the same time they

> intimate a sympathy for what does not fully appear. Political activity is the exploration of that sympathy.[125]

Although civil association is impossible among persons who fail to recognize an adverbial, rule-articulated mode of relationship, no legal system or civil practice is exhaustive or fully reducible to technical formulation. Much as civil association comprises a plurality of individuals, the framework in respect of which they are associated comprises a plurality of practices, institutions, and the agentic resources these components intimate. The practices of civil association always draw upon a capital, a form of life that is actual and enjoyed, but susceptible to deeper understanding and further articulation. Political activity is the exploration, interpretation, contestation, and modification of this capital.

Yet the noninstrumental character that defines civil association limits the forms and directions that politics can properly take. Civil associates are related in terms of a system of adverbial practices, rather than in terms of a substantive religious, moral, or economic condition, and their politics are episodic activities "concerned with an imagined and wished-for condition of *respublica,* a condition in some respect different from its current condition and alleged to be more desirable."[126] That is, Oakeshott pictures the politics of civil association as conversation aimed at clarifying and modifying the terms of association itself, strictly distinguished from activities aimed at promoting or managing a substantive condition such as a moral or economic common good. So imagined, politics are "inherently intermittent activit[ies,] entail[ing] a disciplined imagination" rather than an ongoing plebiscitary or managerial engagements of choosing and pursuing social enterprises.[127] Politics properly understood are thus distinguished from perhaps the majority of activities and concerns commonly labeled political, and the infrequency of the activities Oakeshott describes is no indictment of the vision of politics he articulates. Indeed, his purpose is to illustrate and recommend an often neglected and compromised strain in modern political thought, rather than to sell a normative vision of justice, the common good, or policies instrumental to such ends. He asserts a chastened, pluralistic, modern idiom of politics against the enterprises that have gradually supplanted it in both imagination and practice. As Oakeshott does not suppose that his theory of civil association ever could manifest purely and completely in any modern society, it stands as a view of politics to be explored, rather than as a program or platform to be pursued. And while it no doubt aims to alter how we understand political activity, the object of change is first and foremost how we understand ourselves as agents associated one with another.[128]

Arendt's political theory is likewise chastened and narrowly imagined, insofar as it distinguishes politics properly understood from the many activities that illegitimately claim the title of politics. In Oakeshott's terms, Arendt envisions politics as properly addressed to the creation of and care for a noninstrumental public condition, rather than the management and enjoyment of substantive enterprises. However, whereas Oakeshott characterizes *respublica* in institutional, legalistic, practice-oriented terms, Arendt characterizes the public condition fashioned and maintained through political activity from a phenomenological standpoint. Politics, for Arendt, are not activities enacted through and with respect to certain practices (e.g., deliberation regarding proposed laws and policies), but activities that attain genuine public appearance, that can become the common spectacle, concern, and reality (literally, a common *phenomenon*) for a community of agents.[129] Thus, the public thing is not the practical framework shared by all associates, but what Arendt calls the *world*.

> The term "public" signifies the world itself, in so far as it is common to all of us and distinguished from our privately own place in it. This world, however, is not identical with the earth or with nature, as the limited space of movement of men and the general condition of organic life. It is related, rather, to the human artifact, the fabrication of human hands, as well as the affairs which go on among those who inhabit this man-made world together. To live together in the world means essentially that a world of things is between those who have it in common, as a table is located between those who sit around it; the world, like every in-between, relates and separates men at the same time.
>
> The public realm, as the common world, gathers us together and yet prevents us from falling over each other, so to speak.[130]

The world is thus importantly *contingent* and *relational*—an artifact that serves as the locus of a human community. Insofar as this world is artificial, it is a hard-won accomplishment, tenuously enjoyed, and in need of care if it is to remain shared by a plurality of individuals. Like any other human artifact, and indeed like ourselves, the world is impermanent and frail despite being durable. And insofar as the world is shared by this plurality, it makes a public realm possible, providing a common object of attention that mediates a mode of relationship in respect of its common enjoyment and care.

This account of the robust and ineluctable interrelationship between the world and political activity reveals the privileged place in human affairs that Arendt reserves for politics. As George Kateb traces this relation,

> *Freedom* and *worldliness* can serve as the terms that stand for what Arendt prizes most. She regularly connects them; she sees

> them as dependent on each other. Freedom exists only when men engage in political action. Political action can take place only where there is a common commitment to the reality, beauty, and sufficiency of the world[.] Political action looks to the creation or conservation or augmentation of a suitable world for itself . . . which is the scene and inspiration and source of meaning for political action. . . . [F]reedom and worldliness are the values that alone make life worth living.[131]

This description captures Arendt's valuation of the world, at which the previous passage hinted, and it identifies the essential and unbreakable connection between politics and the world. The world is both the home of politics, and its direct object. Politics makes a world and cares for a world, thereby fashioning a home for itself as the activity through which persons take on public appearance (and thus reality) to one another. As Arendt would have it, when we abandon proper concern for the world, we have not shifted the attention of our politics from the world to something else (e.g., the economy, or the immediate interests of our social class or religious congregation), rather we have abandoned politics for some other kind of activity. Hence, like Oakeshott, Arendt views politics not as an all-purpose mode of activity (e.g., walking or writing), which may be employed indifferently for the sake of any number of objectives (e.g., getting exercise or arriving at a particular destination; expressing one's love or concluding a financial contract), but rather as a mode of activity strictly connected to and limited by its exclusive object of concern. For Oakeshott, the object of politics is *respublica,* for Arendt it is the *world.* For each, politics requires a disciplined imagination, not only if individuals are to continue to enjoy the common condition politics constructs and preserves, but also if proper politics are not to be infiltrated or displaced by activities unsuitable to or parasitic upon the proper object of politics. Oakeshott drew the clearest line between politics and other activities that occupy the imaginations and days of individuals by claiming that politics are addressed to the condition of *respublica* (its content and what it requires of associates), distinguished from activities seeking the realization of substantive conditions or enterprises. As I considered above, this distinction rests upon two different kinds or visions of agency and action—enterprise association presupposes role-performance, whereas civil association presupposes intelligent self-enactment. Similarly, Arendt's distinction between politics and impostors to that title flows from her distinction between three different basic modes of human activity: labor, work, and action.

Labor is the most basic and evanescent of all that humans do. Natural (even when aided by artifacts such as tools) and private (even when undertaken in the company of others), labor serves only the reproduction of biological life. While division, collaboration, and mechanization might allow labor to yield a surplus by which the biological needs of many individuals may be satisfied through the efforts of a few, labor in itself "never 'produces' anything but life," which is likewise evanescent and must be constantly recreated.[132] In distinction from simultaneously and perpetually self-satisfying and self-defeating activity of labor, work is the activity by which individuals fabricate enduring artifacts. Like labor, work is essentially a private and individual activity.[133] The artisan translates her idea into a physical form privately, yet unlike labor, work creates an enduring object capable of appearance to others, and thus capable of the public existence that the products of labor cannot assume. Thus, in the Arendtian schema, the activity of work provides the necessary physical conditions of a common world: objects that can be publicly beheld and that can thus mediate a plurality of distinct persons. The third modality is action, the activity by which individuals "insert [themselves] into the human world" of common artifacts and affairs.[134] There are two great distinctions between action, on the one hand, and labor and work on the other. First, action consists in speech and performance enacted among others, for the sake of caring for the world that individual persons share. Whereas labor is exclusively private no matter how much it is aggregated, and work is essentially private even though it culminates in an object capable of public appearance, action is entirely and exclusively public, "the political activity par excellence," comprising word and deed among others addressed to a public and shared world.[135] Through action, individuals transcend nature by tending to the public artifact of the world, and reveal themselves as distinct persons, "show[ing] who and what they are, reveal[ing] actively their unique personal identities."[136] Second, because of the human discontinuity with nature that it underscores, and its exclusive concern with the public world shared by individual *agents* (rather than individuals as mere producers or members of a biological species), action introduces into the world the "miracle" of natality that Arendt terms freedom.[137] Through action, and its cultivation of and care for a public world that can live on as common object and narrative memory, individuals can achieve both the greatness and the transcendence of mortality that signifies freedom.[138]

As these brief accounts illustrate, Oakeshott and Arendt share several fundamental perspectives regarding the proper conceptual and practical domains of politics. Politics are narrowly defined yet autonomous activities that construct, shape, and maintain a public condition shared among a group of individuals. Both understand this condition (*respublica* for Oakeshott, *world* for Arendt) as, in Oakeshott's phrase, noninstrumental—and consequently "political action is not a means to some end or ends lying outside of itself, like protecting good men, saving souls, [or] insuring progress."[139] What is more, each characterizes politics as a mode of activity that is importantly individual yet also intersubjective. Politics consist of individual agents addressing one another in word and deed in respect of common practices and the public condition they share. Thus, political action (though it is always individual and singular, revealing and enacting persons as individual selves) never takes places in isolation. It is always activity *inter homines*.[140] Above all, Oakeshott and Arendt are prompted to articulate their disciplined images of politics by the sense they shared that "politics" were being broadened to include activities and concerns that human beings cannot get along without, but which do not deserve the title "political."

Nevertheless, substantial differences between their respective views limit how far conversation between them can go before encountering impasse. Though a close examination would yield several relevant distinctions, I shall note only two. First, although each theorizes and valorizes politics as activities in service of the construction, modification, and preservation of a public condition, they characterize this condition in markedly different ways. Arendt's *world* is undoubtedly a more robust and comprehensive condition than Oakeshott's *respublica*. The Arendtian world is both a common object of attention and care, and the common phenomenological space in which a plurality of individuals dwell, whereas Oakeshott's more narrowly characterizes *respublica* as a common normative framework in respect of which such a plurality adjusts their respective plans and actions. In conceiving of the public world in such normatively and existentially privileged terms, Arendt demonstrates her commitment to a civic republican or civic humanist idiom of political thought and practice.[141] The world that politics constructs and cares for is the privileged locus of human life, something without which individuals can enjoy mere life but not the good life. Despite some apparent republican motifs in Oakeshott's political thought, *respublica* is first and last a framework that structures a *modus vivendi* for an association of individuals signifying nothing so grand or profound as a common world that they understand themselves to inhabit. Thus, what one treats as the scene where the highest human potential is realized, the other treats as an artifact of fundamental yet bounded value that is in need of continuous (but not constant) maintenance.

Second, because they envision the objects of politics so differently, Oakeshott and Arendt differ markedly regarding the appropriate style politics ought to take. As has been the overarching theme of this chapter, Oakeshott's political theory is built upon a philosophical account of the individual agent, yet it culminates in a theory of the state. The *respublica* to which politics tends is the state, imagined as the framework of a civil association. Accordingly, politics are the activities that aim to modify or conserve this framework, and its component laws, practices, and institutions.

Thus, politics are activities that narrowly and self-consciously work upon the state, and Oakeshott's political theory is fundamentally state-centered. Arendt, however, articulates what is essentially a theory of the politics of the *polis*.[142] Though scrupulously limited in its domain, political action is categorically the highest form of human activity, aimed at cultivating the highest human achievement—freedom and the transcendence of mortality. Thus, Arendtian politics are a nostalgic gloss upon a classical republican commitment to the *polis* (which, in Arendt's terms, is often synonymous with the world) as the privileged center of human existence, the place in which individuals realize both their fullest humanity and their highest distinction and individuality.[143] Within her theory of politics the state might serve as the stage upon which the drama of politics is performed, or as a prop in such performance, but the inexorable trajectory of political action eclipses the formal-procedural *state* in favor of the phenomenological *world*.[144] Arendtian politics are animated by a *passion* that need not be (and perhaps, at best, ought not to be) present in Oakeshottian politics.[145] The former enable individuals to achieve freedom, greatness, and transcendence—the latter are "limited activit[ies], necessary but second-rate affair[s]," undoubtedly valuable but not the natural or highest fulfillment of the individual.[146] This contrast not only demonstrates the range of forms that a disciplined vision of politics might take, it also prompts an important qualification of Oakeshott's view of the state. While a theory of the state is the centerpiece of Oakeshott's political theory, his attachment to the state is sober, conditional, and skeptical. In addition to the distinction between civil and enterprise association that demonstrates his rejection of the state as a comprehensive mode of association, the account of *respublica* and the politics that cultivate it shows the Hobbesian inclinations of his later thought. The state is a framework in respect of which individuals enact themselves and cultivate individuality or whatever other idiosyncratic goods they value, insofar as these can be reconciled with the noninstrumental character of civil association.[147] The state is not the social totality viewed from a certain angle, it is not the comprehensive, unifying institution of a human community, nor is it an end in itself. The state merely conditions and facilitates certain individual pursuits. While they value the state differently, Oakeshott and Arendt are similarly inclined to recognize its limits.

The Social and the Displacement of Politics

In light of their disciplined views of political activity, Oakeshott and Arendt are in agreement that much of what passes for politics in modern societies is undeserving of the title. Both criticize and even lament the "instrumentalization of action and the degradation of politics into a means for something else."[148] Furthermore, they frequently trace the decline of politics to the same cause, namely the displacement of care for *respublica* or the world by the management of enterprises.

According to Oakeshott's characterization, the emergence of the modern state has been accompanied by the emergence of enterprises clamoring for the services of the state, further displacing the image and guiding ethos of civil association. The state has gradually bowed to the demands of economic prosperity, and modern politics have increasingly taken on a managerial, custodial character. Yet Oakeshott's disdain for these developments does not stem from an ideological commitment to "small government" or the "minimal state." It is precisely here that the terms *liberal* and *conservative* lead readers of Oakeshott to false starts and dead ends. The modern enterprise state earns criticism not because its institutional apparatus is too big or too intrusive, nor because it pursues the wrong policies (such centralized economic regulation and planning rather than the preservation of a free market). Instead, his criticism of the modern enterprise state ends where his theory of the state began: in his account of the individual agent. The imaginary that underlies the modern enterprise state views the individual through the lens of the collective project or purpose she serves.[149] Individuals are treated as less than agents, in the robust sense that Oakeshott champions; they are instead members of a class, or a race, or a nation, or they are sinners, or the faithful, or they are producers and consumers whose activities contribute to or detract from economic growth or prosperity. The modern enterprise state, regardless of its dominant idiom, earns Oakeshott's criticism because it mistakes a contingent dimension of human conduct for its very essence and imposes this image upon politics. The human proclivity for losing oneself in collective purposes and projects becomes the defining criterion of political activity.[150]

Arendt's diagnosis and critique of the drift of modern politics likewise trades in the imagery of displacement and imposition, rendered in terms of her three phenomenological categories of human activity. Genuine politics have suffered in modern times from the rise of what she terms *the social*. Insofar as Arendt's political thought valorizes action above all other modes of human conduct, and by extension elevates care for the *polis*/world over all other human concerns, the social signifies our manifold alienation from action and worldliness.[151] Labor has gradually transformed and displaced action, and care for the world has been eclipsed by "the rise of the "household" (*oika*) or of economic activities [which is] the form in which the fact of mutual dependence for the sake of life and nothing else assumes public significance."[152] Though Arendt finds this state of affairs profoundly disturbing, the first step, both logical and historical, in the process seemed a boon—the mitigation of the pains and toil of labor through rational organization and technological mechanization. However, the physical transformation of labor was accompanied by equally profound transformations in the character of human activities through their relation to labor and its ends.

> [I]n our world the seeming elimination of labor, as the painful effort to which all human life is bound, had first of all the consequence that work is now performed in the mode of laboring, and the products of work, objects for use, are consumed as though they were mere consumer goods. Similarly, the attempt to eliminate action because of its uncertainty and to save human affairs from their frailty by dealing with them as though they were or could be the planned products of human making has . . . resulted in channeling the human capacity for action, for beginning new and spontaneous processes which without men would never come into existence, into an attitude toward nature which up to the latest stage of the modern age had been one of exploring natural laws and fabricating objects out of natural material.[153]

To this diagnosis Oakeshott, Foucault, and Berlin could readily assent. The emergent logics and ends of labor grew into enterprises and ways of living that have interpenetrated and overgrown previous distinctions between domains of life and their values or ends. Here, Arendt recognizes at work the same fundamental forces that Oakeshott and Foucault identified in their genealogies of the modern state.

The confluence of changing circumstances and the rise of the social sciences transformed the language of politics from a language of action and freedom to a language of behavior and necessity.[154] Like Oakeshott, Arendt finds fault with the liberal as well as socialist embrace of political economy, and the practical and theoretical influence of Marxism. Yet she places great causal emphasis upon the French Revolution, which vindicated the notion that

> life is the highest good, and . . . the life process of society is the very center of human endeavor. Thus the role of revolution was no longer to liberate men from the oppression of their fellow men, let alone to found freedom [as in the American Revolution], but to liberate the life process of society from the fetters of scarcity so that it could swell into a stream of abundance. Not freedom but abundance became now the aim of revolution [and of whatever "politics" remain].[155]

Along with the influence of Marxism and the revolutions it informed, the French Revolution sounded the victory of labor over work and action.

Human activity was thereafter understood as serving the biological life process, which at the level of society is termed the economy. Prefiguring the discussions of the same by Oakeshott and Foucault, "What we traditionally call state and government gives place here to pure administration" whose supervision and execution was "put into the hands of experts" motivated and trained by the new social sciences and political ideologies.[156] The eclipse of freedom by necessity, and the public world by the national household, had the effect of displacing the agentic quality that both Oakeshott and Arendt privilege: individuality. The modern state, as the custodian of society and its projects, must interpret the conduct and identity of individuals in terms intelligible and susceptible to its knowledges and apparatus. As with any enterprise association, the modern state has come to value and require conformity—"for society always demands that its members act as though they were members of one enormous family which has only one opinion and one interest."[157] The social organism and the enterprise state have no need for individuality (whose value is inherent and self-justifying), though they crave and praise the instrumentally useful qualities of leadership and innovation. Truly individual tastes and pursuits too often create friction in the smooth processes of production and consumption, and genuine action introduces contingency and instability into systems that can understand only behavior and probable regularities. As has become still more apparent since Oakeshott and Arendt wrote, modern politics have, like the products of work, become assimilated to the character of labor and enterprise. Although their nostalgia for the days when politics were expressions of freedom and the state was a framework in which individuality could be cultivated may be largely convenient fictions, their criticisms of modern politics are none the weaker for it. As with any fruitful critique, theirs do not merely point to the failings of an opponent. Oakeshott and Arendt intimate alternatives, ways in which we and our world could be otherwise. Yet neither falls into utopianism by supposing that the alternative they recommend would be without cost, or would provide all that we truly need and want. We are presented with a choice of worlds, none of which is the best of all possible, but between which intelligent choices can nonetheless be made.

CONCLUSION: OAKESHOTT ON STATE, SOCIETY, AND POLITICS

Oakeshott's thought about the state, society, and politics places him in some of the richest and most fruitful fields of modern political thought. Though this chapter has explored only a few of the threads of conversation in which Oakeshott is at home—sometimes with unlikely interlocutors—it should be enough to demonstrate the breadth of his intellectual interest and reach. Like Hobbes, Oakeshott articulates a state-centered political theory, which is an attempt to make sense of human affairs in light of an image of the individual agent. The theory of the state explored in this chapter is, for Oakeshott, a series of implications and inferences drawn from the accounts of agents and agency explored in the previous two chapters. From two different images of agent and action, Oakeshott derived two different images of association that the modern state variously approximates. Between these two poles, the drama of modern politics continuously plays.

While the modern state comprises practices and institutions, it is in the first and last instance an idea. The institutions of which every actual state is composed, the practices through which it is articulated, the officials and functionaries who are its indispensable human components, all of these operate within the horizon set by ideas—images of the state, models according to which it is built and functions, laws and rules that govern its finest details, and concepts without which none of these other elements would be intelligible or even imaginable. Like Foucault, Oakeshott traces the emergence and development of the most distinctly modern state, the enterprise state, whose apparatus reaches deeper and deeper into the society which it governs and (in a sense) calls into existence. Like Berlin (and, indeed, Hobbes before them), Oakeshott embraces an individualistic view of society. Though inseparable from intersubjective networks of practices and discourses, society is a contingent collection of individuals, and not an organism or corporation defined by natural affinities, or by collective values and ends. Oakeshott recommends civil association because modern societies, properly understood, are ineluctably pluralistic. With Berlin and Foucault, he emphasizes the reality and potency of such plurality, its inherent power to escape and decenter the enterprises managed by the state. Against the backdrop of these images of state and society, politics are a narrowly defined range of activities that work upon the arrangements shared by a multitude of individual associates. With Arendt, Berlin, and Foucault, Oakeshott laments the expanding *imperium* of politics-as-social-management, which is characteristic of the enterprise state (Left as well as Right), and which displaces civil association and the conditions it fosters. In its place he would see the flourishing of a pluralistic, individualistic, association which he describes as a *civitas peregrina*:

> [A]n association, not of pilgrims travelling to a common destination, but of adventurers each responding as best he can to the ordeal of consciousness in a world composed of others of his kind, each the inheritor of the imaginative achievements (moral and intellectual) of those who have gone before and some joined in a variety of prudential practices, but here partners in a practice of civility the rules of which are not devices for satisfying substantive wants and whose obligations create no symbiotic relationship.[158]

Oakeshott's political theory thus mobilizes his underlying views of agency, practice, and tradition in service of this pluralistic yet individualistic image of state, society, and politics. Imbricated and mutually reinforcing, together these aspects of his philosophical and political thought construct a self-standing conceptual edifice that deserves serious attention. Yet Oakeshott's contributions to contemporary political thought exceed the limits imposed by ideological interpretations of his work as conservative or liberal. When read alongside the work of Foucault, Berlin, and Arendt, Oakeshott's political thought breaches the ideological fencing within which it is too commonly presented. By presenting his work in meaningful conversation with a broader range of thinkers and intellectual traditions (even, perhaps, contrary to his own prejudices), I have hoped to show that Oakeshott's thought regarding state, society, and politics speaks to a broader audience than is normally supposed and has, if anything, become even more incisive and relevant for us today.

FOUR

TOWARD A CONVERSATIONAL DEMOCRATIC ETHOS

At the heart of Michael Oakeshott's political thought is a theory of the state, which culminates in his characterization of the dynamic (at times creative, at others destructive) tensions between the nomocratic idiom of civil association and the teleocratic idiom of enterprise association. In a world still dominated by states, and institutions that mimic, attach to, or derive from states, his thought addresses what remains the commonest setting of modern politics. His investigations of the modern state's emergence and character repeatedly encounter what is perhaps the preeminent concept in twentieth and twenty-first-century political thought and practice: *democracy*.[1] Yet democracy never receives the systematic treatment that, for example, *respublica* or the rule of law receives. This relative lacuna is traceable to Oakeshott's disenchantment with the state of twentieth-century democratic thought.

Much like his contemporary, George Orwell, Oakeshott understands democracy to be a "manifold word" that is used (and sometimes abused) to refer to "different sets of ideas," and made to do partisan service for a sometimes perplexing array of ideologies.[2] Apart from the common, unreflective uses of democracy as a term of praise and inclusion (on the one hand) and criticism and exclusion (on the other), meant to rally one's allies and isolate one's adversaries, Oakeshott identifies a number of conceptual problems with the contemporary invocations of democracy. Chief among these problems has been the "corruption of the word 'democracy' in which it has come to mean a method of rule, not a constitutional shape," and accordingly, "[t]he authority of an office of government has been confused" with the character or popularity of its occupants, the alleged wisdom or propriety of their prescriptions, and the institutional apparatus through which political power is exercised.[3] This conceptual confusion, whereby "democratic" becomes a stand-in or equivalent for a host of laudatory adjectives in political discourse, subsequently amplifies practical problems. As he argues in the essay "The Masses in Representative Democracy," a Protean conception of democracy has frequently been wed to projects of expanding and imposing state power (*democratically*) for the sake of producing social conditions believed to be desirable as such. Democratic theory and practice have thus long suffered from a sort of messianic rationalism—democratic government becomes the political panacea, the mechanism through which good social order (properly identified, whether by science, abstract reason, or revealed natural law) can be authoritatively imposed. For these reasons, Oakeshott believes that modern democratic theory stands in need of a "radical restatement" of its principles, which would at least in part clarify these confusions, and thus set democratic theory on sounder, chastened footing.[4] Yet, although Oakeshott is articulate in his analysis of the problem, and although his criticism implies the basic contours of a solution, he never undertakes to deliver the restatement for which he calls. Compared to his treatment of other topics in political theory, his discussions of democracy are few and far between, and are frequently incidental to other themes that occupy a more significant place in his work. This sparseness of treatment, his occasionally mordant criticism of democratic theory and practice, and his insistence upon the stark limits of politics have led some commentators to conclude that Oakeshott either has nothing to contribute to democratic thought, or that he is antidemocratic.[5]

Though he offers no grand, systematic model or theory, and though he is at times stringently critical of democratic theory and practice, Oakeshott's availability and salience to democratic thought has recently been considered more seriously. This new appreciation of Oakeshott generally tracks the boom in democratic theory in the nearly four decades since the publication of *On Human Conduct*. The protest and liberation movements of the 1960s and 1970s, as well as the work of thinkers such as Jürgen Habermas, C. B. MacPherson, and John Rawls, served to reinvigorate democratic theory. The subsequent waves of scholarship have invented or reinvented a wide variety of models or theories of democracy, and have made democratic theory one of the most active fields of political theory as a whole. The search for a democratic Oakeshott responds to the growing sensibility that in order to be a serious modern political thinker, one must have a view of democracy, critical or otherwise. It is a credit to this new avenue of interest in Oakeshott that it has brought to the fore aspects of his work that have languished or that have yet to be scrutinized in terms of their relevance and contribution to democratic theory.

Recent commentators in search of Oakeshott's democratic voice have begun to examine not only his views on civil association and political activity generally, but also his characterization of conversation. These newer approaches generally place Oakeshott's thought in one of two categories. First, some find in him a thoughtful and skeptical critic of modern democracy who nevertheless provides valuable insights for democratic projects. Steven Anthony Gerencser, for example, has suggested that Oakeshott's account of civil authority holds open a circumscribed space for participatory democratic contestation.[6] Oakeshott is thus presented as an incidental democrat, committed to democracy secondarily and in respect of other, more prominent elements of his political thought. Second, there are scholars who read Oakeshott as a committed democratic thinker as such, an approach exemplified by the work of Michael Minch. Looking to Oakeshott's accounts of civil association and conversation, Minch presents Oakeshott's political thought as thoroughly and systematically democratic. Surveying Oakeshott's writings for democratic elements, and subsequently placing him in conversation with several prominent theorists of deliberative democracy, Minch concludes that Oakeshott is a deliberative democrat whose work emphasizes the discursive, participatory registers of democracy.[7]

The interpretation that I shall develop shares the sense that Oakeshott has something significant to say about democracy, but diverges from the readings sketched above in important ways. I concur with Minch's claim that "the idea of open-ended, pluralistic, nonfoundational conversation" is at the heart of Oakeshott's democratic thought.[8] However, I argue that Oakeshott's characterization of conversation in fact challenges several fundamental premises of deliberative democratic theories. Though his understanding of conversational politics is congruent with the general, discursive drift of deliberative democracy, it also illuminates their limits and problematic assumptions. Thus, while Oakeshott's thought is readily conversant with deliberative democratic theory, he ought not to be included among their ranks. Indeed, some of his more notable democratic affinities lay elsewhere.

I begin my characterization of Oakeshott's democratic thought by considering two fundamental features of deliberative democratic theories: (1) their commitment to the goal of consensus, and (2) their epistemic conception of democratic politics. I then discuss Oakeshott's characterization of civil association and conversational politics, and examine their critical bearing on each feature of deliberative democratic theory. I first consider Oakeshott's thought in relation to another critic of deliberative democracy, Chantal Mouffe. Attending to the affinities between Oakeshott and Mouffe, I explore how their respective understandings of plurality contest deliberative ideals of consensus. I then consider Oakeshott's characterization of political conversation, which, I argue, challenges an epistemic assumption that animates and orients deliberative theories. I close with a discussion of the promise and limits of Oakeshott's conversational view. While his understanding of conversation does not furnish a model for democratic institutions, I suggest that it provides an ethos for democratic practice in pluralistic societies. His contribution to contemporary democratic theory is thus both critical and constructive, in that it both chastens and encourages democratic engagement, speaking the language of contemporary democratic theory while staking out a distinctive position within it.

FUNDAMENTAL COMMITMENTS OF DELIBERATIVE DEMOCRACY

The deliberative turn[9] in democratic theory may be considered an outgrowth in political thought of the linguistic turn[10] that originated in early-twentieth-century philosophy and spread throughout the humanities and social sciences. Much as the linguistic turn has emphasized the ways in which practices of language-use affect the meaning and mediate the circulation of concepts within epistemic and practical communities, the deliberative turn has emphasized the ways in which communicative and discursive practices affect and mediate democratic politics. Both rest on the assumption that both practical and conceptual problems generally stem from how we talk about things, and thus solutions to such problems are to be found first by reflecting upon our linguistic practices. Though diverse, theories of deliberative democracy respond to two pervasive phenomena in modern politics. First, deliberative theories respond to the recognition that plurality is an inescapable fact for modern societies and to the problems that difference and disagreement pose for practices of self-government.[11] Second, they respond to a growing sense that democratic institutions have become distanced or insulated from the *demos*, and thus democracy has become merely procedural, soulless in theory and dysfunctional in practice.[12] Within the field of democratic thought, deliberative theories are commonly formulated as alternatives to the aggregative and elite theories of democracy that have dominated postwar political science in the West. These entrenched theories model democracy as an institutionalized mechanism of collective decision whereby citizens' private preferences are registered through voting processes, calculated according to some majoritarian formula, and then either translated into law and policy directly or used to populate legislative bodies. Under such models, private preferences are aggregated through institutional processes that leave the distribution and intensity of those preferences (and the difference and disagreement they manifest) essentially unaltered by public discussion, negotiation, and compromise. Thus, as many critics have argued, aggregative voting procedures are only minimally participatory, with the greatest share of actual politics and governing left to elites. In response to the shortcomings of democracy so conducted, deliberative democrats conceptualize a more robust public sphere in which deeper and more diverse modes of democratic participation and citizenship occur. Rather than merely voting for representatives whose candidacy is often a matter of elite (self-)selection, deliberative theories place practices of collective discussion at the center of politics, in the hopes of facilitating the formation and mobilization of publics that genuinely inform and contribute to governmental policy and action.

While deliberative democratic theories take a number of forms, the family of deliberative theories shares two fundamental, animating commitments. These commitments not only distinguish deliberative theories from other theories of democracy, but also provide points of contrast to Oakeshott's critique of democracy and his own view of democracy as conversation.

Seeking Consensus

Most deliberative democratic theories are committed to facilitating consensus among the citizenry of an otherwise pluralistic society. If deeper and more expansive agreement were not an ultimate goal of democratic politics, then deliberation would scarcely be preferable to either the simple aggregation of private preferences or the rule of experts. The aim is not simply to settle disagreement or institutionalize its fault lines, but to create political conditions in which the content of disagreement can be fundamentally reshaped, common interests can be recognized, and shared identities and sentiments cultivated. This is not to say that deliberative democrats wish or expect to eliminate difference or disagreement altogether. Some deliberative democrats make it a theoretical priority to "embrace difference as well as consensus" and view deliberation as a way to give plurality a genuine voice, rather than reduce it to vote tallies.[13] Yet consensus is nonetheless a regulative ideal and animating principle, a fixed star in the deliberative democratic constellation.

Defenses of consensus generally take two forms. On the one hand, some theorists define deliberation fairly narrowly and recommend restricting the scope and depth of democratic discourse out of a commitment to consensus. They argue that in a democracy, political decisions ought to be justified in terms that those bound by the decisions could in principle accept. Deliberation promotes such legitimacy insofar as it canalizes political contestation into terms and discourses that are "neutral" or "restrained" and, thereby, are more likely to generate consensus.[14] Even when deliberation is restricted in scope and depth, it is restricted for the sake of enhancing the quality of deliberation and its likelihood of generating consensus on political decisions.

On the other hand, there are deliberative theorists who draw inspiration from republican and radical democratic traditions, and emphasize the participatory and transformative of democratic politics.[15] These likewise pin their hopes to the ideal of consensus, contending that consensus on deep political values, identities, and questions is possible and desirable, and that deliberative democratic politics can generate such agreement. Regardless whether they recommend some restrictions on deliberation or seek to foster deep social and political transformation, theorists of deliberative democracy resoundingly aim at discovering, creating, and articulating consensus out of a pluralistic society.

Epistemic Politics

Christian F. Rostbøll has argued that deliberative democratic theories trade upon an underlying "epistemic" premise, and tend to "not only prais[e] the virtues of the procedures of democracy but also believ[e] them to have a tendency to lead to good and rational outcomes."[16] Deliberative democrats "all share a belief that deliberation tends to improve political outcomes" by better aligning political outcomes with some external criterion.[17] Thus, deliberation is desirable not only because of how it produces decisions (i.e., procedurally correct decisions), but also because of the kinds of the decisions it produces (i.e., substantively correct decisions).

One can sort deliberative theories according to the notion of correct decisions that they use. Some theorists value deliberation as a method for *finding* good or correct answers to political questions. Whereas other theorists view deliberation as a method for *constituting* good or correct answers to political questions.

Not all deliberative democrats specify their epistemic commitments, nor are their epistemic premises equally deep and encompassing. Still, deliberative democratic theories generally privilege and seek decisions of a special epistemic character. This epistemic character is sometimes framed in terms of "truth." As Cheryl Misak puts it, deliberative democratic theories treat political and moral questions as "truth-apt"—that is, liable to be more or less true to fact, whether this fact is exogenous or endogenous to democratic deliberation and decision.[18] Other avowedly epistemic deliberative democrats who share Misak's emphasis on truth in politics include David Estlund, Amy Gutmann, Christian Rostbøll, Robert Talisse, and Dennis Thompson. Alternatively, the epistemic character of deliberative outcomes is sometimes framed in terms of "legitimacy," especially by theorists such as Seyla Benhabib, Joshua Cohen, and others who follow the strain of deliberative democratic thought indebted variously to Jürgen Habermas and John Rawls. On this view, deliberative outcomes are better and more legitimate than aggregative or elite-negotiated outcomes, because they "result from the free and unconstrained public deliberation of all about matters of common concern."[19]

Legitimacy may appear prima facie nonepistemic, but there is less difference between truth and legitimacy in deliberative democracy than there may first appear. Both truth-oriented deliberation and legitimacy-oriented deliberation are premised upon the idea that there are objectively better and worse political decisions, and that deliberation facilitates either the finding or the constituting of such decisions. If no such epistemic distinction were invoked between better and worse, or correct and incorrect decisions, then deliberative theories would lose much of their appeal. Regardless whether one considers political outcome *x* the better outcome because it more closely tracks the truth or because it is the legitimate, genuine representation of the will of the people, deliberation (according to theorists of deliberative democracy) produces decisions that are epistemically superior.

The themes of consensus and epistemic politics are central characteristics of deliberative democratic theory, even though individual theorists differ in how explicitly and emphatically they present these themes. In virtue of their commitments to consensus and epistemic politics, I believe that it is unwise to count Oakeshott among the ranks of deliberative democrats, as Michael Minch does. Although Oakeshott's political theory contains an essential discursive dimension (especially but not exclusively with respect to democracy), he constructively challenges these underlying deliberative commitments. While Oakeshott's work neither refutes deliberative democratic theory nor supplies an equally systematic model or theory to supplant it, his own understanding of democracy provides a critical perspective that can inform democratic sensibilities and practices.

PLURALISM AND THE LIMITS OF CONSENSUS

Oakeshott's account of civil association in *On Human Conduct*, the centerpiece of his political thought,[20] characterizes it as a contingent mode of association in which a plurality of individuals "whom chance or choice have brought together" stand related to one another not in terms of shared enterprises or a set of substantive ends (a shared communal identity or *telos*), but in the common recognition of civil authority, the authority of a noninstrumental legal and institutional framework that conditions their choices and actions.[21] In Oakeshott's distinctive twist on a familiar liberal idiom, civil association pictures a society of individuals

> who are joined in no common purpose or engagement, who may be strangers to one another, the objects of whose loves are as various as themselves, and who may lack any . . . allegiance to one another . . . [but] that somewhat "watery" fidelity called civility.[22]

These individuals, who need share only a civil condition (or *respublica*), live as citizens of a "nomocracy whose laws are understood as conditions of conduct, not devices instrumental to the satisfaction of preferred wants."[23] As I discussed in the previous chapter, this conceptual picture forms one of the poles between which the modern European state is perennially stretched, and Oakeshott presents it as the political form that respect for individual agency ideally takes. In the conversation of modern political thought, the institutional form such a nomocracy might take has varied, and a theory of civil association is not per se a theory of democratic politics or institutions. Montesquieu, for instance, theorized monarchical and republican forms of nomocracy, delineating along the way the character of civil association from the types of governmental regime in which civil authority might be vested.[24] Yet within his account of civil association there appears to be some bias in favor of democracy as a constitutional form. With respect to the lives of contemporary Western states, Oakeshott appears to assume that political institutions and practices will most likely be structured along democratic lines. Chantal Mouffe has suggested that Oakeshott's theory of civil association presents an adequate framework for "political association under modern democratic conditions," and thus his account of civil association is adapted to democracy at a conceptual level.[25] Michael Minch insightfully suggests that the fullest realization of the ideal of civil association—"the realization *by* 'agents' that they *are* 'agents'"—under modern conditions requires democratic political institutions.[26] Yet Minch goes a step farther and attributes to Oakeshott a strong normative argument for the superiority of democratic politics generally and deliberative democracy in particular. Though I do not intend to analyze or challenge Minch's position directly here,[27] I shall offer an alternative interpretation of Oakeshott's thoughts on democracy, in part by attending to the conversation between Oakeshott and Mouffe regarding democratic theory and practice. Whereas Oakeshott is a democrat in a qualified but important sense, he is also a thoughtful critic of the two fundamental assumptions of deliberative democracy identified above. The way to both the democratic valences of Oakeshott's thought and his critique of core deliberative ideals is through his application of the concept of conversation to politics.

Oakeshott conceives of conversation as a communicative, dialogical activity in which a plurality of voices and idioms of utterance meet in a mutual exchange.[28] He presents an image of conduct *inter homines* in which parties engage one another in an open-ended interplay of perspectives, ideas, and utterances without "symposiarch or arbiter."[29] So understood, conversation denotes not merely parties exchanging words on specific occasions, but "the appropriate image of human intercourse more generally."[30] It thus serves as a conceptual lens through which to characterize human conduct in its manifold aspects.

Oakeshott suggests that politics, above all other human activities, ought ideally to approximate conversation, manifesting a conversational ethos. As noted above, his theory of civil association gives human plurality and individual agency a great deal of room and his notion of conversation elaborates this form of association, as well as its democratic potential. Building from the notion that plurality is both a standing human condition and a necessary condition for conversation, Oakeshott claims that "the approximation of politics to conversation is . . . the gist and meaning of democracy."[31] In an inexorably pluralistic society, a conversational image of democratic politics as a "hunt without a victim," emphasizing the noninstrumental inclusion of diverse voices and identities, is particularly appropriate and promising.[32]

Oakeshott's conversational ideal of democracy underscores his relevance to contemporary political thought while at the same time complicating some of the normal attempts to classify him as a thinker. Many of Oakeshott's interpreters consider him a liberal because of his views on individuality and civil association, or a conservative because of his views on agency and authority. Thanks to the work of Gerencser, Minch, and Mouffe, Oakeshott's thought has begun to enjoy greater currency in democratic theory, beyond the strictures of such ideological labels. Yet, to my mind, the full character of his contribution to democratic theory has been missed. Minch is correct to emphasize the political valences of Oakeshott's conception of conversation, while excessive in labeling him a deliberative democrat. Mouffe's reading of Oakeshott as recognizing the conditions of plurality that condition democratic politics points toward a more satisfactory understanding of Oakeshott's democratic thought and its place in contemporary debates. Drawn from his accounts of conversation and civil association, his view of democracy resembles that of agonistic democrats in an important, yet qualified sense. To develop this interpretation, I will focus on two main points, which return to themes explored in chapters 1 and 2: (1) Oakeshott's characterization of plurality and shared practices as conditions of democratic politics, and (2) his rejection of consensus as either a goal or a regulative ideal of democratic politics. Although Oakeshott conceives of democracy in discursive terms, I believe that there are good reasons to stop short of counting him a deliberative democrat.

According to Oakeshott, conversation, like any discursive activity, is never entirely unmoored and free-floating. As a mode of human activity, conversation is conditional, built upon an indispensable substrate that shapes the activity. One indispensable condition of conversation is the plurality amid which it takes place. Conversation is "impossible in the absence of a diversity of voices."[33] Yet encounter and play of voices in conversation also requires shared idioms of communication.[34] In order to meet as conversational partners, the parties must share a "stock of emotions, beliefs, images, ideas, manners of thinking, languages, skills, practices and manners of activity" that they draw upon as practical resources in conversation.[35] What is required is not some fixed point of agreement but rough, approximate, or partial attunement in practices that supply bases for mutual intelligibility. Conversation is not premised upon a robust consensus regarding doctrines, final vocabularies, moral values, or even preferred policies or topics. These may remain irresolvably plural, and their reduction to singular agreement signals that conversation has ended and has been replaced by an engagement of an altogether different character. Rather, conversation is premised upon "a flow of sympathy" intelligible to all parties, even as they may vary widely in their interpretations of that common ground, and in their manners of and purposes for exploring it.[36]

Conversational democratic politics thus are not unconditional; they cannot be begun between parties who share no ground of mutual intelligibility and cannot be sustained among parties whose antagonisms are so deep that they relate as enemies. However, within the framework of civil association, such politics picture individuals who share the resources with which to converse and a sense of occasion for which to use them, but who need share little else and who may otherwise be strangers to one another. As a conversational image of democratic politics supposes only some such minimal stratum of attunement, it is emphatically appropriate to modern social conditions, in which increasingly diverse and divided societies struggle both to govern and to understand themselves. Imagined as conversation, democratic politics would embrace rather than bracket or attempt to overcome plurality and difference.

In respect of this image of democracy, it might appear that Oakeshott inclines significantly toward deliberative democratic theory. His conversational view maintains that the deepest essence of democracy is intersubjective discourse rather than isolated actions such as voting, and posits a basis of mutual intelligibility in order for difference and disagreement to be meaningfully expressed in politics, even when mediated by representative or parliamentary institutions. Yet while conversational and deliberative images of democracy appear similar at first blush, there are fundamental differences between the two. In respect of his understanding of plurality and consensus, Oakeshott's conversational image arguably comes closer to agonistic theories of democracy, particularly that of Chantal Mouffe.

Like Oakeshott, Mouffe regards plurality, and its attendant features of difference and disagreement, not as some temporary or contingent obstacle to the Enlightenment dream of ever-widening rational consensus, but as a permanent feature of modern democratic politics.[37] Against what she sees as the dominant liberal democratic tendency (shared by deliberative democrats) to treat plurality as a fact "that we must bear grudgingly or try to reduce," she insists that democratic theorists must instead recognize plurality as "something that we should celebrate and enhance."[38] Democracy, in other words, should be viewed as a meeting of a plurality of voices and identities without the supposition that exchange will gradually narrow or eliminate the difference and disagreement among the parties. In *The Return of the Political*, Mouffe singles out Oakeshott's theory of civil association for its genuine appreciation and embrace of plurality, and regards her own perspective as informed by and conversant with his. Echoes of this conversation are audible in Mouffe's criticism of deliberative democrats on the grounds that they treat plurality as a problem to manage and ultimately solve through the creation of rational consensus. Rather than accept and care for plurality, she sees deliberative democracy as a project of resolving or negating difference and disagreement, in politics and perhaps beyond.

Mouffe's reading of deliberative democratic theory is itself contentious, and contradicts the self-descriptions of many deliberative theories. Many deliberative democrats contend that properly constituted and conducted deliberative practices shall best enable a plurality of voices to be expressed. For instance, John Dryzek, Amy Gutmann and Dennis Thompson, and Seyla Benhabib all strive to reconcile genuine respect for difference with institutions and processes that are designed to promote political consensus. They believe, in other words, that through deliberation disagreement can be resolved without negating or transforming the difference from which it springs. Mouffe, nonetheless, is deeply critical of what she calls the "sacralization of consensus" that inheres in deliberative democratic theories—that is, the deliberative democrat's faith that institutional formulae can cultivate a nonadversarial idiom of political engagement in which the difference and conflict latent in plurality can be "harmonized through dialogue" and transformed into a political nonissue.[39] In her view, theories of deliberative democracy sacralize consensus in two ways.

First, Mouffe claims that deliberative theories treat consensus as a regulative ideal for democratic politics. Whereas aggregative theories of democracy view majority rule as a stand-in for robust consensus, something for which we must be prepared to settle, *faute de mieux*, deliberative theories attempt to enhance majority rule to such an extent that it approximates the consensual ideal of unanimity. Thus, deliberative democracy aims at an ideal of democracy without remainder. Deliberative institutions and practices are to be organized so as to make democratic outcomes the product of the most expansive consensus possible and, furthermore, to ensure that those who are not part of the consensus have, in effect, excluded themselves. Even when designed to be inclusive, deliberative theories inherently risk stigmatizing residual disagreement, as if only those who are unreasonable, irrational, or intolerant will fail to come to agreement (e.g., on account of clinging to the narrow interests of partisanship or pursuing private rather than public good). Although attempts to craft such consensus-building practices and institutions face a number of empirical obstacles, Mouffe believes that the primary problem with the ideal of consensus is conceptual, not empirical.[40] The conceptual danger is that in our haste to secure consensus and to enjoy a politics without adversaries, we will "negate the ineradicable character of antagonism" that saturates social life and that is the very condition of the political.[41] On Mouffe's agonistic view, the consensual goal of deliberative democracy endangers plurality and makes sense only against the background of a philosophical anthropology that is fundamentally mistaken.

Second, Mouffe contends that theorists of deliberative democracy insert the ideal of consensus at both ends of democratic politics. Consensus is the goal and guiding ideal of deliberation, yet it is also presumed to exist already. By positing regulative principles for democratic deliberation (such as reasonableness, reciprocity, or neutrality), deliberative democrats risk either imputing to or requiring of citizens a degree of prepolitical agreement that makes the next step to political consensus seem almost automatic, and the demand for it irresistible. It is as if disagreement is merely manifestation of misunderstanding about some underlying register of agreement, misunderstanding that properly conceived and enacted deliberation can correct. Even if deliberative theories disavow notions of unanimous or stable consensus at the end of deliberation, they rely upon front-end consensus as a condition for entry into the deliberative forum.[42] Mouffe charges deliberative democratic theories with imposing and presupposing just the sort of moral and political agreement that deliberation is meant to cultivate. Though some measure of common ground and mutual intelligibility is necessary for democratic contestation to take place, deliberative theories trade upon the dubious assumption that "one will in fact approach the good society by acting as if one had already arrived there."[43] The result is what Stuart Hampshire has called "harmony within the liberal stockade," a façade of consensus constructed at the expense of plurality.[44]

Oakeshott's characterization of conversation dovetails with Mouffe's critique of deliberative democracy. Rather than seeking consensus as an end or adopting consensus as a regulative ideal, in conversation, "different universes of discourse meet, acknowledge each other and enjoy an oblique relationship which neither requires nor forecasts their being assimilated to one another."[45] This is not to say that conversation cannot lead to greater mutual understanding and perhaps agreement between parties. Nor should such a result be avoided or lamented. Yet as the purpose of conversation is not to achieve consensus, judging the conduct and outcome of conversation against a metric of consensus is out of place.

The application of Oakeshott's concept of conversation to modern democracy pictures politics in modern societies not as the search for bipartisanship, the conversion of opponents to common ground (whether that ground is fashioned or discovered already to exist), or the triumph of one program over another. Democratic politics signify one possible way to tend to and modify the political arrangements of a pluralistic society—"the pursuit of [its] intimations" conducted as "a conversation, not an argument."[46] The minimal agreement or attunement that conversation presupposes need not prejudice discussion toward a particular consensual end, nor must it silence claims and bracket identities that might destabilize consensus.

Thus imagined, democratic politics require a "shared symbolic space" in which parties meet, even as adversaries, as well as commitment to and competence in using the conceptual and institutional resources of civil association.[47] Participants need not share profound identities, substantive traditions, or initial consensus upon either fundamental values or the ultimate aims of political discourse. They need only be initiates into the same intersubjective capital of practices, willing and able to speak in common idioms. Some deliberative theorists admittedly strive to articulate a similar kind of minimal threshold, such as Gutmann and Thompson's argument for reciprocity as a regulative principle for deliberative democratic politics. However, as Mouffe and Oakeshott contend in their distinct ways, to picture democratic politics as a quest for consensus (even if only as a regulative ideal to be approximated) is to labor under an impoverished political imagination. Contestation can be productive without being transformed into settlement, and conversation can sustain democratic politics without either expecting or demanding convergence of positions. Reaching a modicum of consensus in agonistic contestation or democratic conversation may be worthwhile and desirable, but taking consensus as the *telos* of democratic engagement is liable to disfigure both democratic politics and its participants.

Despite the significant affinities between Mouffe and Oakeshott regarding plurality and consensus, there are, of course, limits to how far their commonalities ought to be pushed. Influenced by Carl Schmitt's critique of liberal democracy, Mouffe criticizes Oakeshott for not adequately recognizing "division and antagonism" in his account of civil association.[48] She correctly observes that division and antagonism are peripheral considerations for Oakeshott, which he does little to address systematically. Much as his analysis of the state tends toward myopia, eliding the potency of nonstate and substate institutions, he pictures the politics of civil association as somewhat too civil, elevated above the agonistic fray.[49] What is more, his underlying account of conversation likewise conveys an image of plurality without significant antagonism, in which difference manifests lightly and without friction. The significant worth of Oakeshott's conversational vision of democratic politics must be weighed against this shortcoming. The ideal of democracy as conversation is presented within a fairly narrowly imagined society in which plurality abounds, but in which genuine, intractable antagonism is all but absent. However, while this may count against the completeness of Oakeshott's position, it is not fatal to his insights. Even as he constructs this conversational ideal, Oakeshott remains an attentive reader of Hobbes and is under no illusions about the turbulent and even dangerous aspects of plurality. In his account of the emergence of the modern European state, Oakeshott remarks that "[a]ll European states began as mixed and miscellaneous collections of human beings precariously held together, disturbed by what they swallowed and were unable to digest, and distracted by plausible or fancied *irredènta*."[50] Politics, of any description, are the activities of tending to the arrangements of a pluralistic society so conceived, and Oakeshott presents his political thought against this background. Hence, while antagonism and conflict do not receive systematic discussion, he is certainly not naive with respect to them. On account of his keen sense of plurality and the contingency of political order, Oakeshott's views on politics overlap at several points with those of agonistic democrats. This shared perspective is often obscured by scholars who label Oakeshott simply as a liberal or a conservative.

In addition, Mouffe and Oakeshott differ in regard to the practical status of their respective visions of democracy. Mouffe envisions agonistic democratic politics as a possible form that everyday contestation might take. Hers is a theory of normal politics, enacted or waged almost continuously. Oakeshott, however, presents his conversational image of democracy as an ideal type rather than an everyday form of political activity. In respect of its open disposition toward plurality and its inherent hesitancy toward decision, conversational democracy is arguably suitable for good times and all but unattainable in times of crisis. Conversational politics are thus "inherently intermittent activities," rather than an ongoing plebiscite or the daily bread of social life.[51] As Oakeshott no doubt recognized, except when it appears in compromised and admixed forms, democracy of this sort will be "as rare as it is excellent."[52]

CONVERSATION AND THE LIMITS OF ARGUMENT

Although Oakeshott does not develop a systematic model of conversational democracy, he does offer several important claims about its character and conduct. When combined, these claims articulate a conversational ethos suitable to inform and inspire democratic politics in modern pluralistic societies. Once again, despite picturing democracy in discursive terms, the democratic ethos Oakeshott articulates stands in sharp contrast to deliberative democratic theories on several fundamental points. Tracing these lines of distinction between conversational and deliberative ideals shows Oakeshott to offer a critical voice as well as a constructive vision.

Deliberation and Argument, Deliberation as Argument

Oakeshott's relevance to democratic theory (and his critical perspective on deliberative theories) arises not only from his conceptions of civil association and conversation, but also from another central theme that informs his political thought and has received perhaps the greatest share of attention in the secondary literature: his critique of rationalism. Oakeshott describes rationalism as an intuitively appealing, yet ultimately self-defeating, rebellion of the human intellect against human finitude, which manifests differently in different domains of thought and action. In all its forms rationalism seeks to impose "the sovereignty of technique," pursuant to the conviction that the human reason can grasp all things, and that what can be known can be controlled.[53] Yet thought and action do not become rationalistic in this sense merely when it is supposed that reason has a privileged place in human understanding and conduct. This attitude is in some ways inherent to all systematic reflection and deliberate action. Rather, rationalism signifies a cultivated faith that whatever does not fit the ideal (often a priori) schemes of reason must be false, meaningless, misguided, or immoral, and thus discarded as ignorance or superstition. Philosophy was the midwife of this attitude, and still remains its natural partner, yet it has spread farther. In the domain of modern science, rationalism manifests in the belief that the world is susceptible to reduction without remainder to the formulae and laws science has fashioned for itself, as if the fully rational mind were indeed the undistorted and infallible mirror of nature. And in politics rationalism is conviction that institutions, policies, and problems admit of designs and solutions deducible from rationally certified principles (empirical or conceptual). Subjected to the sovereignty of technique, political life is imagined as a domain of clearly delineated truth and falsehood, in which knowledge, rather than skill, is the needful trait. According to Oakeshott's most elaborate discussions of the topic, partisans of rationalistic politics imagine society as a collection of objective facts and institutional arrangements that are amenable to management and transformation through technical solutions. Politics are undertaken as enterprises of fashioning and implementing policies that will arrange social facts and institutions in patterns and that will maximize some particular ideal. Although his criticisms of rationalism in politics were most often directed against projects by Left governments in postwar states to impose central economic and social planning of various scopes, he also believed that rigid anti-planning, "free market" alternatives fell prey to the same seductions and flaws.[54] The important, but often forgotten, lesson is that rationalism is a style of thought rather than a concrete set of policies, and therefore can manifest anywhere on contemporary political spectra.

Deliberative democratic theories bear a complex relationship to rationalism. On the one hand, theorists of deliberative democracy often criticize the elitism and rule of experts that characterize many modern representative democracies. Much of what recommends deliberative democracy is the vision of a participatory public sphere, in which politics is neither managed nor mitigated by elites, or by centrally devised and administered institutions. Yet, on the other hand, insofar as they view and value democratic politics in epistemic terms, deliberative theorists demonstrate a characteristic of the rationalistic habit of mind.

The trace of rationalism rests upon the epistemic character of deliberative democracy. Deliberative theories picture moral and political questions as truth-apt, and democratic politics as argumentative engagements that will arrive at better or more correct beliefs, principles, and policies. Yet deliberative theories fall under the scope of Oakeshott's critique not on account of their aspirations for better politics, but because of the way in which such politics are imagined and pursued. Oakeshott does not label "rationalism" all systematic endeavors to improve the human condition. He never suggests that merely having a thoughtful plan or a bright idea convicts one of rationalism and its ills. Rather, rationalism participates in the belief that most if not all genuine questions and problems admit of technical answers and solutions, which is to say that contingency can be not merely abated through our practices, but conquered through the imposition of systems. Deliberative theories hinge on the notion that properly constituted argumentative procedures can provide an epistemically privileged forum, through which answers to political questions can be found or generated. The contingency of political life would be rendered transparent and manageable by way of systematic procedures that steer political action toward consensus around authoritatively valid outcomes. Admittedly, deliberative theories vary significantly in terms of how fully and explicitly they elaborate the institutional dimensions of deliberation. Some theorists, such as David Estlund and Jürgen Habermas, develop systematic theories without specifying in great detail the institutional mechanics of deliberative democratic politics, whereas others, such as Benjamin Barber, offer detailed institutional structure, ascending from local to national levels.[55] Nonetheless, despite such variation these theories necessary stand committed to some vision of systematic, epistemically privileged deliberation, otherwise such theories become little more than exhortations to talk more, regardless of what is said, how it is said, or what issues at the conclusion.

The rationalistic commitments and aspirations of deliberative democratic theory are readily apparent in the deliberative aim to find or generate consensus among citizens on what Rostbøll calls "good and rational" decisions—outcomes that are not just procedurally legitimate but epistemically optimal. This rationalistic spirit is especially well illustrated by the neopragmatist theories of Cheryl Misak and Robert Talisse. Employing a Peircean conception of "inquiry" as their epistemological foundation, Misak and Talisse both respectively envision democratic deliberation as a large-scale political manifestation of the discipline-transcending argumentative search for truth. Misak contends that the very attempt to undertake deliberation is animated by "a hope of reaching the truth"; thus, there is no truly non-epistemic form of deliberation.[56] Although she lauds deliberative theories that are based on her favored conception of inquiry as a regulative principle, the epistemic core that she identifies is common to deliberative theories generally. Talisse likewise characterizes deliberation as the political practice of inquiry, yet he equates the spirit of inquiry with the spirit of modern democracy itself, claiming that "at the core of [constitutional] democracy is the belief that *reasoned argument* is possible, even among people who are very deeply divided over moral and religious doctrines."[57] Deliberative democracy attempts to perfect and institutionalize this fundamental epistemic commitment. So conceived, deliberation aims at truth defined as "a belief that would be forever assertable . . . were inquiry pursued as far as it could fruitfully go."[58] It achieves this end through a process of argumentation in which epistemically privileged procedures of inquiry discover or produce epistemically optimal outcomes—that is, truth and rational consensus around it.

Although the Peircean idiom they employ is foreign to many deliberative democrats, Misak and Talisse insightfully foreground an essential element common to many deliberative theories. The overarching aim of deliberation, as opposed to mere majoritarian aggregation of preferences, is to arrive at consensual decisions that have a superior epistemic character. Conducted as an inquiry into and an argument about the truth, deliberation consists in offering truth claims, or propositions purported to be true about moral and political questions (including the question of what is the true will of the democratic public). Other deliberative democrats, such as Dryzek, have insisted that deliberation should welcome other modes of discourse, including "rhetoric, humour, emotion, testimony or storytelling, and gossip."[59] This more expansive vision appears, prima facie, to loosen the deliberative constraints that theorists such as Misak and Talisse impose. Yet, the inclusion of such additional modes of discourse can be misleading. Within the larger deliberative project, rhetoric or narrative are valuable only insofar as these help advance premises or provide evidence in the context of a propositional argument about political truth. Deliberative democratic politics do not merely determine which parties win or lose in policy debates. They also differentiate right and wrong, true and false answers, regardless of whether the truth sought is about a moral or political fact, or about the genuine content of the will of the engaged public.

This is not to say that public deliberation is either worse or no better than any other ways of conducting democratic politics. From an Oakeshottian perspective, it is certainly *pro tanto* desirable that citizens who are bound by democratically taken decisions view these decisions as true to the relevant facts, or legitimate, and that they have an opportunity to participate directly or indirectly in decision-making processes. Insofar as it fosters such understanding and engagement, deliberative democracy breaks from the classic rationalistic tendency to leave political decisions in the hands of experts or elites who know best how to answer the questions of political life. Perhaps deliberative democracy is even less strongly, or at least less narrowly, epistemic than some representative or elite models of democracy. However, from an Oakeshottian perspective, deliberative democracy remains tied to a rationalistic ethos and presumes that decisions crafted through suitably framed and conducted deliberation possess a superior epistemic character.

Deliberation, Rhetoric, and Conversation

Often in response to criticisms about implicit rationalism, a number of deliberative democrats have widened the discursive net beyond argument and inquiry as construed above, and have included rhetoric as a mode of democratic engagement. In the words of one of its advocates, rhetoric is a discursive mode that "persuades rather than proves,"[60] and thus its inclusion in deliberative democratic theory and practice appears to at least broaden the repertoire of politics. Yet even though the turn to rhetoric in democratic theory is often meant to make deliberation more inclusive of different kinds of utterance, the appeal of rhetoric ultimately lies in its potential to complement the underlying consensual and/or epistemic aims of deliberative theories. Rhetoric is thus added to the deliberative mix, rather than presented as an alternative or competitor.

It may appear that the inclusion of rhetoric tempers the rationalistic edge of deliberation, pushing it closer to the open play of voices that characterizes Oakeshottian conversation. However, while greater attention to rhetoric and persuasion perhaps enriches theories of deliberative democracy by providing a more realistic and robust image of deliberation at various social and institutional registers, the resulting image of political discourse still differs markedly from Oakeshott's conversational image. The apparent similarity between conversation and rhetoric lies primarily in the emphases of voice and expressive style alongside (and perhaps even above) content.

For Oakeshott, conversation is characterized not by the impersonal search for conclusion or settlement, but by ongoing practices of self-enactment and intersubjective acknowledgment and response. In conversation, individuals are not merely proxies for argumentative positions, but auto-poetic persons who themselves are *in* the conversation. Similarly, rhetoric engages and expresses the situatedness of the speaker, even if the purpose of rhetorical utterance is to advance an argument (by persuasion rather than proof). In rhetoric, as in conversation, who one is and where one stands may attain significance that is irrelevant in propositional argument about truth. Yet, there are important differences between conversation and rhetoric. Simone Chambers has raised the concern (which dates to Plato and Aristotle and has resurfaced in contemporary analyses of partisan politics in representative democracies) that rhetoric is, on the one hand, often monological rather dialogical and is, on the other hand, liable to a "plebiscitary" mode that is tantamount to demagogic manipulation.[61] In the first case, political rhetoric often eschews the search for common ground and thus amounts to an individual or group addressing itself while talking past its interlocutors. The performative dimension of rhetorical utterance can overwhelm the communicative dimension. In the second case, the rhetorical mode, as it plays upon persuasion, invites discourse that is calculated to produce certain emotive or affective states that ultimately enable the speaker to manipulate his or her audience. Both types of criticism reveal the complex and strained relation between rhetoric and deliberation, and also illustrate the partial disconnection between rhetoric and conversation. Conversation and deliberation entail more than mere persuasion, regardless of the rhetorical tools that are employed to persuade. The epistemic characteristic of deliberation and the pluralistic dimension of conversation preclude their equation with rhetoric, which is ultimately committed to neither epistemically optimal outcomes nor the recognition and expression of plurality.

Yet this is not to deny rhetoric a valid or desirable place in either deliberation or conversation. Here a Wittgensteinian idiom may clarify the positive role that rhetoric might play. Conversation and deliberation can be viewed as two different language-games, whereas different modes of discourse (such as argument or rhetoric) can be recognized as different kinds of moves that participants might make. Oakeshott contends that conversation will contain rhetoric and occasionally will thrive upon the virtuosity of persuasive utterance. Some deliberative democrats, such as Dryzek, likewise recognize that rhetoric can sometimes prove to be a welcome and useful move in deliberative practices. But neither for Oakeshott nor for the deliberative democrats is rhetoric the entire game. Reducing either conversation or deliberation to rhetoric is to conflate a language-game with a move that one might make in that game. Argument (whose aim is to discover, demonstrate, or prove) constitutes another kind of move that one might employ in language-games of democratic politics. Furthermore, as I have shown, deliberative democracy is an essentially argumentative endeavor, animated by an argumentative ethos. Rhetoric can have a place in deliberation, if it serves to demonstrate a larger argument—in deliberation, persuasion and proof are never entirely distinct. Oakeshott, however, distinguishes conversation from argument and inquiry, and thereby from deliberation. Conversation may contain moments of rhetoric or argument, but the purpose of conversation is neither argumentative (aimed at proving) nor rhetorical (aimed at persuading).

Because the games of deliberation and conversation differ, rhetoric plays a different role in each. At the conclusion of deliberation, the parties might find themselves persuaded of a particular claim, or induced to endorse a policy they had not previously supported, or convinced of the validity of a particular argument. Likewise, at moments of arrest in conversation the interlocutors might be persuaded, convinced, or converted. Yet, unlike conversation, the *purpose* of deliberation is to produce such effects, to demonstrate the epistemic superiority of a particular decision or policy and generate consensus around it.[62] Rhetoric is at most a move employed for this epistemic end, and if deliberation does not achieve these goals, it has by definition failed. Oakeshott grants that one might make use of argument and rhetoric in conversation, but conversation itself is neither a persuasive or argumentative discourse. Conversation might lead to persuasion, conversion, or proof; but these are its side effects, not its purpose. Like the framework of civil association in which Oakeshott believes such politics would thrive, conversation is self-justifying rather than instrumental to some end or enterprise beyond itself.

Conversation as a Democratic Ethos

Oakeshott's characterization of the communicative soul of modern, pluralistic democracy is his positive contribution to democratic theory. In lieu of an argumentative ethos that strives to get politics right or true to fact, Oakeshott proposes a conversational ethos that holds less promise to settle political questions cleanly, decisively, or ultimately, but that is less prone to transform difference and disagreement into a battle between truth and error. His view of conversation as the proper ethos for democratic politics (whatever their institutional form) arises both from his favorable characterization and estimation of conversation, and from his distinctive characterization of politics.

Oakeshott's most succinct characterization of conversation appears in "The Voice of Poetry in the Conversation of Mankind." He states that in a conversation

> the participants are not engaged in an inquiry or a debate; there is no "truth" to be discovered, no proposition to be proved, no conclusion sought. They are not concerned to inform, to persuade, or to refute one another, and therefore the cogency of their utterances does not depend upon them all speaking the same idiom; they may differ without disagreeing. Of course, a conversation may have passages of argument and a speaker is not forbidden to be demonstrative; but reasoning is neither sovereign nor alone, and the conversation does not itself compose an argument.[63]

Here Oakeshott expresses his sense of the inexorability and interconnection of plurality and contingency in human affairs, and presents conversation as a way of imagining social space that doesn't strive to condense, unify, or fix. This characterization of voices in conversation, which speak to one another in different idioms without any one idiom coming to dominate, is akin to Jean-François Lyotard's claim that the "social universe is formed by a plurality of [language] games without any one of them being able to claim that it can say all the others."[64] Conversation—as a way of imagining human conduct and as an ethos for democratic politics—favors the open over the closed, the plural over the singular, and the tentative over the conclusive. None of this runs contrary to the notion of democratic self-government, but it gives the pursuits of self-government distinctive, pluralistic inflections that mitigate tendencies in politics toward monotonous pursuit of decision or argumentative closure.

Some might judge this characterization of conversation as a dead end for democratic politics, which undoubtedly entail the making of decisions, the imposition of settlement, and, therefore, the foreclosure of further exchange. Deliberative theorists have criticized agonistic democrats, such as Mouffe, on precisely these grounds, claiming that it is desirable or even necessary for some contestations to come to an end and not be waged further.[65] Oakeshott, likewise, might be criticized on the grounds that endless conversation would either undermine or paralyze democratic politics.

This criticism might be mitigated, though certainly not refuted, by appeal to Oakeshott's general sense of politics. As I considered in the previous chapter, Oakeshott understands politics as activities by which individuals collectedly apply their intelligence to the arrangements of their society. In a pluralistic society imagined as a civil association, politics are the episodic activities by which civil associates reimagine, negotiate, and contest the form and content of their legal and political practices and institutions. This undertaking is intermittent, yet ongoing. It is essentially discursive, but neither demonstrative nor merely persuasive. Decisions are made, but there is no such thing as "proof" in political discourse; institutional changes are temporarily settled upon and implemented, but there is no once-and-for-all conclusion on any political matter.[66] One might say that such openness and restlessness is substantially what demarcates politics from other activities. When politics are understood in these terms, it is somewhat easier to imagine democracy as the political manifestation of an ongoing conversation, because politics need not be understood as antithetical to the ethos of conversation.

Nevertheless, Oakeshott's conversational view of democracy is aspirational. He pictures democratic politics as "neither a search for 'truth' nor the propagation of a belief," but as a pluralistic discursive engagement in which "[s]uccess does not lie in the conclusion of the discussion by some unanswerable pronouncement" but instead consists in "keep[ing] the conversation going . . . among persons who have a propensity not always to be conversible."[67] This is not an institutional model or a policy program, but an imaginative vision of politics whose intimations are yet unrealized. Despite this sanguine vision of democracy, Oakeshott is far from a dewy-eyed optimist; and he never suggests that democratic politics could or should be nothing but conversation. He is expressly critical of plebiscitary dreams of continuous, collective talk, and is skeptical of concentrated and unrestrained political power linked to radical participatory politics of any finer description. In his view, politics involves making decisions, and every decision is an arrest in democratic conversation. Yet he seeks a conversational ethos that recognizes and remains sensitive to the tension between self-government and pluralism within society. Pluralism leads to perpetual questioning and to the destabilization of the identity and decisions of the "people" that governs itself. Yet when animated by a conversational ethos, democratic politics can accept the necessity of temporary breaks in the conversation and of momentary impositions of tentative priorities, without converting arrest into foreclosure or hegemony into exclusion. This image of democratic politics best reflects what Oakeshott considers the origins of modern democratic thought and practice—a healthy practical skepticism of ideals and "the determination not to allow human life to be perverted by the tyranny of a person or fixed by the tyranny of an idea."[68]

CRITICISMS AND APOLOGIES: ELITISM, POWER, AND IRRESPONSIBILITY

Despite its promise as a conceptual picture of democracy, Oakeshott's conversational view is exposed to salient criticisms. Some such criticisms address discursive (rather than aggregative or elite) theories generally, including both deliberative and conversational variants. Yet others may speak quite directly to Oakeshott's conversational view. I shall consider three possible criticisms for the purpose of assessing how valid they are when applied to a conversational view of democracy, as well as to further weigh conversational and deliberative theories against one another. When properly understood, even in respect of its limitations, Oakeshott's conversational view of democracy is a promising alternative or amendment to other democratic theories, both aggregative and discursive.

Elitism

One familiar criticism to which both deliberative and conversational views of democracy might be exposed is that they are elitist. Both deliberative and conversational theories are open to the charge of expecting or demanding too much of participants, requiring information, resources, social capital, and discursive qualifications and skills that few members of a modern society can acquire. As a purely practical matter, this is likely true of all forms of modern democracy. Even the most minimal forms of political participation—for example, checking a box on a ballot—require or presume that a number of qualifying conditions be met (including adequate time, resources, and interest for a voter to acquire both information and legal proof of eligibility). No conception of democracy can escape every conceivable charge of exclusion, though the richer the vision of political participation it embraces, the more susceptible it is to charges of elitism in theory and in practice. Replacing the isolated act of voting with participation in ongoing public discourse appears to raise the threshold conditions for engagement in democratic politics by orders of magnitude, leaving more and more citizens out.

However, Oakeshott's vision seems especially vulnerable to this line of criticism, as participation in political conversation appears to require not only information and resources but a significant measure of aristocratic traits.[69] One might challenge Oakeshott's conversational view on the grounds that it presumes or demands of each conversant an intellectual, moral, and even aesthetic bearing that is the privilege (or misfortune) of the few, and that is not likely evenly or widely distributed in pluralistic societies. Accordingly, it might appear that conversational democracy is in fact elite or managed democracy under a different guise and according to different criteria. Thus, the distinctiveness and elevation of conversational democracy is likely (and perhaps rightly) lost on those excluded from the conversation. This criticism undoubtedly carries weight, as projects aimed at cultivating democratic conversation could be used to privilege and exclude different voices. Yet conversation is no more (and perhaps even less) exposed to the charge of elitism than is deliberation, particularly with the latter's emphases upon consensus, truth, and the argumentative and rhetorical competence necessary to arrive at them. What is more, the taint of elitism appears greatest when one pictures conversation in a way that Oakeshott perhaps unwittingly invited,[70] as sophisticated banter among artists or university professors.[71] Yet if one looks beyond the coloration that Oakeshott sometimes gives to his description, conversation welcomes such cultivation, as it welcomes much besides, but it presupposes neither any particular cultural heritage nor any relative standing within society. Much as Wittgenstein described a level of linguistic attunement that is the condition of our nonetheless genuine and deep disagreements and differences, Oakeshott in fact describes individual conversants as initiates into shared grammars and idioms of self-enactment who, nonetheless, may differ and disagree in their understandings and uses of the shared language. Shared idioms make conversation possible, without denying the plurality and contingency of modern societies and politics. While not all individuals will find themselves ideally disposed or equipped to participate in conversation (as could likewise be said about deliberation, or even the minimal act of voting), the concept of conversation (in respect of emphasizing the irreducible plurality of human voices and perspectives) is congenitally equipped to accommodate any willing to hazard joining the engagement. The charge of elitism may be thus mitigated because conversation is in principle no more exclusionary than other discursive forms of democracy, and is perhaps even more inclusive of eccentric identities, styles, and doctrines than more narrowly focused deliberative theories. If democratic politics are not construed as the popular election of self-selected elites or as the search for consensus upon truth or the public will, elitism may find less fertile soil in which to take root.

Discourse and Power

A second and closely related criticism, familiar from its application to deliberative theories by agonistic democrats and Foucauldians, maintains that the guiding ethos of conversation obscures or elides the power relations latent in every discursive context. Participatory, discursive theories promise greater popular access to political institutions and power, but in practice new routes of political action are variously coopted or diverted, leaving the newly discursively enfranchised no better off than before. Much as it appears that deliberation and conversation risk letting elitism in through the back door, it may appear that new deliberative or conversational spaces are merely echo chambers for the same discourses of power imposed upon the people under other institutional frameworks.[72] If, as Michel Foucault argued, a fundamental problem of modern political thought and practice is to recognize "the effects of power attached to the true" and the "political role" of such regimes of truth, then Oakeshott's image of democracy may appear unable to escape the gravity of existing power structures.[73] Despite overtly emphasizing plurality, conversation might covertly deliver old wine in new bottles. This line of criticism is more difficult to respond to than the charge of elitism, in part because the critics assert that power relations tend to mask themselves, and so the appearance of new forms of freedom and agency likely harbor either new or old forms of control and oppression.

If there is any truth to such criticisms of contemporary democratic politics, then distinguishing between different visions of democracy in terms of which escape existing networks of power relations and which do not is a misguided endeavor. The meaningful distinctions will be of degree, rather than kind, reckoned in terms of the ways in which democratic institutions and practices admit of reflexive challenges to the power relations that are interwoven throughout them. Here a significant distinction may be drawn between deliberative and conversational views of democracy. Like many theorists of deliberative democracy, Oakeshott imagines political conversation occurring in multiple sites throughout society and regards this multiplicity as going some way toward gaining critical purchase upon sedimented political ideologies and institutions. Though his conversational ideal is nested within his view that traditions and shared practices are the lifeblood of any genuine politics, he does not take this to the extreme of embracing what exists simply because it is so. While Oakeshott was no radical, he advocated reflexive, critical politics as the best realistic alternative. Consonant with his commitments to individuality and agency, to civil association, and to his critique of rationalism, political power ought to be institutionally dispersed and decentralized rather than held or mediated primarily by elites.[74] Here there is in fact significant affinity between Oakeshott's democratic prescriptions and Michel Foucault's analyses of power, in which discourses of truth are concentrated nodes of power relations bound up in the state but extending beyond it.[75] Rather than imagining that democracy of any sort can be liberated from power relations, both recognize that democracy ideally multiplies sites at which critical reflection and resistance can gain footing. Built upon a robust sense of irreducible plurality, Oakeshott's conversational theory is primed to sustain critical political practices.

Deliberative democrats are not altogether insensitive to considerations of power. Dryzek, Rostbøll, and Talisse, for instance, explicitly respond to concerns about how deliberative practices interact with relationships of subordination, domination, and discipline. Each views properly conceived and conducted deliberation as escaping or destabilizing the entrenched power relations of conventional democratic politics. However, the epistemic commitments of deliberative theories at least partially undermine the critical purchase of deliberative practices, keeping discourses of truth at the heart of democracy. If the critiques of Foucault, Mouffe, and others accurately describe the distribution and operation of power in modern societies, then epistemically oriented deliberation may in fact lead us deeper into the very domains of power from which participatory democratic politics were meant to free us.

Though no discursive conception of democracy can altogether avoid these problematics, theories can still be differentiated with respect to how porous and reversible the networks and relations of power they rely upon happen to be. Here a conversational view likely fares better than do deliberative theories. Oakeshott's critique of rationalism and his advocacy of conversation as the essential ethos of modern democracy converge in the recognition that where demonstration and truth are at stake, and politics are pursued as argument, power relations are at their thickest and most sedimented. Though conversation is neither neutral with regard to power relations, nor does it necessarily act as a discursive solvent, it does at least foreswear the rationalistic, epistemic ideal of truth-through-argument in democratic politics. Hence, when compared to other discursive theories, Oakeshottian conversation is a distinct and promising pluralistic alternative.

Responsible and Irresponsible Conversation

Even if the concept of conversation makes a meaningful contribution to democratic thought and practice, and even if conversation achieves a comparatively favorable standing among discursive democratic theories in the face of criticisms rooted in concerns about elitism and power, it might still be objected that Oakeshott's conception of conversation is less suitable to democratic politics than some other. In this vein, Stephen Mulhall argues that conversation is indeed the appropriate ethos for democratic politics, but criticizes Oakeshott's (as well as Richard Rorty's) conception of conversation as irresponsible. Mulhall turns instead to Stanley Cavell's conception of conversation with its emphasis upon the breadth and depth of moral responsibility and responsiveness that differentiates conversation from other discursive modes.[76] Deeply indebted to the work of Ludwig Wittgenstein, Cavell describes political community as a community of speakers engaged in articulating and inhabiting "a way of life together."[77] Democratic politics are bound up in this conversational engagement, what Cavell calls "the conversation of justice"; citizens in a democratically constituted and governed community are always speakers and hearers, parties to an ongoing public conversation about who they are (individually and together), what they believe, accept, hope for, deny, reject, and fear. So pictured, democratic politics consist in negotiations and explorations of what it means to belong, of how membership in political community is acquired and accepted, of how profound are the community's claims upon the individual, and vice versa.[78] At the heart of this picture of democratic politics are the twin commitments to moral responsibility and moral responsiveness—to be willing to mean and stand for what one says, to genuinely enter conversation with others, which conversely requires that one recognize one's exposure to the words of others. The individual's political standing as a citizen, and her moral standing as a person, are not facts of some juridical code and thus settled in advance, but positions taken up or denied, shaped and articulated, in the ongoing engagements of speaking and listening in one's community. Insofar as it draws upon Wittgensteinian themes about language and agency, this conception of conversation resonates with Oakeshott's understanding of agency, action, and practices, which I explored in chapter 1. However, Cavell self-consciously invests conversation with a distinctive moral gravity that binds one to one's words and their eventual effects, and to the words of others and the demands they make of one as an individual. The conversation of justice is inseparable from the moral (which is not to say moralized or moralistic) life of a democratic society; its conduct constructs the moral character of the community and its individual members.

Embracing Cavell's view that democracy is properly epitomized in the conversation of justice, and that undertaking this conversation requires and elicits a dimension of moral seriousness and commitment, Mulhall criticizes Oakeshott's conception on moral grounds. He reads Oakeshott as giving novelty and inconsequence free rein in conversation, indeed a privileged place, and thus claims that Oakeshott's conception "risks conjuring an image of mere play—of a conversation whose key tone is one of frivolity and superficiality, in which nothing real is at stake, and in which the significance of its outcomes is as nothing in comparison with immersion in the process."[79] Much as Cavell criticizes John Rawls for tending to reduce justice to unresponsive and even condescending practices of calling moral balls and strikes, Mulhall criticizes Oakeshott for tending to reduce conversation to self-indulgent utterance for its own sake, without the seriousness that the articulation of genuine moral and political community requires. Hence, while Oakeshott is correct to embrace pluralistic conversation rather than rather epistemic argument as the discursive mode appropriate to democratic politics, he overshoots the mark and articulates a conception of conversation that is not so much immoral as morally vacuous, that welcomes and defends abstention from political and moral commitment.[80] If this is so, Oakeshott's conception now seems hemmed in from two different sides. The charge of elitism criticizes Oakeshottian conversation for excluding certain persons and voices from participation, whereas the charge of irresponsibility criticizes it for allowing participants and their utterances to circulate too casually, without meaning what they say, without regard for the moral standing of the conversational enterprise itself and of the community it continually articulates.

The purpose of this section, as should now be apparent, is not to absolve Oakeshott of faults or shortcomings, but to arrive at balanced and realistic appreciation of their grounds, severity, and implications. Granting Mulhall the substance of his criticism, which includes granting him a more complete and satisfying textual discussion of Oakeshottian conversation than he in fact offers,[81] it is still possible to affect some reconciliation between these two conceptions of conversation. In particular, it is possible to grant to Cavell and Mulhall the moral weight of conversation and thus the moral dimension of conversational democracy while identifying in Oakeshott's conception a richer basis for moral commitment than Mulhall, or perhaps Oakeshott himself, supposes. A deeper Oakeshottian conception of conversation and its application to democratic thought and practice rests upon three primary considerations.

First, as has been explored from a number of vantage points in this and earlier chapters, Oakeshott turns to the conceptual picture of conversation in order to render an account of human conduct that satisfactorily acknowledges and expresses care for the plurality of persons, idioms of conduct and thought, and traditions of living together that populate the human world. Mulhall is correct that, at least compared to Cavell, Oakeshott presents a lighter, less explicitly moral conception of conversation. Yet if one considers the object of Cavell's moral seriousness, Oakeshott's view may in fact approach the same object from a different angle. Cavell utilizes the concept of conversation as a way to imagine a democratic society in order to avoid the Rawlsian notion of cooperation, which characteristically "suggests the idea of society as a whole either as having a project, or, at the other extreme, as being a neutral field in which each can pursue his or her own projects."[82] The first sense, both Cavell and Oakeshott reject—Cavell through his criticism of a certain image of social contract theory that fixes an index of social and political goods and rules for their distribution so as to leave those who lack them without ground for criticism or recourse, and Oakeshott through his critique of teleocratic, enterprise association as a model or ideal for a pluralistic political community. The second sense, I believe the two likewise reject, though this assessment may strike some readers of Oakeshott as surprising. Cavell inveighs against Rawls for offering a view of political community that narrows and inhibits an essential moral dimension. Cavell maintains that in democratic political community, even settled claims to social and political goods must be open to challenges, and that these challenges can legitimately demand responses even from those who have played by the rules. Rawls, he supposes, hedges such conversational engagement in with schemes of rights that are specified in advance, the uses of which must be accepted virtually regardless of their consequences. Oakeshott, even in his more classically liberal moments, challenges the idea that the terms of a scheme of social cooperation (e.g., a full and satisfactory scheme of rights) can be drafted in such a way as to both certify their ultimate justice and eliminate the need or grounds for their responsiveness to experience (an idea that smacks of rationalism). He turns to conversation in part to leave space in political as well as moral life for a greater sensitivity to and appreciation for the contingency of our places in a world that is itself contingent. The very thing that Mulhall criticizes—privileging immersion in the process of conversation over the conclusions it reaches—is part and parcel of Oakeshott's emphasis upon our practices and what their actual uses intimate over attempts to impose or extract simple and rigid structures that can fully abate the contingencies that destabilize our best laid plans. That is, Oakeshottian conversation is parasitic upon two of the most potent political threats to human plurality: the imposition of sovereign enterprises and the imposition of sovereign techniques. Mulhall's charge of frivolity thus rests upon a failure to appreciate the substantive commitments of Oakeshott's conception.

Second, in their respective conceptions of conversation, both Cavell and Oakeshott strive to acknowledge and care for the dignity and moral weight of the agent, which is inseparable from her standing as a speaker in an ongoing conversation. There is thus a sense of moral gravity to Oakeshott's conception as well. Whereas Cavell places the greater emphasis upon the ties that bind the individual to others in community, and how these are continuously and intimately negotiated, Oakeshott places greater emphasis on the irreducibility of the individual to any given or contingent set of ties.[83] When Oakeshott says that individuals have a history but no nature, that they each are what they (in doing) become, he challenges the very idea that an individual's relationship to others (individually or in notional community) can be specified in some sort of empirical list of facts or in some sort of abstract theoretical formula.[84] Conversation provides a conceptual framework for this way of fitting together the contingency of individual identity with the notion of a community whose members contingently share a common life through their common practices. Oakeshott's use of the concept of conversation to get a clearer view of how contingency fundamentally shapes and animates the lives of individuals both singly and together preserves a sense of seriousness with regard to the contingent grounds upon which moral agents stand. The openness and playfulness of conversation expresses doubt regarding the givenness or finality of any individual or communal identity. That this is not the precise *kind* of moral sensibility that Mulhall expects is no demonstration that Oakeshottian conversation lacks a moral sensibility altogether, and it may very well complement the moral sensibility manifest in Cavell's conception.

Third, readers of Oakeshott would do well to take seriously Mulhall's caution against valuing the practice of conversation irrespective of its conclusions or implications. There is, in Oakeshott's account, a tendency to present conversation as a self-justifying practice whose value is solely inherent and whose end is self-perpetuation. However, his conception of conversation does possess a sense of moral consequence, both with regard to human plurality and the individuals whose live give plurality its texture. Furthermore, without some sense that immersion in the engagement is valuable regardless of its outcomes, it may become difficult to sustain conversation in precisely those moments when we enter upon difficult moral and political terrain. Oakeshott's valuation of conversation might preserve a commitment to conversation, precisely in those moments when we find our interlocutors least conversible or most in need of demonstrative correction by argument. As Oakeshott realized, arrests in conversation invite a return to argumentative idioms, in which the end sought is unanswerable (and thus unresponsive and irresponsible) truth. Although it would be misguided to suppose that conversation always delivers the goods, a basic sense of commitment to the endeavor (even in its less consequential moments) promotes an idiom of democratic politics that admits of passages of argument and of the various arrests that accompany decision, but which is nonetheless resistant to foreclosure by either epistemic or communal force. This, one could say, is how Oakeshott imagines public life in a society that is deeply pluralistic despite its shared networks of intersubjective practices. Far from lacking responsiveness or responsibility, his vision of conversational democracy depicts the politics of civil associates who need be united in neither more nor less than practices and idioms of utterance and action.

CONCLUSION: APPROACHING A VANISHING IDEAL

In the wake of the revival in democratic theory in recent decades, one of the principal measures of a political thinker is what he or she has to say about democracy. Despite his rigorous thought about the modern state, its conditions, emergence, and contingent shapes, Oakeshott was not a theory builder. His extensive writings on politics are flush with theoretical insights, but are almost wholly devoid of programs, policy prescriptions, or models to be operationalized and implemented. Even his theorization of enterprise and civil association is meant as a lens through which to view the dominant, conflicting tendencies manifest in modern politics. At no point does he offer a blueprint for institutional design or a handbook for activists. Principled, skeptical avoidance of political programs should be counted among both the weaknesses and the strengths of Oakeshott's work. In respect of its sparseness and aspirational tone, Oakeshott's conversational ideal appears to lack theoretical rigor and practical purchase. In comparison to robust theoretical models and institutional programs, conversational democracy is likely to appear little more than a vague suggestion, a high-minded critique, or a thought-provoking idea with little or no empirical application.

Though institutional models often enjoy pride of place in contemporary democratic thought, the salience of ethos in democracy should not be underestimated. Even in its classical Athenian origins, which possessed a complex institutional structure, democracy was as much the manifestation of an ethos as of a model. The most fundamental democratic ideal—that the people (*dēmos*) hold and exercise power (*kratos*)—specifies no model or even theory of democracy, but it certainly expresses a political ethos. Similarly, although Oakeshott's conversational view contains no concrete model or ready-to-operationalize theory, it formulates a nuanced ethos that is not limited in imagination or application in the ways that rigorous models and theories necessarily are. It may seem slight praise to say of a political thinker that his or her democratic thought is vague enough to be flexible, but actual democratic politics tend to be hybrids cobbled together out of practices of diverse provenance. Hence, the absence of systematic scope and programmatic rigor does not foreclose either the theoretical or the practical significance of Oakeshott's work. Much as his reflections on the ideal type he calls civil association can inform our political thought and practice without presenting a concrete institutional pattern, his discussion of conversation and its democratic potential can enrich our political imagination and bolster our aspirations without being reduced to a set of policies or slogans.

Without formulating a single, detailed model, one can imagine how a conversational ethos could find a place in present-day democratic practices. Mouffe provides a useful characterization, akin to Oakeshott's, when she suggests that even though the complete realization of the ideal of consensus is conceptually impossible and would undermine modern pluralistic democracy, "it should be conceived as a good that exists as good only as long as it cannot be reached."[85] Applied to Oakeshott's view of conversation, one might say that even if the complete realization of conversational politics would amount to a fruitless and interminable politics without decision, an asymptotic approximation might nonetheless be both realistic and beneficial. It is certainly possible that democratic politics could admit of a greater diversity of discursive idioms, and there is good reason to believe that such diversity would better reflect the actual human plurality that is the source and frame of our politics.

This, I believe, is the most faithful reading of Oakeshott's vision of conversation in democratic politics. The central insight of his democratic thought is that the proper yet hopeful way to imagine a democratic society is as a plurality of individuals who share in an authoritative institutional framework engaged in conversation, perhaps punctuated by argument, but not obsessed or dominated by it. His vision thus speaks to the most fundamental levels of our political imagination and self-understanding, provides a fresh way to view our actual politics, and suggests what might lie just beyond them.

CONCLUSION

Hearing Voices

[I]t has rhythms which remain when the words are forgotten.

—Michael Oakeshott, *On Human Conduct*

A theory of agency, or tradition, or the state, or democracy—indeed, of anything at all—is a body of discrete ideas and sentiments whose elements engage one another and hang together more or less systematically. Although such elements harmonize at some level, they need not, and often do not, constitute an undifferentiated unity, and while they collectedly eventuate in something not reducible to any one element, each offers its own distinct contribution. Viewed from a certain angle, a theory thus resembles a conversation: a circumstantial intercourse of a plurality of ideas and sentiments, expressed in diverse idioms and conveying varied perspectives. While some theories (their structures, aims, components, and presuppositions) are such that conversation among them may be difficult, limited, or prone to *aporia*, it is naive or dogmatic to suppose that such conversation is ever altogether fruitless or impossible. Even angels and devils have something to talk about, if only their profound differences. Most theories, of course, are separated by less.

This book is an assemblage of conversations, or at least it has been my intention to construct such an assemblage. As an approach to political theory, a style or disposition of thought, conversation is recommended by its openness. Oakeshott had such a role in mind when he characterized conversation as "the appropriate image of human intercourse—appropriate because it recognizes the qualities, the diversities, and the proper relationships of human utterances," and as a pluralistic engagement in which "different universes of discourse meet, acknowledge each other and enjoy an oblique relationship which neither requires nor forecasts their being assimilated to one another."[1] There is no doubt that this is an optimistic image of human thought and communication, but its aspirations are tempered by a healthy skepticism. Out of plurality we should expect plurality—out of the meeting of many voices and perspectives should emerge many voices and perspectives. Insofar as plurality is a feature of the human condition, conversation recommends itself as a viable and valuable ethos. Unlike argument—which seeks to demonstrate and convince, whittling the field of ideas and perspectives down to the smallest domain possible, leaving no respectable alternative—conversation invites exchange without competition as well as competition without triumph or defeat, and thus invites us to loosen slightly the grip with which we hold our doctrines, or with which they hold us. The point is not to abandon conviction, but to see it always as our own, as contingent as ourselves, and at home in a pluralistic world of persons and ideas. In conversation a plurality of voices meet, recognize their affinities and differences, pursue passages of persuasion and argument, but in the end none is either leader or follower, victor or vanquished.

A distinct advantage of such an approach to political theory is that it invites the recognition at the level of theory of what Arendt posited at the level of human subjectivity.[2] We and our ideas exist in narrative webs or, one might say, suspended in the fluid media of language, history, experience, and understanding. Our conversational engagements ineluctably reflect the distinctness and plurality of ourselves; in conversation we shall find affinities as well as discrepancies, moments of arrest or friction as well as moments of consensus and harmony. The distinction of conversation as a discursive ethos resides in its openness to the fruits of plurality and contingency, and its unwillingness to demand their reduction to one voice or perspective. Placing thinkers and their ideas in a conversation invites the discovery and appreciation of such affinities and discrepancies, and in hearing what the several voices say we shall likely hear new resonances within each.

My aim has been to elicit such a conversation around Oakeshott's political thought, prompted by my sense that (despite the efforts of his interpreters) he remains a more insightful and relevant philosopher and political thinker than is often appreciated, and that the way to a better appreciation is through his concept of conversation. His work has suffered the fate that became common during the second half of the twentieth century—it was sorted into ideological categories such as "liberal" and "conservative," which are useful to a point, but always abridgments of something more nuanced. For his own part, Oakeshott self-consciously resisted ideological labels, seeing them as a manifestation of the rationalism that he believed had infected too much of modern politics. He was often beloved of postwar British conservatives, but refused to become an ideological spokesperson.[3] He wrote in praise of the disposition of conservatism in politics, but rarely of its ideological or policy commitments. What is more, important aspects of Oakeshott's work fall within the scope of liberal political thought yet he is also not a "liberal theorist" in any straightforward or doctrinaire sense. His philosophical and political thought is systematic, sometimes to a fault, but the system is distinctly his own.

It is in virtue of the irreducibility of Oakeshott's thought that the concept of conversation is so uniquely appropriate as a guide to its study and appreciation. He praised conversation, both as the proper image by which to imagine human conduct generally and as the appropriate ethos for politics. His characterization of agents presents them as persons eminently fit for, and inexorably fated to, conversation with others of their kind. His understanding of tradition valorizes the collected yet individual endeavors of understanding and self-enactment, viewing tradition as a kind of ongoing, auto-poetic conversation, rather than as the endless repetition of a script or the unfolding of some latent *telos*. His account of civil association and critique of enterprise association apply this conversational ethos to the modern state and politics, sketching a form of association in which individuals meet as conversants rather than as comrades or opponents. Finally, his characterization of democracy closes the circle, as it were, gesturing toward how a plurality of individual agents might address the common arrangements of their *respublica* through politics embodying a conversational ethos. Thus, our understanding of Oakeshott's thought in its own terms benefits from following his lead, taking seriously his own overarching conception of conversation. This already takes us beyond several of the barriers to understanding posed by renderings of Oakeshott's thought in terms of philosophical and political labels that he never so much as embraced or that he eschewed altogether.

In exploring Oakeshott's thought by placing it in conversation with a selection of twentieth-century thinkers, I have hoped to highlight some unexpected or unconventional affinities that are lost or obscured when his thought is read through ideological lenses. By challenging some of the commonplaces regarding his work, I have attempted to situate him within a larger context of modern political thought. While my conversational treatment of Oakeshott is perhaps in itself worthwhile as an exercise in intellectual ecumenism, I believe that it takes seriously dimensions of his work that have been muted or mitigated, intentionally or not, in decades of scholarship. My hope is that the recognized circle in which Oakeshott's thought travels will have grown slightly, not just adding to our appreciation and understanding of his work, but underscoring his continued significance to modern political thought.

NOTES

INTRODUCTION

1. In addition to the spate of previously unpublished or uncollected works by Oakeshott, more than twenty books (both monographs and edited volumes) and an even greater number of articles and book chapters have been published expressly on the work of Michael Oakeshott. A significant number of these appear in the Oakeshott Studies series published by Imprint Academic, and have recently been joined by edited companions from Cambridge University Press and Pennsylvania State University Press.

2. Book-length synoptic treatments include works by Wendell John Coats Jr., Paul Franco, Robert Grant, Stuart Isaacs, Terry Nardin, Edmund Neill, and Efraim Podoksik.

3. A sample of more narrowly topical treatments include books by Aryeh Botwinick and Steven Anthony Gerencser (skepticism), Roy Tseng (skepticism and idealism), Michael Minch (democracy), Debra Candreva (rationalism), Elizabeth Corey and Glenn Worthington (religion and aesthetics), Luke O'Sullivan (history), Robert Devigne and Anthony Farr (conservatism), Ian Tregenza (Oakeshott's understanding of Thomas Hobbes), Paul Franco, W. H. Greenleaf, Eric Steven Kos, Kenneth McIntyre, and Suvi Soininen (political philosophy and practice), Kevin Williams (education), and Andrew Sullivan (practice).

4. Examples of how labels tend to both refine and distort understanding of Oakeshott are furnished by Corey Abel, ed., *The Meanings of Michael Oakeshott's Conservatism* (Charlottesville, VA: Imprint Academic, 2010).

5. Michael Oakeshott, "The Voice of Conversation in the Education of Mankind," in *What is History? and Other Essays*, ed. Luke O'Sullivan (Charlottesville, VA: Imprint Academic, 2004), 187–99; and "The Voice of Poetry in the Conversation of Mankind," in *Rationalism in Politics and Other Essays*, rev. ed. (Indianapolis: Liberty Fund, 1991), 488–541.

6. For discussions of Oakeshott's recognition and embrace of plurality, see Richard E. Flathman, *Pluralism and Liberal Democracy* (Baltimore: Johns Hopkins University Press, 2005), 109–61; Paige Digeser and Richard Flathman, "Oakeshott's *On Human Conduct*," in *The Cambridge Companion to Oakeshott*, ed. Efraim Podoksik (Cambridge: Cambridge University Press, 2012), 199–221; and Efraim Podoksik, *In Defense of Modernity: Vision and Philosophy in Michael Oakeshott* (Charlottesville, VA: Imprint Academic, 2003).

7. E.g., Michael Oakeshott, "Political Education," in *Rationalism in Politics*, 58 (where Oakeshott characterizes "the pursuit of intimations" that is the heart of politics as "conversation") and Michael Oakeshott, *On Human Conduct* (Oxford: Clarendon Press, 1975), 238.

8. Oakeshott, "The Voice of Poetry in the Conversation of Mankind," 490.

9. Oakeshott, *On Human Conduct*, 59.

10. Thus, Oakeshott maintains that in conversation "[s]uccess does not lie in the conclusion of the discussion by some unanswerable pronouncement; that is failure. Success is to maintain this delicate aerial equilibrium [between the plurality of voices and utterances], to keep alive what has miraculously been given life." Oakeshott, "The Voice of Conversation in the Education of Mankind," 190.

11. Michael Oakeshott, "Rationalism in Politics," in *Rationalism in Politics*, 22.

12. Ibid., 20; Oakeshott, "The Voice of Poetry in the Conversation of Mankind," 489.

13. Oakeshott, "The Voice of Poetry in the Conversation of Mankind," 490.

14. Oakeshott, *On Human Conduct*, 58–59.

15. Oakeshott, "The Voice of Poetry in the Conversation of Mankind," 490.

16. This latter notion was initially developed in *Experience and Its Modes*, but was carried forward in different terms into the conversation essays, *On Human Conduct*, and two essays published in *On History and Other Essays* (Indianapolis: Liberty Fund, 1999): "The Rule of Law" (129–78) and the second essay given the title "The Tower of Babel." (179–210).

17. Ibid., 489; Oakeshott, "The Voice of Conversation in the Education of Mankind," 187–88.

18. Oakeshott, *On Human Conduct*, 2–3.

19. This is the stated and manifest purpose of both *Experience and Its Modes* (Cambridge: Cambridge University Press, 1933), where Oakeshott strives to defend experience against reduction to the modes of thought through which it is partially and conditionally understood, and *On Human Conduct*, where he strives to defend the intelligence and freedom of human conduct against doctrines that dismiss or overstate them.

20. Numerous secondary works describe or appeal to Oakeshott's "voice" and his concept of conversation, yet none pursue the course that I am suggesting and many engage in the synoptic, topical, and classificatory approaches that I aim to avoid.

21. Bhikhu Parekh, "Oakeshott's Theory of Civil Association," *Ethics* 106 (Oct. 1995): 158. Paul Franco makes a fundamentally similar claim in *The Political Philosophy of Michael Oakeshott* (New Haven: Yale University Press, 1990), 1. While my treatment of Oakeshott in respect of such "misunderstanding" is generally sympathetic, I do not mean to absolve him of all responsibility for the bold labels attributed to his thought.

22. David Boucher and Stuart Isaacs each identify aspects of this tendency, noting the trend of offering "ideological" or "political" readings of Oakeshott's *corpus* that interpret his varied thought through the lenses of conservatism, liberalism, or similar limiting categories. See David Boucher, "Politics in a Different Mode: An Appreciation of Michael Oakeshott 1901–1990," *History of Political Thought* XII, no.4

(Winter 1991): 717–28; Stuart Isaacs, *The Politics and Philosophy of Michael Oakeshott* (London: Routledge, 2006), 2.

23. I would be clear that although it is useful and important to identify Oakeshott's recognition of and commitments to plurality, I do not mean to present him as a "pluralist" in the way that he is often presented as an "idealist" or "liberal." His notions of conversation and plurality are not exclusive or ideological in the sense required for such labels to stick.

24. The theme of continuity or discontinuity from Oakeshott's early to later works is a staple in the secondary literature and takes many forms. Works exemplary of the other themes are: Paul Franco, *The Political Philosophy of Michael Oakeshott* (conservative to liberal); Suvi Soininen, *From a "Necessary Evil" to an Art of Contingency: Michael Oakeshott's Conception of Political Activity* (Charlottesville, VA: Imprint Academic, 2005) (apolitical to political); Steven Anthony Gerencser, *The Skeptic's Oakeshott* (New York: St. Martin's Press, 2000) (idealist to skeptical); Ian Tregenza, *Michael Oakeshott on Hobbes* (Charlottesville, VA: Imprint Academic, 2003) (from Hegel and Bradley to Hobbes).

25. Wendell John Coats Jr., *Oakeshott and His Contemporaries* (Selinsgrove, PA: Susquehanna University Press, 2000).

26. It is clear from textual evidence that Oakeshott was familiar with some of the work of Ludwig Wittgenstein and Hannah Arendt, and he knew personally Isaiah Berlin. As he was also a voracious reader on a wide variety of subjects, it is certain that his familiarity far exceeds his explicit acknowledgment.

27. Two outstanding examples are Paul Franco, *Michael Oakeshott: An Introduction* (New Haven: Yale University Press, 2004), and Terry Nardin, *The Philosophy of Michael Oakeshott* (University Park: Pennsylvania State University Press, 2001).

28. Oakeshott, "The Voice of Conversation in the Education of Mankind," 194.

CHAPTER ONE. LANGUAGE, PRACTICE, AND INDIVIDUAL AGENCY

1. Oakeshott, *Experience and Its Modes*, 14.

2. Michael Oakeshott, *On Human Conduct*, 234–42; Michael Oakeshott, "The Masses in Representative Democracy," in *Rationalism in Politics*, 363–83.

3. Oakeshott, *On Human Conduct*, 59.

4. See, for instance, Aryeh Botwinick, *Michael Oakeshott's Skepticism* (Princeton: Princeton University Press, 2011); Stuart Isaacs, *The Politics and Philosophy of Michael Oakeshott*; Terry Nardin, *The Philosophy of Michael Oakeshott*; and Richard Rorty, *Philosophy and the Mirror of Nature* (Princeton: Princeton University Press, 1979).

5. Richard E. Flathman, *The Practice of Political Authority* (Chicago: University of Chicago Press, 1980); *Toward a Liberalism* (Ithaca: Cornell University Press, 1989), esp. 14–64; *Reflections of a Would-be Anarchist* (Minneapolis: University of Minnesota Press, 1998), esp. 49–77; and *Freedom and Its Conditions* (London: Routledge, 2003).

6. The ascription of the label *conservative* is widespread with regard to Oakeshott. See, for instance, Robert Devigne, *Recasting Conservatism: Oakeshott, Strauss, and the Response to Postmodernism* (New Haven: Yale University Press, 1994); Gertrude Himmelfarb, "The Conservative Imagination," *The American Scholar* 44, no. 3 (Summer 1975): 405–20; John Kekes, "What Is Conservatism?," *Philosophy* 72, No. 281 (July 1997): 351–74; Hanna F. Pitkin, "The Roots of Conservatism: Michael Oakeshott and the Denial of Politics," *Dissent* (Fall 1973): 496–525; Anthony Quinton, *The Politics of Imperfection: The Religious and Secular Traditions of Conservative Thought in England from Hooker to Oakeshott* (London: Faber and Faber, 1978). The ascription is somewhat more varied and contested with regard to Wittgenstein. As I will explore below, David Bloor and J. C. Nyíri are among the most thoroughgoing advocates of Wittgenstein's conservatism, with the latter suggesting that Wittgenstein and Oakeshott have precisely this in common. Such a position is also taken, with a variety of qualifications and inflections, by Dean C. Hammer, "Meaning & Tradition," *Polity* 24, No. 4 (Summer 1992): 551–67; John Kekes, "What Is Conservatism?"; Richard Rorty, *Contingency, Irony, and Solidarity* (Cambridge: Cambridge University Press, 1989) (esp. ch. 3); and Richard Rorty, "Postmodernist Bourgeois Liberalism," *Journal of Philosophy* 80, no. 10 (Oct. 1983): 583–89.

7. David Bloor, *Wittgenstein: A Social Theory of Knowledge* (New York: Columbia University Press, 1983) and *Wittgenstein, Rules and Institutions* (London: Routledge, 1997); J. C. Nyíri, "Wittgenstein's New Traditionalism," *Acta Philosophica Fennica* 28 (1976): 501–12 and "Wittgenstein's Later Work in Relation to Conservatism," in *Wittgenstein and his Times*, ed. Brian McGuinness (Chicago: University of Chicago Press, 1982), 44–68. Yet, as Andrew Norris suggests, Richard Rorty approvingly attributes a similar view of agency, community, and membership to Wittgenstein and Oakeshott in *Contingency, Irony, and Solidarity*, 58–60. Andrew Norris, "'La chaîne des raisons a une fin.' Wittgenstein et Oakeshott sur le rationalisme et la pratique," *Cités: Philosophie, Politique, Histoire* 38 (2009): 95–108. I thank the author for sharing the original essay on which the French translation was based.

8. For the sake of terminological economy and consistency I will use the term *theories of agency* to cover both theoretical accounts of agency (understood as a capacity to act) and of action (understood as a particular kind of event authored by or attributable to an agent).

9. E.g., Anthony Downs, *An Economic Theory of Democracy* (New York: Harper, 1957); John Rawls, *A Theory of Justice*, rev. ed. (Cambridge: Belknap Press of Harvard University Press, 1999); William H. Riker, *Liberalism Against Populism: A Confrontation Between the Theory of Democracy and the Theory of Social Choice* (San Francisco: W. H. Freeman, 1982); Joseph A. Schumpeter, *Capitalism, Socialism, and Democracy* (New York: Harper and Row, 1962).

10. E.g., the work of conservative sociologists (such as Erving Goffman and Karl Mannheim), communitarian political and moral theorists (such as Alasdair MacIntyre, Michael Sandel, and Charles Taylor), and Left political and social thinkers influenced by Karl Marx, Friedrich Nietzsche, and Martin Heidegger (such as Michel Foucault and Gilles Deleuze).

11. There is no clear indication that the two ever met during their overlapping time at Cambridge, and the extent of their textual engagement with one anoth-

er is exhausted by a single oblique quotation from the *Tractatus Logico-Philosophicus* in Oakeshott's 1929 essay "The Authority of the State," in *Religion, Politics, and the Moral Life*, ed. Timothy Fuller (New Haven: Yale University Press, 1993), 79. See Kenneth Minogue, "The History of Political Thought Seminar," in *The Achievement of Michael Oakeshott*, ed. Jesse Norman (London: Duckworth, 1993), 96.

12. Oakeshott's pursuit of this theme stretches from *Experience and Its Modes*, through *Rationalism in Politics*, to *On Human Conduct*. As I shall illustrate below, Wittgenstein embraces and explores similar views throughout his later works.

13. Ludwig Wittgenstein, *Philosophical Investigations*, 3rd ed., trans. G. E. M. Anscombe (Upper Saddle River, NJ: Prentice-Hall, 1958), §199.

14. Oakeshott, *On Human Conduct*, 55.

15. Ibid., 59.

16. Wittgenstein speaks of a language-game as grounding and structuring agential "capacity" (*Können*) in *Zettel*, ed. G. E. M. Anscombe and G. H. von Wright, trans. G. E. M. Anscombe (Berkeley: University of California Press, 1970), §421; see also *Philosophical Investigations*, §199.

17. Oakeshott, *On Human Conduct*, 58.

18. Wittgenstein, *Philosophical Investigations*, §241–42. As with language-games, Wittgenstein stops short of fully specifying or defining "forms of life" (*Lebensformen*), though he variously illustrates aspects of the concept. Stanley Cavell provides a useful statement, faithful to the breadth and scope of Wittgenstein's discussions of forms of life and what it means to be "attuned" or "in agreement" in respect of them. As Cavell puts it,

> We learn and teach words in certain contexts, and then we are expected, and expect others, to be able to project them into further contexts. Nothing insures that this projection will take place (in particular, not the grasping of universals nor the grasping of books of rules), just as nothing insures that we will make, and understand, the same projections. That on the whole we do is a matter of our sharing routes of interest and feeling, modes of response, senses of humor and of significance and of fulfillment, of what is outrageous, of what is similar to what else, what a rebuke, what forgiveness, of when an utterance is an assertion, when an appeal, when an explanation—all the whirl of organism Wittgenstein calls "forms of life." Human speech and activity, sanity and community, rest upon nothing more, but nothing less, than this.

Stanley Cavell, *Must We Mean What We Say?*, 2nd ed. (Cambridge: Cambridge University Press, 2002), 52.

19. Wittgenstein, *Philosophial Investigations*, §§5–9; Oakeshott, *On Human Conduct*, 57.

20. E.g., Oakeshott, *On Human Conduct*, 88–107.

21. For further discussion of this learning process as Wittgenstein presents it, see Cavell, *The Claim of Reason*, 2nd ed. (Oxford: Oxford University Press, 1999), esp. 168–90.

22. Oakeshott, *On Human Conduct*, 53.

23. Peter Winch describes Wittgenstein's view in this way, yet accuses Oakeshott of disregarding the importance of rules and their role in reflection. Peter Winch, *The Idea of a Social Science and Its Relation to Philosophy*, 2nd ed. (London: Routledge, 1990), 62. However, Oakeshott's more complete position published in *On Human Conduct* almost two decades after Winch's original assessment is quite consistent with Wittgenstein's.

24. Wittgenstein, *Philosophical Investigations*, §§80–90; 150–243.

25. Ibid., §244–318. Many attributions to Wittgenstein of a social theory of agency draw extensively upon his discussion of rules and rule-following. The common argumentative thread in the secondary literature is that agency manifests in following rules in speech and action; rule-following is a social activity; hence, agency is derivative of conformity to intersubjective conventions. See Bloor, *Wittgenstein, Rules, and Institutions*; Saul Kripke, *Wittgenstein on Rules and Private Language* (Cambridge: Harvard University Press, 1982), e.g., 96; and Richard Rorty, *Contingency, Irony, and Solidarity* and "Postmodernist Bourgeois Liberalism."

26. Ludwig Wittgenstein, *On Certainty*, ed. G. E. M. Anscombe and G. H. von Wright, trans. Denis Paul and G. E. M. Anscombe (New York: Harper and Row, 1972), §229.

27. Michael Oakeshott, "The Study of 'Politics' in a University," in *Rationalism in Politics and Other Essays*, 184–218.

28. Oakeshott, *On Human Conduct*, 59.

29. Such interpretations flourish among thinkers who enlist or classify Wittgenstein and Oakeshott as conservative figures (e.g., Bloor, Nyíri, Kekes, Hammer), as well as among thinkers who employ Wittgenstein and Oakeshott as iconoclastic or even radical figures in larger debates about the individual and society (e.g., Pitkin, Rorty, Winch).

30. I draw what immediately follows from J. C. Nyíri and David Bloor, see *supra* 4.

31. Bloor, *Wittgenstein, Rules, and Institutions*, 30; Wittgenstein, *Philosophical Investigations*, §§185–219; Oakeshott, "Rationalism in Politics" and "Political Education," in *Rationalism in Politics*, 5–42 and 43–69 respectively. The conservative reading thus understands a "form of life" as a complex of empirical patterns of behavior that felicitous individual action follows and reproduces. Alice Crary argues that Rorty's reading of Wittgenstein (and, I would add, of Oakeshott) arrives at similar conclusions by way of similar, if more sophisticated, claims. See Alice Crary, "Wittgenstein's Philosophy in Relation to Political Thought," in *The New Wittgenstein*, ed. Alice Crary and Rupert Read (London: Routledge, 2000), 118–45; esp. 119–30; also Norris, "'La chaîne des raisons a une fin.'"

32. Nyíri, "Wittgenstein's Later Work," 58.

33. Wittgenstein, *On Certainty*, §§449, 344; see also Oakeshott, "Political Education," 62.

34. Bloor, *Wittgenstein: A Social Theory of Knowledge*, 1; Nyíri, "Wittgenstein's Later Work," 59.

35. Nyíri, "Wittgenstein's Later Work," 58–59. The apparent force of this conclusion stems from a highly questionable conflation of agreements of truly basic and rudimentary conceptual kinds (e.g., agreements on the proper practice of addition)

and agreements of highly complex and ambiguous conceptual kinds (e.g., agreements on the proper meaning of freedom or equality or obligation). Identifying and challenging this conflation, see K. Jones, "Is Wittgenstein a Conservative Philosopher?," *Philosophical Investigations* 9, no. 4 (Oct. 1986): 274–87, esp. 285.

36. Bloor, *Wittgenstein: A Social Theory of Knowledge*, 166. Similar claims, some indebted to Wittgenstein and Oakeshott, some not, have been carried forward in social and political thought by Richard Rorty and by a number of postmodern thinkers who, in their attempt to reject certain universalistic doctrines of the Enlightenment, slide into a form of relativism that is often closely akin to the conservatism articulated by Bloor and Nyíri. George Kateb traces this philosophical Laffer Curve in *The Inner Ocean* (Ithaca: Cornell University Press, 1992), 222–39 and in *Patriotism and Other Mistakes* (New Haven: Yale University Press, 2006), 3–20.

37. Nyíri, "Wittgenstein's New Traditionalism," 505.

38. Cressida J. Heyes presents an informative overview of the debate surrounding this reading in her introduction to *The Grammar of Politics: Wittgenstein and Political Philosophy*, ed. Cressida J. Heyes (Ithaca: Cornell University Press, 2003), 1–13; esp. 3–6.

39. Crary, "Wittgenstein's Philosophy in Relation to Political Thought," 140.

40. Bernard Williams, "Pluralism, Community, and Left Wittgensteinianism," in *In the Beginning Was the Deed*, ed. Geoffrey Hawthorn (Princeton: Princeton University Press, 2005), 29–39; 35.

41. Wittgenstein, *On Certainty*, §609.

42. Williams, "Left Wittgensteinianism," 36.

43. Wittgenstein, *On Certainty*, §519.

44. Williams, "Left Wittgensteinianism," 36–37.

45. Oakeshott, "The Study of 'Politics' in a University," 187, and *On Human Conduct*, 120.

46. See William E. Connolly, *The Terms of Political Discourse*, 3rd ed. (Princeton: Princeton University Press, 1993). Looking to Connolly in his discussion of political contestation in a Wittgensteinian idiom, Allan Janik states that Connolly "demonstrate[s] that these conceptual conflicts are the very stuff of political life." Janik, "Notes on the Natural History of Politics," in *The Grammar of Politics*, 99–116; 105.

47. Oakeshott, "Political Education," 57–69.

48. Ferdinand de Saussure, *Course in General Linguistics*, ed. Charles Bally and Albert Sechehay, trans. Wade Baskin (New York: Philosophical Library, 1959), 9–17. Interesting similarities withstanding, I should not like to press the analogy between Wittgenstein and Saussure too far, first, because Saussure regards the individuality of utterance to be "accessory and more or less accidental" to the reproduction of the language of the speaker (Saussure, *Course*, 14) and, second, because Saussure does not recognize as fully as Wittgenstein and Oakeshott the way in which language and concepts penetrate word and deed. I believe that these potential points of disanalogy can be explained by the social-scientific approach taken by Saussure, as distinct from the analytic-philosophical approach taken by Wittgenstein. Each approach carries with it conceptual pictures that foreground certain aspects of language-use while obscuring others. Without adjudicating between Saussure and Wittgenstein, I

suppose Wittgenstein to offer a distinctive and adequate picture. For a more extensive discussion of Wittgenstein and Saussure, see Roy Harris, *Language, Saussure, and Wittgenstein: How to Play Games with Words* (London: Routledge, 1990).

49. E.g., Wittgenstein, *On Certainty*, §§128–30, 140; Oakeshott, *On Human Conduct*, 87.

50. The notional "we-say" entailed by all language-use may be understood as akin to the transcendental "I-think" that Kant believed must be able to accompany all of one's mental representations—that is, a formal condition of possibility but not an ever-present empirical fact or event. Taking the "we-say" too literally and empirically, as the conservative reading demands that we do, leaves us unable to account for eccentric utterance and action that nonetheless *works*. See Bernard Williams, "Wittgenstein and Idealism," in *Moral Luck* (Cambridge: Cambridge University Press 1981), 144–63.

51. Hilary Putnam, "Rules, Attunement, and 'Applying Words to the World': The Struggle to Understand Wittgenstein's Vision of Language," in *The Legacy of Wittgenstein: Pragmatism or Deconstruction*, ed. Chantal Mouffe and Ludwig Nagl (Frankfurt am Main: Peter Lang, 2001), 9–25; 21.

52. A telling passage from Wittgenstein is:

> And does this mean e.g. that the definition of "same" would be this: same is what all or most human beings with one voice take for the same? —Of course not.
>
> For of course I don't make use of the agreement of human beings to affirm identity. What criterion do you use, then? None at all.

Remarks on the Foundations of Mathematics, ed. G. H von Wright, Rush Rhees, and G. E. M. Anscombe, trans. G. E. M. Anscombe (Oxford: Basil Blackwell, 1956), VII, §40.

53. Wittgenstein, *Philosophical Investigations*, §219.

54. Wittgenstein, *Philosophical Investigations*, §325; Colin McGinn, *Wittgenstein on Meaning: An Interpretation and Evaluation* (Oxford: Basil Blackwell, 1984), 23.

55. On this point Bloor and Nyíri are joined by Richard Rorty.

56. Stanley Cavell offers a similar, yet more consensual, interpretation of "This is simply what I do," claiming that "[w]hat justifies what I say and do is, I feel like saying, *me*—the fact that I can respond to an indefinite range of responses of the other, and that the other, for my spade not to be stopped, must respond to me." *Conditions Handsome and Unhandsome: The Constitution of Emersonian Perfectionism* (Chicago: University of Chicago Press, 1990), 77.

57. Ludwig Wittgenstein, *Culture and Value*, ed. G. H. Von Wright, trans. Peter Winch (Chicago: University of Chicago Press, 1980), 16e.

58. This insight may also find some analogue in Saussure's claim that "[a] mong all the individuals that are linked together by speech, some sort of average will be set up: all will reproduce—not exactly of course, but approximately—the same signs united with the same concepts" (*Course in General Linguistics*, 13). I am not entirely confident, however, that the Saussurean gap between conventional language

and individual speech admits the sort of genuine critical agency that Wittgenstein and Oakeshott recognize.

59. Wittgenstein, *Philosophical Investigations*, §§67–77.

60. Wittgenstein, *On Certainty*, §281. Not only does this emphasis of the first-person singular pronoun exist in Wittgenstein's original German, it is even capitalized, contrary to the normal German orthography: "aber *Ich* stimme mit ihnen überein." The emphasis, it seems, is on the individual who agrees rather than on the community with whom the individual agrees.

61. Richard E. Flathman, *The Philosophy and Politics of Freedom* (Chicago: University of Chicago Press, 1987), 23; See Janik, "Notes on the Natural History of Politics," 104.

62. McGinn, *Wittgenstein on Meaning*, 200. That Oakeshott also falls on the individualist side of this issue is clear from his treatment of understanding and action in Essays I and II of *On Human Conduct*.

63. Such projects have been fruitfully undertaken by Richard Flathman, Andrew Norris, Hanna Pitkin, Gaile Polhaus and John Wright, Christopher C. Robinson, James Tully, and Bernard Williams.

64. This, I suggest, is the principal shortcoming of Polhaus and Wright's interpretation of Wittgenstein (which is indebted primarily to their reading of Stanley Cavell). See Gaile Polhaus and John R. Wright, "Using Wittgenstein Critically: A Political Approach to Philosophy," *Political Theory* 30 (Dec. 2002): 800–27.

65. Wittgenstein, *On Certainty*, §§341, 343.

66. Ibid., §344; see also §403. As Oakeshott put this idea, "You will never get anywhere by questioning everything at the same time." Michael Oakeshott, "On Misunderstanding Human Conduct," *Political Theory* 4 (Aug. 1976): 353. Also published in Michael Oakeshott, *The Vocabulary of a Modern European State*, ed. Luke O'Sullivan (Charlottesville, VA: Imprint Academic, 2008), 267. He discusses extensively the conditionality of understanding, agency, and action in *On Human Conduct*.

67. Nyíri and Bloor are not alone, however. Though more nuanced and measured in its formulations, Rorty's reading of Wittgenstein and Oakeshott ultimately arrives at these conclusions as well. Criticism of our practices (e.g., of democracy) can ultimately be nothing more than ironic, as we are already committed to them at a level more fundamental than criticism can reach.

68. Wittgenstein, *Zettel*, §425.

69. Rorty, *Contingency, Irony, and Solidarity*, 18. Crary discusses Rorty's position in different terms and for different reasons in "Wittgenstein's Philosophy in Relation to Political Thought," 125–26.

70. This dimension of criticism, in and out of politics, is discussed in David R. Cerbone, "The Limits of Conservatism: Wittgenstein on 'Our Life' and 'Our Concepts,'" in *The Grammar of Politics*, 58–59; and Janik, "Notes on the Natural History of Politics," 101. This connection between thinking and doing is also at the heart of Oakeshott's discussions of morality and politics in "Rationalism in Politics" and "Political Education," and it is a persistent theme in the discussion of practice in the first essay of *On Human Conduct*, esp. 31–107.

71. Wittgenstein, *Zettel*, §430.

72. Wittgenstein, *Philosophical Investigations*, §107.

73. Ibid., §124.

74. Oakeshott develops this perspective most elaborately and comprehensively in *Experience and its Modes*, but he employs it elsewhere. His praise of theory (properly understood) and polemic against attempts to deduce practical maxims from abstract philosophy in *On Human Conduct* is drawn from the same well.

75. Oakeshott, *On Human Conduct*, 6–31.

76. Wittgenstein, *Philosophical Investigations*, §90; see also Wittgenstein, *Culture and Value*, 10e.

77. Polhaus and Wright describe and embrace such instrumentalization in terms of politicizing philosophy, and they read Wittgenstein as justifying and informing this very endeavor. See *supra* 64.

78. Wittgenstein, *Philosophical Investigations*, §309.

79. Oakeshott draws this limit to the practical reach of philosophy most explicitly and emphatically, both in his critique of rationalism and in his critique of the "theoretician" in the first essay of *On Human Conduct*.

80. For commentary regarding the possibility consistently manifesting widely differing dispositions of thought or action in different domains of life, see Oakeshott, *The Vocabulary of a Modern European State*, 83.

CHAPTER TWO. INDIVIDUALITY BETWEEN TRADITION AND CONTINGENCY

1. Michael Oakeshott, *On Human Conduct*, 41. As my concern in this chapter is to consider how Oakeshott constructs an account of self-enacted individuality, I shall have to consider his account of agency and action in some measure of depth. However, I shall not undertake a full philosophical analysis of his view of agency and action. Terry Nardin offers an especially relevant discussion that goes into greater depth in *The Philosophy of Michael Oakeshott*, 73–99.

2. Michael Oakeshott, "The Masses in Representative Democracy," in *Rationalism in Politics*, 363–83; Oakeshott, *On Human Conduct*, 237.

3. I shall maintain no technical distinction between tradition and its various cognates in ordinary speech, such as custom or convention, and will use these interchangeably. I shall, however, maintain a distinction between tradition and practice in Oakeshott's technical sense of the latter term, though this distinction will serve primarily to underscore the broad inclusiveness of "practice."

4. Oakeshott, *On Human Conduct*, 1.

5. Ibid., 1; see also, Oakeshott, *Experience and Its Modes*, 13–16.

6. Oakeshott, *On Human Conduct*, 2. Oakeshott renders a similar theme in terms with a somewhat Platonic or Kantian flavor in the earlier essay "Political Philosophy," published posthumously in *Religion, Politics, and the Moral Life*, ed. Fuller, 142–44.

7. Michael Oakeshott, "Education: The Engagement and Its Frustration," in *The Voice of Liberal Learning: Michael Oakeshott on Education*, ed. Timothy Fuller (New Haven: Yale University Press, 1989), 65.

8. As Oakeshott remarks, "The notion of an unconditional or definitive understanding may hover in the background, but it has no part in the adventure" (*On Human Conduct*, 3). Which is to say, in terms popularized by analytic philosophy, that the "view from nowhere" may be an intelligible ideal and may inform the strivings of individuals to understand their world, but this ideal is never fully attainable and ought not to be taken as the highest or sole criterion of validity in understanding. Cf. Thomas Nagel, *The View from Nowhere* (Oxford: Oxford University Press, 1986).

9. Oakeshott, *On Human Conduct*, 43–46; Oakeshott, *Experience and Its Modes*, 260–61.

10. Though even in recognizing both terms of this relation, Oakeshott is most anxious to avoid overemphasis of the seemingly impersonal dimensions of an agent's situation. The conceptual core of agency is an individual's self-understanding, and thus Oakeshott rejects out of hand reduction of agency and action to the impersonal, determining forces of biology, genetics, or social and historical forces. Oakeshott, *On Human Conduct*, 38–41, 234–35.

11. Ibid., 59.

12. I shall not retrace the formal contours of this intersubjective background here. For more discussion, see the previous chapter.

13. For a related discussion, see Nardin, *The Philosophy of Michael Oakeshott*, 76.

14. Blaise Pascal, *Pensées*, ed. Anthony Levi, trans. Honor Levi (Oxford: Oxford University Press, 1995), 39.

15. Hannah Arendt, *The Human Condition*, 2nd ed. (Chicago: University of Chicago Press, 1998), 9.

16. Edward Shils, *Tradition* (Chicago: University of Chicago Press, 1981), 12–13.

17. Karl Mannheim, "Conservative Thought," in *Essays on Sociology and Social Psychology*, ed. Paul Kecskemeti (London: Routledge and Kegan Paul, 1953), 99.

18. Alasdair MacIntyre, *After Virtue*, 2nd ed. (Notre Dame: University of Notre Dame Press, 1984), 220–21. It is significant that Oakeshott characterizes the now defunct order of feudalism in almost identical terms in "The Masses in Representative Democracy," 365: "To know oneself as the member of a family, a group, a corporation, a church, a village community . . . had been, for the vast majority, the circumstantially possible sum of self-knowledge. Not only were ordinary activities, those concerned with getting a living, communal in character, but so also were decisions, rights and responsibilities. Relationships and allegiances normally sprang from status and rarely extricated themselves from the analogy of kinship. For the most part anonymity prevailed; individual human character was rarely observed because it was not there to be observed. What differentiated one man from another was insignificant when compared with what was enjoyed in common as members of a group of some sort."

19. Alasdair MacIntyre, *Whose Justice? Which Rationality?* (Notre Dame: University of Notre Dame Press, 1988), 12–13.

20. Sandra Laugier, "Wittgenstein and Cavell: Anthropology, Skepticism, and Politics," in *The Claim to Community: Essays on Stanley Cavell and Political Philosophy*,

ed. Andrew Norris (Stanford: Stanford University Press, 2006), 28. Laugier offers this description of MacIntyre's view in a discussion of the affinities between his views of tradition and J. C. Nyíri's interpretation of Wittgenstein (against which I argued in the previous chapter).

21. MacIntyre, *After Virtue*, 221–22. MacIntyre's primary criticism regards not the normative standing or claims of tradition, but the smooth, uncontested façade that Burke characterizes. As a thinker and defender of a Catholic moral and intellectual tradition, MacIntyre sees both internal and external disputation as natural features of any tradition.

22. Charles Taylor, *Sources of the Self* (Cambridge: Harvard University Press, 1989), 27. As Taylor sees it, this tradition-articulated horizon is essential to being a human person in the fullest sense, of being capable of taking a stand both on one's world and on one's self. See, for instance, Charles Taylor "What Is Human Agency?" and "Self-Interpreting Animals," in *Philosophical Papers, Vol. I: Human Agency and Language* (Cambridge: Cambridge University Press, 1985), 15–44 and 45–76 respectively.

23. Taylor, *Sources of the Self*, 112.

24. MacIntyre, *After Virtue*, 221.

25. Ibid., 33–34. See also, Taylor, "Introduction," in *Philosophical Papers, Vol. II: Philosophy and the Human Sciences* (Cambridge: Cambridge University Press, 1985), 8.

26. MacIntyre, *Whose Justice? Which Rationality?* 11.

27. Ibid., 174–75; Alasdair MacIntyre, *Three Rival Versions of Moral Inquiry: Encyclopaedia, Genealogy, and Tradition* (Notre Dame: University of Notre Dame Press, 1990), 142. With suitable qualification, Oakeshott makes similar claims in both *Rationalism in Politics* and *On Human Conduct* insofar as he rejects the notion that a tradition or a practice can be reduced to the simplicity of a rulebook. Yet his purpose is to vindicate the intelligent individual agency which is the *conditio sine qua non* and *conditio per quam* for the use of a practice or observance of a tradition.

28. MacIntyre, *Whose Justice? Which Rationality?* 326–48; Taylor, *Sources of the Self*, 143–58; Charles Taylor, "Atomism," in *Philosophical Papers, Vol. II: Philosophy and the Human Sciences*, 187–210.

29. In addition to MacIntyre and Taylor, such arguments have been pursued by George Allan, *The Importances of the Past: A Meditation on the Authority of Tradition* (Albany: State University of New York Press, 1986), Allan Bloom, *The Closing of the American Mind: How Higher Education Has Failed Democracy and Impoverished the Souls of Today's Students* (New York: Simon and Schuster, 1987), and by Robert Bellah et al., *Habits of the Heart: Individualism and Commitment in American Life* (Berkeley: University of California Press, 1984) and *The Good Society* (New York: Vintage Books, 1992).

30. Edmund Burke, *Reflections on the Revolution in France*, ed. J. G. A. Pocock (Indianapolis: Hackett, 1987).

31. G. W. F. Hegel, *Phenomenology of Spirit*, trans. A. V. Miller (Oxford: Oxford University Press, 1977), §352, 214, quoted by F. H. Bradley in *Ethical Studies*, 2nd ed. (Oxford: Oxford University Press, 1962) at 173 and 187. The quotations differ slightly as the latter is drawn from the *Phänomenologie des Geistes* (1842)

whereas the former is drawn from a nearly identical passage in Hegel's *Philosophische Abhandlungen* (1832).

32. In this literature, tradition is often implicit in discussions of related concepts such as community. See, for instance, Michael J. Sandel, *Liberalism and the Limits of Justice*, 2nd ed. (Cambridge: Cambridge University Press, 1998). As I noted in the previous chapter, there is also an affinity between the constitutive view of tradition and some of the most radical philosophical analyses and critiques of the individual subject, which reduce the individual to a function of relations of power or assemblages of affect.

33. J. C. Nyíri, "Wittgenstein's Later Work in Relation to Conservatism," in *Wittgenstein and his Times*, ed. Brian McGuinness (Chicago: University of Chicago Press, 1982), 58–59. I dispute Nyíri's reading of Oakeshott directly in chapter I of the present volume.

34. J. G. A. Pocock offers such a characterization of Oakeshott's *Rationalism in Politics*. See Pocock's "Time, Institutions and Action: An Essay on Traditions and Their Understanding," in *Politics, Language, and Time: Essays on Political Thought and History*, rev. ed. (Chicago: University of Chicago Press, 1989), 233–72. Dana Villa makes a similar assessment. Dana Villa, "Oakeshott and the Cold War Critique of Political Rationalism," in *The Cambridge Companion to Oakeshott*, ed. Efraim Podoksik (Cambridge: Cambridge University Press, 2012), 325–26.

35. Andrew Gamble, "Oakeshott's Ideological Politics: Conservative or Liberal?" in *The Cambridge Companion to Oakeshott*, 153–76; 173. Paul Franco, who generally counts Oakeshott (with qualification) as a liberal, nonetheless claims that Oakeshott's critique of rationalism offers in its place "a defense of the not terribly liberal notion of 'tradition.'" See Paul Franco, "Michael Oakeshott as Liberal Theorist," *Political Theory* 18 (August 1990): 412. For a committed critique of Oakeshott on these grounds, see Hanna Pitkin, "The Roots of Conservatism": 496–525. Pitkin was forced to change the angle of her critique in light of the change of conceptual vocabulary in *On Human Conduct*, but maintained the same spirit, charging Oakeshott with using the concept of "authority" to evacuate all political content from public life, leaving nothing but rule following akin to the uncritical reproduction of traditions. See Hanna Pitkin, "Inhuman Conduct and Unpolitical Theory: Michael Oakeshott's *On Human Conduct*," *Political Theory* 4 (1976): 301–17.

36. Michael Oakeshott, "Rationalism in Politics," in *Rationalism in Politics and Other Essays*, 22.

37. Indeed, as early the 1920s Oakeshott criticized treatments of tradition (be they backward-looking and conservative, or forward-looking and even radical) that understand tradition as something static, a permanence to be either worshipped or escaped. See Michael Oakeshott, "Religion and the World," in *Religion, Politics, and the Moral Life*, 30–33.

38. Oakeshott, *On Human Conduct*, 59; 58.

39. Oakeshott, "Education: The Engagement and Its Frustration," 64–65.

40. Michael Oakeshott, "The Study of 'Politics' in a University," in *Rationalism in Politics and Other Essays*, 187.

41. Michael Oakeshott, "Political Education," in *Rationalism in Politics and Other Essays*, 60.

42. Michael Oakeshott, "Rationalism in Politics: A Reply to Professor Raphael," in *The Vocabulary of a Modern European State*, ed. Luke O'Sullivan (Charlottesville, VA: Imprint Academic, 2008), 184.

43. Oakeshott, "Political Education," 59.

44. Edward Shils, "Tradition and Liberty: Antinomy and Interdependence," *Ethics* 68 (April 1958): 156.

45. Oakeshott's account is capacious enough to incorporate the finer distinctions that John Searle has made between regulative and constitutive rules, and that Andrei Marmor (drawing largely upon Searle) has made between deep and surface conventions or between constitutive and coordinating conventions. See John Searle, *Speech Acts* (Cambridge: Cambridge University Press, 1969), 33–35; Andrei Marmor, *Social Conventions: From Language to Law* (Princeton: Princeton University Press, 2009), especially chs. 2 and 3.

46. Shils, "Tradition and Liberty: Antinomy and Interdependence," 157.

47. Oakeshott, *On Human Conduct*, 57–58.

48. Friedrich Nietzsche, *The Will to Power*, ed. Walter Kaufmann, trans. Walter Kaufmann and R. J. Hollingdale (New York: Vintage Books, 1968), §767, 403. See MacIntye, *Three Rival Versions of Moral Enquiry*, 37, as well as his use of Nietzsche as a foil/villain throughout *After Virtue*.

49. Oakeshott emphasizes the naturalness of such drift and change when he notes of a tradition or practice that "like other languages . . . it is not the creation of grammarians; it is made by speakers." Oakeshott, *On Human Conduct*, 78.

50. Ibid., 86–87.

51. Ibid., 56.

52. Oakeshott, "Political Education," 61.

53. Taylor, *Sources of the Self*, 21; Michael Sandel, "The Procedural Republic and the Unencumbered Self," *Political Theory* 12 (Feb. 1984): 81–96.

54. This is not to deny that Oakeshott bears substantial affinities to numerous dimensions of liberal political theory, only to note that he was self-consciously hesitant to embrace liberalism as such. I address further grounds for distinction in the following chapter. For a thoughtful assessment see Franco, "Oakeshott as Liberal Theorist."

55. Hilary Putnam, *Reason, Truth, and History* (Cambridge: Cambridge University Press, 1981), 215; Oakeshott, *On Human Conduct*, 1–8.

56. Oakeshott, *On Human Conduct*, 37.

57. Ibid., 32.

58. Ibid., 1–2. In his later works, Oakeshott's account of this interpretive process goes beyond a residually idealist exploration of experience and its conditions, and begins to incorporate genuinely phenomenological dimensions.

59. This is a central theme in both *Experience and Its Modes* (e.g., 9–48) and Essay I of *On Human Conduct*. See Wilfrid Sellars, *Empiricism and the Philosophy of Mind* (Cambridge: Harvard University Press, 1997); Byron Kaldis, "Worlds of Experience: Science," in *The Cambridge Companion to Oakeshott*, ed. Efraim Podoksik (Cambridge: Cambridge University Press, 2012), 78–82.

60. Oakeshott, *On Human Conduct*, 74.

61. Ibid., 100.

62. There is some apparent tension between Oakeshott's late views regarding contingency, formulated most elaborately in *On Human Conduct* and in the first three essays of *On History and Other Essays*, and some of the idealist themes in his earlier works, including his approving quotation of Bradley's statement that "[t]he world is the best of all possible worlds, and *everything* in it is a necessary evil." See "Political Education," 66. Yet in its context the quotation is not meant as a denial of contingency, but to underscore Oakeshott's argument that all politics necessarily spring from *some* tradition of behavior. Such traditions he nevertheless recognizes to be contingent in a sense similar to that explored in his later works.

63. Richard Rorty, *Contingency, Irony, and Solidarity*, 22.

64. Oakeshott, *On Human Conduct*, 101.

65. Ibid., 38, 41.

66. Ibid., 104.

67. Ibid., 105.

68. Cast in terms of conditionality and contingency, Oakeshott's account of agency harmonizes with themes developed by Hubert L. Dreyfus in *What Computers Still Can't Do: a Critique of Artificial Reason* (Cambridge: MIT Press, 1992).

69. Oakeshott, *On Human Conduct*, 105.

70. Ibid., 235.

71. Franco, "Michael Oakeshott as Liberal Theorist," 420–21; also Franco, *The Political Philosophy of Michael Oakeshott*, 167.

72. Oakeshott, *On Human Conduct*, 36–37.

73. Efraim Podoksik, "Oakeshott's Theory of Freedom as Recognized Contingency," *European Journal of Political Theory* 2 (2003): 61.

74. For the now classic formulation of the negative/positive distinction, see Isaiah Berlin, "Two Concepts of Liberty," in *Four Essays on Liberty* (Oxford: Oxford University Press, 1969), 118–72.

75. Michael Oakeshott, "The Vocabulary of a Modern European State," in *The Vocabulary of a Modern European State*, 258.

76. See, for instance, Charles Taylor, "What's Wrong with Negative Liberty," in *Philosophical Papers, Vol. II: Philosophy and the Human Sciences*, 211–29; and Harry G. Frankfurt, *The Importance of What We Care About* (Cambridge: Cambridge University Press, 1988).

77. Oakeshott, "Political Education," 54.

78. Michael Oakeshott, "The Political Economy of Freedom," in *Rationalism in Politics and Other Essays*, 388.

79. Oakeshott, *On Human Conduct*, 158.

80. Oakeshott, "The Masses in Representative Democracy," 366.

81. Oakeshott, *On Human Conduct*, 236–37.

82. Oakeshott discusses these characters in both "The Masses in Representative Democracy," 370–83 and *On Human Conduct*, 276–79.

83. Oakeshott, *On Human Conduct*, 241.

84. George Kateb, *The Inner Ocean: Individualism and Democratic Culture* (Ithaca: Cornell University Press, 1992), 34. Kateb explores this theme further in "The Idea of Individual Infinitude," *The Hedgehog Review* 7 (Summer 2005): 42–54, esp. 52–54.

85. Kateb, *The Inner Ocean*, 5.

CHAPTER THREE. IMAGINING THE MODERN STATE

1. Michael Oakeshott, "Introduction to *Leviathan*," in *Rationalism in Politics and Other Essays*, 223. See also Oakeshott, *On Human Conduct*, 252.

2. In taking this interpretive position, I am in the company of Richard E. Flathman and Steven Anthony Gerencser, both of whom find the influence of Hobbes to be deep and pervasive with regard to both philosophical outlook (via Oakeshott's skepticism) and political theory (via Oakeshott's theory of civil association).

3. Oakeshott, "Introduction to *Leviathan*," 234.

4. Thomas Hobbes, *Leviathan*, ed. Edwin Curley (Indianapolis: Hackett, 1994), ch. I, 6.

5. For present purposes I need not take a position regarding the ultimate accuracy or felicity of the reading of Hobbes that informs *On Human Conduct*. Oakeshott is widely regarded as an insightful Hobbes scholar, yet his reading and reception of Hobbes is subject to some dispute. E.g., William A. Galston, "Oakeshott's Political Theory: Recapitulation and Criticisms," in *The Cambridge Companion to Oakeshott*, ed. Efraim Podoksik (Cambridge: Cambridge University Press, 2012), 236–40.

6. See, for instance, Michael Oakeshott, "The Masses in Representative Democracy," in *Rationalism in Politics and Other Essays*, 366–70.

7. Oakeshott, *On Human Conduct*, 185.

8. Michael Oakeshott, "*Leviathan*: a Myth," in *Hobbes on Civil Association* (Indianapolis: Liberty Fund, 1975), 159–60.

9. This was discussed in the previous chapter, where both Oakeshott and Charles Taylor were shown to view human beings as (in Taylor's phrase) "self-interpreting animals."

10. Michael Oakeshott, "Political Education," in *Rationalism in Politics*, 44; Oakeshott, "*Leviathan*: a Myth," 163. Benedict Anderson characterizes the *nation* in fundamentally similar terms. See his *Imagined Communities*, 2nd ed. (London: Verso, 2006), 5–7. Oakeshott self-consciously offers images of the *state* as the focal point, as he regards the nation as an infelicitous image for modern politics for a variety of reasons, the greatest of which being the denial of human plurality that such imaginaries require. See Oakeshott, *On Human Conduct*, 188.

11. While most receptions have been mixed in these terms, Hanna Pitkin's assessment of *On Human Conduct* represents it as old conservative wine poured into new conceptual bottles, while Paul Franco and John Gray have received the work as more or less squarely in the liberal tradition. See Hannah F. Pitkin, "Inhuman Conduct and Unpolitical Theory": 301–17; Franco, "Oakeshott as Liberal Theorist"; John Gray, *Liberalisms* (London: Routledge, 1989), 199–216.

12. Arendt, *The Human Condition*, 5.

13. Oakeshott's project to elicit these ideal characters rests upon the premise that every modern state "has a 'character' to be investigated," where a 'character' is "a rut or channel which has been excavated by human choices [and which] establishes itself by long-continued movement which gradually chisels out its own restrictions, each absence of deviation contributing to a balance of dispositions which in the course of time discloses itself." Michael Oakeshott, *Morality and Politics in Modern Europe*, ed. Shirley Robin Letwin (New Haven: Yale University Press, 1993), 31.

14. Oakeshott, *On Human Conduct*, 114.

15. Ibid., 115. For a broader characterization of the ways that such an engagement has been imagined, see Michael Oakeshott, *Lectures in the History of Political Thought*, ed. Terry Nardin and Luke O'Sullivan (Charlottesville, VA: Imprint Academic, 2006), 469–82.

16. Ibid., 315.

17. From this perspective, Augustine's elaborate theory of the divided-yet-free will is an extremely robust instance of the phenomenon of sour grapes.

18. Charles Taylor describes the tendency toward (or perhaps inevitability of) such assimilation in his account of individual identity as inseparable from one's orientation in "moral space" defined by some notion of "incomparably higher" goods. See *Sources of the Self* (Cambridge: Harvard University Press, 1989), especially chs. 1 through 4. A different yet related account of this phenomenon and its inexorability is given by Harry G. Frankfurt in *The Importance of What We Care About* (Cambridge: Cambridge University Press, 1988), especially the title essay.

19. Oakeshott, *On Human Conduct*, 215.

20. Ibid., 264.

21. Ibid., 205.

22. Franco, *The Political Philosophy of Michael Oakeshott*, 158.

23. Flathman, *Pluralism and Liberal Democracy*, 159; Galston, "Oakeshott's Political Theory," 232.

24. The most exalted of these goods is individuality, which flourishes best (and perhaps only) under conditions that civil association secures. Civil association also permits the private pursuit of any number of enterprises as well, and so does not strictly trade off with the goods that enterprise associations might provide.

25. *On Human Conduct*, 58.

26. Ibid., 60–78. It may be unfortunate that Oakeshott chooses "moral" as a complementary (if not strictly synonymous) term for "noninstrumental." This choice, which is perhaps justified in the context of Essay I of *On Human Conduct*, has a variety of confusing consequences for readers more accustomed to uses that equate "moral" with "instrumental to the achievement of some independently valuable end" (even if this end is Kantian respect for the moral law itself).

What Oakeshott calls non-instrumental or moral action is, of course, teleological in the weak and local sense that all genuine actions (distinguished from mechanical behaviors) are teleological. Every action undertaken by an agent is performed for a reason, however simplistic, dimly understood or even misunderstood. That is, every action is performed in order that some state of affairs be realized, yet action itself entails no more than this weak, nearsighted teleology. This view is clearest in *On Human Conduct*, but even at the early extremes of his idealism Oakeshott affirmed no more than this weak and local sense of purpose inherent in action. E.g., *Experience and Its Modes*, 274, 288–90.

27. Ibid., 122, 75.

28. Hanna F. Pitkin, "Inhuman Conduct and Unpolitical Theory": 301–20; Galston, "Oakeshott's Political Theory," 236–40. Attempts to grapple, sympathetically, with the idea of noninstrumental, adverbial action, rules, and association include: Richard Friedman, "Michael Oakeshott and the Elusive Identity of the

Rule of Law," in *The Intellectual Legacy of Michael Oakeshott*, ed. Cory Abel and Timothy Fuller (Charlottesville, VA: Imprint Academic, 2005), 160–80 and "What Is a Non-Instrumental Law?" *Political Science Reviewer* 21 (Spring 1992): 81–98; David Mapel, "Purpose and Politics: Can There Be a Non-Instrumental Civil Association?" *Political Science Reviewer* 21 (Spring 1992): 63–80.

29. E.g., Oakeshott, *On Human Conduct*, 120–21; "The Study of 'Politics' in a University," in *Rationalism and Politics*, 187.

30. Oakeshott, "The Masses in Representative Democracy," 366.

31. David Mapel, "Civil Association and the Idea of Contingency," *Political Theory* 18 (August 1990): 393.

32. Richard Flathman, *Willful Liberalism: Voluntarism and Individuality in Political Theory and Practice* (Ithaca: Cornell University Press, 1992), 88.

33. On the idea of such a *modus vivendi*, and Oakeshott's intellectual relation to it, see John Gray, *Two Faces of Liberalism* (New York: The New Press, 2000).

34. John Rawls, *A Theory of Justice*, 3. For Oakeshott's view of justice as a formal property rather than a substantive virtue, see *On Human Conduct*, 253, 313–14.

35. Oakeshott, *On Human Conduct*, 129; 147. See also Oakeshott, "The Rule of Law," in *On History and Other Essays*, 148.

36. Oakeshott, *On Human Conduct*, 174–76.

37. Yet as civil association is not premised upon a robust moral doctrine (e.g., natural rights) and is not defined in terms of the range of functions it performs, it is distinct from the "minimal state" advocated as a "framework for utopia" by Robert Nozick in *Anarchy, State, and Utopia* (New York: Basic Books, 1974).

38. Benjamin Barber, *Strong Democracy: Participatory Politics for a New Age* (Berkeley: University of California Press, 1984), 20–21.

39. Oakeshott, *On Human Conduct*, 164.

40. For Oakeshott's most imaginative treatment of this theme, see "Tower of Babel," in *On History and Other Essays*, 179–210.

41. Rousseau proudly expressed the essence of this relationship between the enterprise state and its comrades or wards in saying that although "it is good to know how to deal with men as they are, it is much better to make them what there is need that they should be." Jean-Jacques Rousseau, "A Discourse on Political Economy," in *The Social Contract and Discourses*, trans. G. D. H. Cole (London: Everyman, 1994), 139. In *Emile* this maxim is applied to education, in *The Social Contract* it is applied to law and politics.

42. Oakeshott, *On Human Conduct*, 200–201.

43. This antagonism between civil and enterprise association, described in *On Human Conduct*, marks a clear distinction between these two images of the state and Oakeshott's earlier characterization of "the politics of faith" and "the politics of scepticism" as opposed yet mutually correcting political dispositions. Though there are analogues between "faith" and "enterprise," on the one hand, and between "scepticism" and "civility," on the other, Oakeshott's mature political theory differs in a significant way from his earlier reflections that remained unpublished in his lifetime. See Michael Oakeshott, *The Politics of Faith and the Politics of Scepticism*, ed. Timothy Fuller (New Haven: Yale University Press, 1996), 92.

44. Michel Foucault, *Discipline and Punish: The Birth of the Prison*, trans. Alan Sheridan (New York: Vintage Books, 1977), 194, 217.

45. See for instance Aryeh Botwinick, *Michael Oakeshott's Skepticism*, 38 (briefly noting intellectual affinity between the two as part of a separate line of discussion); Franco, *Michael Oakeshott: An Introduction*, 169 (drawing a line between Oakeshott and Foucault, charging the latter with a "one-sidedly pessimistic and monolithic account of modernity"); Stuart Isaacs, *The Politics and Philosophy of Michael Oakeshott*, 118–22 (marking a dismissive distinction between their respective views of history); Suvi Soininen, *From a 'Necessary Evil' to an Art of Contingency*, 86–87 (recognizing only shallow and inconsequential affinities between the two). Those who have recognized deeper affinities between Oakeshott and Foucault have not pursued the insight systematically. See David Mapel, "Civil Association and the Idea of Contingency" (recognizing similar theoretical perspectives on the emergence of the modern state) and Jacob Segal, "Michel Foucault and Michael Oakeshott: The Politics of the Virtuosity of Individuality," *Foucault Studies* 18 (2014) (forthcoming) (exploring affinities between Oakeshott's and Foucault's accounts of individuality).

46. For instance, *On Human Conduct*, "The Masses in Representative Democracy," *The Politics of Faith and the Politics of Scepticism*, *Morality and Politics in Modern Europe*, and "The Rule of Law."

47. Oakeshott, *Lectures in the History of Political Thought*, 388.

48. For the sake of terminological economy I will speak of the medieval state and modern state, recognizing that in important ways the "medieval state" is an anachronism. See Quentin Skinner, "The State," in *Political Innovation and Conceptual Change*, ed. Terrence Ball, James Farr, and Russell L. Hanson (Cambridge: Cambridge University Press, 1989), 90–131.

49. Michel Foucault, "The Confession of the Flesh," in *Power/Knowledge: Selected Interviews and Other Writings, 1972–1977*, ed. Colin Gordon, trans. Colin Gordon (New York: Pantheon, 1980), 194.

50. I mean this term in the sense given it by Ian Hacking, in connection to Foucault. See *Historical Ontology* (Cambridge: Harvard University Press, 2002), especially the title essay.

51. Oakeshott, *On Human Conduct*, 109; Michel Foucault, *The Birth of Biopolitics: Lectures at the Collège de France, 1978–1979*, ed. Michel Senellart, trans. Graham Burchell (New York: Palgrave Macmillan, 2008), 19, 76–77.

52. Oakeshott, *On Human Conduct*, 214; see also Oakeshott "The Masses in Representative Democracy," 365–68.

53. Ibid., 223.

54. Ibid., 218; also Oakeshott, *The Politics of Faith and the Politics of Scepticism*, 48.

55. Ibid., 194, 224–31, 267.

56. Michel Foucault, *Security, Territory, Population: Lectures at the Collège de France, 1977–1978*, ed. Michel Senellart, trans. Graham Burchell (New York: Palgrave Macmillan, 2007), 88–89.

57. Foucault, *Discipline and Punish*, 90.

58. Ibid., 214.

59. Max Weber arrived at fundamentally similar (if conceptually distinguishable) conclusions regarding the emergence of modern state bureaucracies and the processes of rationalization in politics and government. E.g., Max Weber, *From Max Weber: Essays in Sociology*, trans. and ed. H. H. Gerth and C. Wright Mills (Oxford: Oxford University Press, 1958), 196–243, 253–61; Hubert J. Dreyfus and Paul Rabinow, *Michel Foucault: Beyond Structuralism and Hermeneutics*, 2nd ed. (Chicago: University of Chicago Press, 1983), 166; John O'Neill, "The Disciplinary Society: From Weber to Foucault," *The British Journal of Sociology* XXXVII, no. 1 (March 1986): 42–60.

60. Foucault, *Discipline and Punish*, 228.

61. Foucault, *Security, Territory, Population*, 108–109, 234–37; Oakeshott, *On Human Conduct*, 267.

62. Oakeshott, "The Masses in Representative Democracy," 366–70; Oakeshott, *On Human Conduct*, 263–66.

63. Oakeshott, *On Human Conduct*, 153.

64. Ibid., 270. It is significant that despite the resemblances between Oakeshott's image of civil association and a number of liberal images of the state, he considers much liberal political theory to embrace an image tantamount to enterprise association. This is particularly true when liberal political theory presents the state as a custodian or manager of the economy in some substantial capacity.

65. Ibid., 279–88; Foucault, *Security, Territory, Population*, 125–26.

66. Foucault, *Security, Territory, Population*, 128.

67. To religious-spiritual and economic idioms of enterprise one might add a republican idiom, which (despite its interweaving with elements of the other two idioms) has appeared here and there as a distinguishable image in which the enterprise pursued is active citizenship and self-government of some description. Classical examples are presented by Machiavelli in his *Discourses*, Harrington in *Oceana*, and Rousseau in *The Social Contract*, whereas contemporary democratic theory abounds with participatory and deliberative theories indebted substantially to the republican vision of the enterprise state.

68. Foucault, *Security, Territory, Population*, 67–75; see also Oakeshott, "The Conservative Opportunity," in *The Vocabulary of a Modern European State*, 189.

69. Isaiah Berlin suggests that in virtue of his technological-economic analysis of society and politics Henri de St. Simon was the single most prescient prophet of the twentieth century (including the developments that Oakeshott and Foucault diagnose), whose vision is as much an article of faith in capitalist societies as socialist societies. See Isaiah Berlin, *Freedom and Its Betrayal: Six Enemies of Human Liberty*, ed. Henry Hardy (Princeton: Princeton University Press, 2002), 105–30. On Oakeshott's telling of the story, productivists from St. Simon to Marx built upon foundations laid by Bacon.

70. Oakeshott, *The Politics of Faith and the Politics of Scepticism*, 53. Theodor Adorno and Max Horkheimer similarly consider Bacon the patron saint of the rationalizing forces of "enlightenment," and trace the path from capitalist (though, myopically, only capitalist) productivism and consumerism back to him. See Adorno and Horkheimer, *The Dialectic of Enlightenment*, trans. John Cumming (London: Verso, 1978), 1–34.

71. Foucault, *Security, Territory, Population*, 68–69; Michael Oakeshott, "The Rule of Law," 166–67.

72. Foucault, *Security, Territory, Population*, 300–302; Foucault, *Discipline and Punish*, throughout; Michel Foucault, *"Society Must Be Defended": Lectures at the Collège de France:1975–1976*, ed. Mauro Bertani and Alessandro Fontana, trans. David Macey (New York: Picador, 2003), 267; Oakeshott, *On Human Conduct*, 274, 311; Michael Oakeshott, "Contemporary British Politics," *Cambridge Journal* 1 (1947–48): 477; Michael Oakeshott, "The Universities," in *The Voice of Liberal Learning*, ed. Timothy Fuller (New Haven: Yale University Press, 1989), 115–17.

73. Oakeshott, *On Human Conduct*, 287–88; see also Foucault, *Security, Territory, Population*, 74, 350.

74. Foucault, *Discipline and Punish*, 138.

75. Foucault, *Security, Territory, Population*, 76–79; see also Foucault's discussion of the shift from the classical to the modern *episteme* in *The Order of Things: An Archaeology of the Human Sciences*, trans. (New York: Vintage Books, 1973).

76. Foucault, *The Birth of Biopolitics*, 13–16. Foucault defines "political economy" as including not only "strict and limited analysis of the production and circulation of wealth" but also "any method of government that can procure the nation's prosperity" and (following Rousseau's popularization of the term in the eighteenth century) "general reflection on the organization, distribution, and limitation of powers in society" (13). In this sense, political economy is literally a fusion of the concerns of economics and politics, taking the one to be inexorably interwoven with the other. A point that both Oakeshott and Foucault stress is that the belief that such an interweaving is possible, let alone inevitable or even natural, is the contemporary of the modern state apparatus.

77. Foucault, *Security, Territory, Population*, 110.

78. Michel Foucault, *The History of Sexuality, Volume I: An Introduction*, trans. Robert Hurley (New York: Vintage Books, 1978), 135–45; Foucault, *"Society Must Be Defended,"* 239–44.

79. Paul Franco, *Michael Oakeshott: An Introduction*, 83. One finds the same basic formulation in Nardin, *The Philosophy of Michael Oakeshott*, 92, 103. See also Michael Oakeshott, "Rationalism in Politics," in *Rationalism in Politics and Other Essays*, 5–42; Michael Oakeshott, "Scientific Politics," in *Religion, Politics, and the Moral Life*, ed. Fuller, 97–110.

80. Oakeshott, *On Human Conduct*, 51–56.

81. The first phrase is found in Oakeshott, "Rationalism in Politics," 16, 22; the second, in Foucault, *Security, Territory, Population*, 99. See also Oakeshott, *On Human Conduct*, 195.

82. Oakeshott, *On Human Conduct*, 161; Foucault, *The Birth of Biopolitics*, 13–16.

83. For Oakeshott's recognition of both faces, see *On Human Conduct*, 292–296; for Foucault's, see, for instance, *Security, Territory, Population*, 77.

84. In addition to the essays contained in *Rationalism in Politics*, and the description of modern politics in *The Politics of Faith and the Politics of Scepticism*, see "A Reminder from Leviathan," in *The Vocabulary of a Modern European State*, ed. Luke O'Sullivan (Charlottesville, VA: Imprint Academic, 2008), 38–40.

85. Oakeshott, *On Human Conduct*, 192, 261. Richard Flathman provides an extensive analysis (and partial critique) of the distinction Oakeshott invokes in *The Practice of Political Authority* (Chicago: University of Chicago Press, 1980), especially 13–70. In Flathman's terms, Oakeshott attributes to civil association a "formal-procedural" conception of authority and to enterprise association a "substantive-purposive" conception.

86. Michel Foucault, "Truth and Power," in *Power/Knowledge*, 121.

87. Fear of too much government, as a subcategory of a larger phenomenon of "state-phobia," is a recurrent theme in Foucault's description of liberalism in *The Birth of Biopolitics*.

88. Foucault, *Security, Territory, Population*, 12. This is also a dominant trope in *Discipline and Punish*.

89. For a characterization and critique of this "liberal individual" in its Rawlsian instance, see Michael Sandel, "The Procedural Republic and the Unencumbered Self," *Political Theory* 12, no. 1 (Feb. 1984): 81–96. Broadly related critiques of the detached, liberal individual can be found in Charles Taylor's *Sources of the Self* and in Richard Rorty, *Philosophy and the Mirror of Nature*, as well as *Contingency, Irony, and Solidarity*.

90. Foucault, "Truth and Power," 122.

91. For instance, Michel Foucault, "The Ethics of the Concern for Self as a Practice of Freedom," trans. Phillis Aranov and Dan McGrawth, in *Foucault Live: Collected Interviews, 1961–1984*, ed. Sylvère Lotringer (New York: Semiotext(e), 1996), 432–49 and "Space, Knowledge, and Power," trans. Christian Hubert, in *The Foucault Reader*, ed. Paul Rabinow (New York: Pantheon Books, 1984), 239–56.

92. Foucault, *Discipline and Punish*, especially 170–94.

93. See, for instance, Charles Taylor, "Foucault on Freedom and Truth," in *Philosophical Papers Vol. II: Philosophy and the Human Sciences* (Cambridge: Cambridge University Press, 1985), 152–84.

94. Flathman, *Pluralism and Liberal Democracy*, 109–61; Paul Franco, "Oakeshott, Berlin, and Liberalism," *Political Theory* 31, no. 4 (Aug. 2003): 484–507; Efraim Podoksik, *In Defense of Modernity*.

95. Franco, "Oakeshott, Berlin, and Liberalism," 491; Flathman, *Pluralism and Liberal Democracy*, 111. Such attributions of significance to Oakeshott's idealism are often problematic for two, intersecting reasons. First, the very term *idealism* is given a number of inflections in philosophical and political contexts, and, when unmodified, can include a range of thinkers as otherwise diverse as Plato, Berkeley, Kant, Emerson, Hegel, Bradley, Wittgenstein, and Oakeshott. Second, Oakeshott's idealism is itself a moving target. His early thought was a variation on the British idealism of the early twentieth century, whereas the idealism of his later works bears precious few affinities of style or substance to the work of Hegel or Bradley or McTaggart. Despite this fairly obvious fact of the development of Oakeshott's thought, commentators often present *Experience and its Modes* (1933) as the paradigm of Oakeshott's lifelong idealism, despite the fact that the style of idealism of *On Human Conduct* (1975) is shorn of the majority of the tropes and conclusions of the earlier work. David Boucher claims such unbroken continuity in "The Victim of Thought: The Idealist Inheritance," in *A Companion to Michael Oakeshott*, ed. Paul Franco and

Leslie Marsh (University Park: Pennsylvania State University Press, 2012), 47–69. Though I recognize strands that run throughout Oakeshott's career, I would dissent from the common, if waning, approach, which presents the programmatic Absolute Idealism of *Experience and its Modes* as the lens through which to read all of his later works.

96. Isaiah Berlin, "The Pursuit of the Ideal," in *The Cooked Timber of Humanity: Chapters in the History of Ideas*, ed. Henry Hardy (New York: Knopf, 1991), 11–13.

97. John Gray, *Isaiah Berlin* (Princeton: Princeton University Press, 1996), 43. Berlin himself famously illustrated such internal plurality to the concept of liberty in his "Two Concepts of Liberty," in *Four Essays on Liberty* (Oxford: Oxford University Press, 1969), 118–72, whereas Michael Walzer illustrated such plurality within the concept of equality in *Spheres of Justice: A Defense of Pluralism and Equality* (New York: Basic Books, 1983).

98. Isaiah Berlin, "The Originality of Machiavelli," in *The Proper Study of Mankind*, ed. Henry Hardy and Roger Hausheer (New York: Farrar, Straus, and Giroux, 1998), 269–325; Isaiah Berlin, *Vico and Herder: Two Studies in the History of Ideas* (New York: Vintage Books, 1977).

99. Oakeshott, *Experience and Its Modes*, 6.

100. Francis Herbert Bradley, *Ethical Studies*, 2nd ed. (Oxford: Oxford University Press, 1962), esp. 58–84 and 160–213. Bradley claims that "[t]here is nothing better than [one's] station and its duties, nor anything higher or more truly beautiful" because he views the individual as situated in a unified social/political/ethical fabric in which plurality of values is merely apparent, and is in the final instance always reconciled to the whole. (201).

101. Oakeshott, *On Human Conduct*, 87.

102. Oakeshott, "The Vocabulary of a Modern European State," in *The Vocabulary of a Modern European State*, 253.

103. Oakeshott, *On Human Conduct*, 88; see also 98.

104. Ibid, 24.

105. Podoksik, *In Defense of Modernity*, 209; emphasis added.

106. Oakeshott, *Experience and Its Modes*, 355.

107. See, for instance, F. H. Bradley, *Ethical Studies*, 160–213; Crispin Wright, "The Moral Organism," in *The Philosophy of F. H Bradley*, ed. Anthony Manser and Guy Stock (Oxford: Oxford University Press, 1984), 77–97. Although Oakeshott never seemed to embrace (or at any rate, to explore) this trope fully, traces are apparent in the 1929 essay "The Authority of the State," in *Religion, Politics, and the Moral Life*, ed. Fuller, 74–90.

108. Oakeshott puts his view in these terms in "Rationalism in Politics," but he develops it systematically in *On Human Conduct*. Michael Oakeshott, "Rationalism in Politics," in *Rationalism in Politics and Other Essays*, 41.

109. Oakeshott, *On Human Conduct*, 129.

110. Richard Flathman offers a similar assessment from a different perspective, characterizing Oakeshott as an "agency liberal" rather than a "virtue liberal." See Richard E. Flathman, "Strains in and around Liberal Theory: An Overview from a Strong Voluntarist Perspective," in *Reflections of a Would-be Anarchist* (Minneapolis: University of Minnesota Press, 1998), 3–16.

111. I specifically have in mind the interpretation of Arendt offered by George Kateb, which informs the following discussion.

112. George Kateb, "Hannah Arendt: Alienation and America," *Raritan* 3 (Summer 1983): 4.

113. The same sense of loss is palpable in *The Politics of Faith and the Politics of Scepticism*, 90–115.

114. Oakeshott approvingly offers this summary of Arendt's overarching claim in the eight essays of her *Beyond Past and Future: Eight Exercises in Political Thought* (New York: Penguin Books, 1977). Michael Oakeshott, "Between Past and Future," in *What is History? and Other Essays*, ed. Luke O'Sullivan (Charlottesville, VA: Imprint Academic, 2004), 316.

115. Lisa Jane Disch, *Hannah Arendt and the Limits of Philosophy* (Ithaca: Cornell University Press, 1994), 23.

116. Arendt, *The Human Condition*, 7. See Oakeshott, *On Human Conduct*, 86–88.

117. Oakeshott, "Political Education," 44.

118. On this basic theme in Arendt and Oakeshott, see Arendt, *The Human Condition*, 52; George Kateb, "Freedom and Worldliness in the Thought of Hannah Arendt," *Political Theory* 5 (May 1977): 141–82; Oakeshott, "Political Education," especially 56–60; Oakeshott, *On Human Conduct*, Essay II generally.

119. For instance, Arendt, *The Human Condition*, 188–90; Oakeshott, *On Human Conduct*, 161–73.

120. Oakeshott, *On Human Conduct*, 180; compare Arendt on the "greatness" of action, in *The Human Condition*, 205.

121. Oakeshott, *On Human Conduct*, 70.

122. Ibid., 66, 126, 177.

123. Ibid., 147–48. Beyond the use of the Latin term *respublica* in its literal sense of the concern or property of the public, there are perhaps other echoes of classical republican themes in Oakeshott's political theory—though the quoted passage sets distinct limits to such affinity. For treatments of this theme, see David Boucher, "Oakeshott, Freedom and Republicanism," *British Journal of Politics and International Relations* 7 (2005): 81–96. Wendell John Coats Jr., "Some Correspondences Between Oakeshott's "Civil Condition" and the Republican Tradition," *Political Science Reviewer* 21 (Spring 1992): 99–115.

124. As Oakeshott characterizes this kind of association: "The laws of civil association . . . relate to the miscellaneous, unforeseeable choices and transactions of agents each concerned to live [the lives they each desire, such as they understand their own horizons], who are joined in no common purpose or engagement, who may be strangers to one another, the objects of whose loves are as various as themselves, and who may lack any but this moral [i.e. noninstrumental] allegiance to one another" (*On Human Conduct*, 129).

125. Oakeshott, "Political Education," 56–57.

126. Oakeshott, *On Human Conduct*, 168. See also Oakeshott, "The Vocabulary of a Modern European State," 260–64. While Oakeshott admits that enterprises (such as businesses, clubs, or churches) have their own "politics," so to speak, none-

such are properly political in the civil sense he articulates. See Oakeshott, "Political Education," 44–45 and *On Human Conduct*, 162.

127. Ibid., 166; 164. Imagined civilly, even the ongoing activity of *ruling* (which Oakeshott, like Arendt, is careful to distinguish from *politics*) consists essentially in the circumstantial interpretation of the content of *respublica* and the adjudication of disputes that arise under it.

128. In virtue of placing an adverbial idiom of association above substantive projects and the techniques for pursuing them, Oakeshott envisions civil association and its politics as an alternative and corrective to ideological and rationalistic modes that sacralize substantive ideals (e.g., economic prosperity or distributive egalitarianism) and technical methods (e.g., utilitarian calculation or scientific planning).

129. As Arendt declares (in terms not altogether unambiguous) "For us, appearance—something that is seen and heard by everybody—constitutes reality." Arendt, *The Human Condition*, 50. Peter Fuss offers this gloss on Arendt's understanding of appearance: "From a human point of view, what does not appear is not real. In fact, intersubjective confirmation is the ground of our assurance that anything whatever—ourselves, our fellow men, the world of natural objects and the world of man-made things—is real." Peter Fuss, "Hannah Arendt's Conception of Political Community," in *Hannah Arendt: the Recovery of the Public World*, ed. Melvyn A. Hill (New York: St. Martin's Press, 1979), 164. Other treatments of Arendt's thought that are attentive its phenomenological dimension include Bhikhu Parekh, *Hannah Arendt and the Search for a New Political Philosophy* (London: The MacMillan Press, 1981) and Dana R. Villa, *Arendt and Heidegger: the Fate of the Political* (Princeton: Princeton University Press, 1996).

130. Arendt, *The Human Condition*, 52. There exists a fundamental ambiguity regarding whether Arendt's concept of "world" properly takes a definite or indefinite article. As the quoted passage illustrates, she variously mixes references to *the* world with references to *a* world or *this* world, leaving some doubt as to whether only one such world exists (or can exist at once), or whether it is but one of many (possible or actual) worlds. On the whole, her commonest phrasings and conceptual emphases speak of *the* world, in the all-encompassing, definite singular. Yet given her account of how any world is created and maintained through action, this manner of speaking is suspect insofar as it implies that there exists or could exist but one such public condition, which is either shared by all humanity, or enjoyed by some while others lack such a condition altogether. It is appropriate to note that Oakeshott's account of *respublica* does not fall into similar ambiguity, as both his use and his conceptual definition clearly indicate that *respublica* is the framework of rules and institutions shared by a particular, definite, identifiable group of individuals.

131. Kateb, "Freedom and Worldliness in the Thought of Hannah Arendt," 142–43.

132. Arendt, *The Human Condition*, 88. Kateb draws from Arendt's account of labor the agent-centered claim that "[t]he laborer lives only to die; he turns everything, including what is meant to last, into the stuff of consumption. He devours the world [or, perhaps more correctly, the earth]; time devours him." Kateb, "Freedom and Worldliness in the Thought of Hannah Arendt," 144. Arendt's definition of

labor and her exclusion of labor from the proper concerns and conduct of politics demonstrate her adverse stance toward Marxism, which likewise bears a remarkable affinity to Oakeshott's. See *On Human Conduct* and Michael Oakeshott, "Review of *Socialism and Ethics*," in *The Concept of a Philosophical Jurisprudence: Essays and Reviews 1926–1951*, ed. Luke O'Sullivan (Charlottesville, VA: Imprint Academic, 2007), 271–74. Yet Oakeshott and Arendt oppose Marxism for reasons deeper than ideology, and criticize both the capitalist and socialist idioms that the fixation on labor and its concerns takes in activities commonly branded "politics."

133. Arendt, *The Human Condition*, 162.

134. Ibid., 176.

135. Ibid., 9.

136. Ibid., 179; see also 179–81.

137. Ibid., 178; 246–47; Hannah Arendt, "What is Freedom?," in *Between Past and Future*, 143–71.

138. Arendt, *The Human Condition*, 9, 175–92; Arendt, "What is Freedom?," 153; Kateb, "Freedom and Worldliness in the Thought of Hannah Arendt," 160.

139. Kateb, "Freedom and Worldliness in the Thought of Hannah Arendt," 158. Kateb's words, and what they exclude from "political action," equally characterize Oakeshott's view.

140. For this reason, along with her strongly phenomenological interpretation of publicity, Arendt denies individual acts of conscientious objection or civil disobedience (such as Henry David Thoreau's refusal to pay his taxes) the title "political," claiming that "the civil disobedient . . . never exists as an individual; he can function and survive only as a member of a group." Hannah Arendt, "Civil Disobedience," in *Crises of the Republic* (New York: Harcourt Brace, 1972), 55. On Oakeshott's view of political action, individual acts (such as Thoreau's writings regarding his withdrawal to Walden Pond and his refusal to pay his taxes) could indeed constitute political acts, insofar as they recommend a wished-for condition of *respublica* (such as the repeal of the Fugitive Slave Act). I have elsewhere argued for the circumstantial inclusion of withdrawal and silence in the canon of genuine (if thin and ambiguous) political acts. See Luke Philip Plotica, "Public and Private: the Sense of the Political in Wittgenstein and Arendt," *Cadernos de Filosofia* 19/20 (2006): 305–19, esp. 316–19.

141. See, for instance, Margaret Canovan, *Hannah Arendt: a Reinterpretation of Her Political Thought* (Cambridge: Cambridge University Press, 1992), esp. 201–52 and Dana Villa, "The Philosopher versus the Citizen: Arendt, Strauss and Socrates," *Political Theory* 26 (April 1998): 147–72.

142. E.g., Arendt, *The Human Condition*, 28–37, 192–99, 201. For a discussion and qualification of her commitment to the classical image of *polis* and politics, see Roy T. Tsao, "Arendt against Athens: Rereading *The Human Condition*," *Political Theory* 30, no. 1 (Feb. 2002): 97–123.

143. Oakeshott understands individuality as possible in every domain, every form of action, whereas Arendt sees individuality as only possible in politics. See Arendt, *The Human Condition*, 175–81 and George Kateb, "Arendt and Individualism," *Social Research* 61 (Winter 1994): 783–84.

144. Arendt's view of the state can be elicited from her treatment of founding and foundations in "What is Authority?," in *Between Past and Future*, 91–141 and *On Revolution* (New York: Viking Press, 1963).

145. Yet while Oakeshott's state-centric view is emphatically procedural it is not inhumanly or implausibly circumscribed. Despite the limits to proper politics, "there is . . . no want that may not set going a project to change *respublica*." See Oakeshott, *On Human Conduct*, 169.

146. Oakeshott, "Contemporary British Politics," 486. See also, Soininen, *From a "Necessary Evil" to an Art of Contingency: Michael Oakeshott's Conception of Political Activity*.

147. For these themes in Oakeshott's reading of Hobbes, see Michael Oakeshott, "Introduction to *Leviathan*," and "The Moral Life in the Writings of Thomas Hobbes," both in *Rationalism in Politics and Other Essays*, 221–94 and 295–350 respectively. For a reading of Hobbes that further develops the place of individuality in his political and moral thought, see Richard E. Flathman, *Thomas Hobbes: Skepticism, Individuality, and Chastened Politics* (Newbury Park, CA: Sage, 1993).

148. Arendt, *The Human Condition*, 230. While this point of affinity has been recognized, it has been little discussed. See Franco, *The Political Philosophy of Michael Oakeshott*, 213; Stuart Isaacs, *The Politics and Philosophy of Michael Oakeshott*, 150–51.

149. The modern enterprise state thus appeals to an account of agency akin to that drawn from the conservative reading of Wittgenstein and Oakeshott with which I dispensed in chapter 1.

150. Here, Oakeshott's criticism of the enterprise state runs parallel to Kenneth Minogue's criticism of postwar liberal ideology. See Kenneth R. Minogue, *The Liberal Mind* (New York: Vintage Books, 1968).

151. Both George Kateb and Hanna Pitkin pose Arendt's treatment of politics and the social in terms of alienation. See Kateb, "Hannah Arendt: Alienation and America" and Hanna Fenichel Pitkin, *The Attack of the Blob: Hannah Arendt's Concept of the Social* (Chicago: University of Chicago Press, 1998), e.g., 177.

152. Arendt, *The Human Condition*, 33, 46.

153. Ibid., 230–31.

154. Ibid., 40–49. Compare Oakeshott, "The Masses in Representative Democracy," 370–83 and *On Human Conduct*, 276–79, 289–313.

155. Hannah Arendt, *On Revolution* (New York: The Viking Press, 1963), 58.

156. Arendt, *The Human Condition*, 45; Arendt, *On Revolution*, 86.

157. Arendt, *The Human Condition*, 39.

158. Oakeshott, *On Human Conduct*, 243.

CHAPTER FOUR. TOWARD A CONVERSATIONAL DEMOCRATIC ETHOS

1. See, for instance, the treatment of democracy in Claude Lefort, *Democracy and Political Theory*, trans. David Macey (Minneapolis: University of Minnesota Press, 1988).

2. Oakeshott, *The Politics of Faith and the Politics of Scepticism*, 130–31; George Orwell, "Politics and the English Language," in *Critical Essays*, ed. George Packer (London: Harvill Secker, 2009), 272–86, esp. 276.

3. Oakeshott, "The Vocabulary of a Modern European State," 248–49. The same theme is also developed in *On Human Conduct*, 192–93; *The Politics of Faith and the Politics of Scepticism*, 130–32; and "The Masses in Representative Democracy," in *Rationalism in Politics*, 363–83.

4. Michael Oakeshott, ed. *The Social and Political Doctrines of Contemporary Europe* (Cambridge: Cambridge University Press, 1939), xvi. See also George Feaver, "Regimes of Liberty: Michael Oakeshott on Representative Democracy," in *The Intellectual Legacy of Michael Oakeshott*, ed. Corey Abel and Timothy Fuller (Charlottesville, VA: Imprint Academic, 2005), 136.

5. Paul Franco, despite his praise of Oakeshott as a critical and refreshing voice in liberal political thought, concludes that some of Oakeshott's fundamental commitments regarding tradition and practice are "profoundly anachronistic[, aristocratic and] irrelevant to democratic societies." Franco, *Michael Oakeshott: An Introduction*, 96. Chapters 1 and 2 of this volume contain my contrary assessment. Hanna Pitkin exemplifies the estimation of Oakeshott as antidemocratic as well as (and perhaps because he is) antipolitical. Pitkin, "Inhuman Conduct and Unpolitical Theory" and "The Roots of Conservatism." Pitkin's discussion of Oakeshott is somewhat more positive, though qualified in its scope, in *Wittgenstein and Justice* (Berkeley: University of California Press, 1972).

6. Steven Anthony Gerencser, "A Democratic Oakeshott?" *Political Research Quarterly* 52 (Dec. 1999): 845–65. Gerencser's skeptical yet democratic assessment of Oakeshott's political theory broadly comports with those of Richard Flathman, in *The Practice of Political Authority* and *Towards a Liberalism*; David Mapel, in "Civil Association and the Idea of Contingency," *Political Theory* 18 (Aug. 1990): 392–410 and "Purpose and Politics: Can There Be a Non-Instrumental Civil Association?" *Political Science Reviewer* 21 (Spring 1992): 63–80; Chantal Mouffe, in *The Return of the Political* (London: Verso, 1993); and Richard Rorty in *Contingency, Irony, and Solidarity*.

7. Michael Minch, *The Democratic Theory of Michael Oakeshott* (Charlottesville, VA: Imprint Academic, 2009). Much of Minch's argument rests upon Oakeshott's frequent use of the term *deliberation* to describe political activity within civil association. Below, I shall suggest that the leap from Oakeshott's characterization of politics as a deliberative activity to the conclusion that he is a "deliberative democrat" in the currently fashionable sense of that term is unwarranted and misleading.

8. Ibid., 25–26.

9. By deliberative democracy I mean to identify a group of democratic theories that emphasize various forms of citizen participation, more or less active and direct, in which collective self-government is conducted through discursive, communicative practices of a certain character. Hence, deliberative theories belong to the larger families of participatory and discursive democracy. In what follows, I specify features of deliberative democracy that distinguish it from other participatory and discursive theories of democracy.

10. By this I mean the twentieth-century movement to treat philosophical problems as first and foremost problems of language and language-use. See Richard Rorty, ed., *The Linguistic Turn: Recent Essays in Philosophical Method* (Chicago: The University of Chicago Press, 1967) and Richard J. Bernstein, *The Pragmatic Turn* (Cambridge: Polity, 2010), ch. 6.

11. For instance, Amy Gutmann and Dennis Thompson take this as the conceptual starting point for their thinking about deliberative democracy. See *Democracy and Disagreement* (Cambridge: Belknap Press of the Harvard University Press, 1996).

12. Two of the most articulate diagnoses of these deficiencies remain Benjamin Barber's *Strong Democracy: Participatory Politics for a New Age* (Berkeley: University of California Press, 1984) and C. B. MacPherson's *The Life and Times of Liberal Democracy* (Oxford: Oxford University Press, 1977). A more recent and somewhat more foreboding discussion is Sheldon Wolin's *Democracy Incorporated: Managed Democracy and the Specter of Inverted Totalitarianism* (Princeton: Princeton University Press, 2008).

13. John S. Dryzek, *Deliberative Democracy and Beyond: Liberals, Critics, Contestations* (Oxford: Oxford University Press, 2000), 175. On the value of difference for democracy, see Iris Marion Young, "Difference as a Resource for Democratic Communication," in *Deliberative Democracy: Essays on Reason and Politics*, ed. James Bohman and William Rehg (Cambridge: MIT Press, 1997), 383–406.

14. For a "neutral" vision of deliberation, see Amy Gutmann and Dennis Thompson, *Democracy and Disagreement* and *Why Deliberative Democracy?* (Princeton: Princeton University Press, 2004). For a "restrained" vision, see Bruce Ackerman, "Why Dialogue?," *The Journal of Philosophy* 86 (Jan. 1989): 5–22.

15. Barber, *Strong Democracy*; Mark Warren, "What Should We Expect from More Democracy?: Radically Democratic Responses to Politics," *Political Theory* 24 (May 1996): 241–70. Recent work on the concept of representation approaches many of the same issues, although from a different direction. See Lisa Jane Disch, "Towards a Mobilization Conception of Democratic Representation," *American Political Science Review* 105 (Feb. 2011): 100–14; Jane Mansbridge, "Clarifying the Concept of Political Representation," *American Political Science Review* 105 (Aug. 2011): 621–30; and Andrew Rehfeld, "The Concepts of Representation," *American Political Science Review* 105 (Aug. 2011): 631–41. Yet not all democratic theories in the republican tradition advocate deliberative democracy. Philip Pettit offers a republican theory of democracy that, by emphasizing mediating institutions and unintentional modes of popular influence upon government, treats dissensus as "entirely acceptable, even desirable." See *On the People's Terms: A Republican Theory and Model of Democracy* (Cambridge: Cambridge University Press, 2012), 268, and chs. 4 and 5 generally.

16. Christian F. Rostbøll, *Deliberative Freedom: Deliberative Democracy as Critical Theory* (Albany: State University of New York Press, 2008), 180.

17. Ibid., 274, n17.

18. Cheryl Misak, *Truth, Politics, and Morality: Pragmatism and Deliberation* (London: Routledge, 2000), 3. For another neopragmatist account of deliberative democracy that closely aligns with Misak's, see Robert B. Talisse, *Democracy after Liberalism: Pragmatism and Deliberative Politics* (London: Routledge, 2005), *A Pragmatist*

Philosophy of Democracy (London: Routledge, 2007), and *Democracy and Moral Conflict* (Cambridge: Cambridge University Press, 2009). For a related claim regarding the truth-seeking epistemic character of deliberative democracy, see Benedetto Fontana, Cary J. Nederman, and Gary Remer, "Introduction: Deliberative Democracy and the Rhetorical Turn," in *Talking Democracy: Historical Perspectives on Rhetoric and Democracy*, ed. Benedetto Fontana, Cary J. Nederman, and Gary Remer (University Park: Pennsylvania State University Press, 2004), 1–25.

19. Seyla Benhabib, "Toward a Deliberative Model of Democratic Legitimacy," in *Democracy and Difference: Contesting the Boundaries of the Political*, ed. Seyla Benhabib (Princeton: Princeton University Press, 1996), 68. See also Joshua Cohen, "Deliberation and Democratic Legitimacy," in Bohman and Rehg, *Deliberative Democracy: Essays on Reason and Politics*, 67–91.

20. The resemblances between the form and matter of *On Human Conduct* and earlier works, such as the essays collected in *Rationalism in Politics*, are readily apparent. Yet the extent to which this reconciliation is complete or successful, and the adjustments by which it is accomplished, are open questions addressed extensively in the secondary literature on Oakeshott. Oakeshott's own understanding of the relation between *On Human Conduct* and his earlier works can be gleaned from the early pages of the work itself, as well as from his reply to his critics after the book's publication. See Michael Oakeshott, "On Misunderstanding Human Conduct," *Political Theory* 4, no. 3 (Aug. 1976): 353–67.

21. Michael Oakeshott, "Political Education," in *Rationalism in Politics*, 44. Oakeshott discusses civil association systematically in Essays II and III of *On Human Conduct* and in slightly different terms in "The Rule of Law," in *On History and Other Essays*, ed. Timothy Fuller (Indianapolis: Liberty Fund, 1999), 129–78, and "The Vocabulary of a Modern European State," in *The Vocabulary of a Modern European State*. For a thoughtful discussion of Oakeshott's pluralism, both philosophical and political, see Flathman, *Pluralism and Liberal Democracy*, 109–61.

22. Oakeshott, *On Human Conduct*, 129, 147.

23. Ibid., 203.

24. Ibid., 247–51.

25. Mouffe, *The Return of the Political*, 67.

26. Minch, *The Democratic Theory of Michael Oakeshott*, esp. 133–57. The quoted formulation of the agent-centered ideal of civil association, with which Minch concurs, comes from David Mapel, "Civil Association and the Idea of Contingency," 393.

27. For a direct critical analysis of Minch's position see Luke Philip Plotica, "Michael Oakeshott's Democratic Voice," *Anamnesis* 2 (Fall 2013): 144–57.

28. Oakeshott discusses conversation in "The Voice of Conversation in the Education of Mankind," 187–99, and "The Voice of Poetry in the Conversation of Mankind," 488–541.

29. Oakeshott, "Voice of Poetry," 490.

30. Ibid., 490. See Fred Dallmayr's invocation of Oakeshott's view in "Conversation Across Boundaries," in *Dialogue Among Civilizations* (New York: Palgrave Macmillan, 2002), 31–47.

31. Oakeshott, "Voice of Conversation," 194.

32. Ibid., 187.

33. Oakeshott, "Voice of Poetry," 490.

34. Ibid.

35. Michael Oakeshott, "The Study of 'Politics' in a University," in *Rationalism in Politics*, 187. A relevant analogue is the attunement regarding civil authority presupposed by civil association. See Oakeshott, *On Human Conduct*, 147–63 and Gerencser, "A Democratic Oakeshott?" 856–64.

36. Oakeshott, "Political Education," 59.

37. Mouffe pursues this theme in *The Return of the Political* and *The Democratic Paradox* (London: Verso, 2000). Oakeshott's clearest statements to this effect can be found in the third essay of *On Human Conduct* and in "The Masses in Representative Democracy."

38. Mouffe, *The Democratic Paradox*, 19.

39. Ibid., 113, 111.

40. There is evidence that deliberation may face a number of empirical obstacles as well. Social science literature on group polarization—the phenomenon by which discussion tends to reinforce rather than change the pre-discussion opinions of participants—suggests that deliberation may in fact reinforce disagreement along initial lines. See Noah E. Friedkin, "Choice Shift and Group Polarization," *American Sociological Review* 64 (1999): 856–75 and Cass R. Sunstein, "The Law of Group Polarization," *The Journal of Political Philosophy* 10, no. 2 (2002): 175–95.

41. Mouffe, *The Democratic Paradox*, 22.

42. Stanley Fish has similarly criticized deliberative democrats for crafting a deliberative forum that is a tool of exclusion: in order to play the game one must accept rules that privilege certain outcomes. See Stanley Fish, "Mutual Respect as a Device of Exclusion," in *Deliberative Politics: Essays on Democracy and Disagreement*, ed. Stephen Macedo (Oxford: Oxford University Press, 1999), 96–99. See also Lynn M. Sanders, "Against Deliberation," *Political Theory* 25 (June 1997): 347–76.

43. Jon Elster, "The Market and the Forum: Three Varieties of Political Theory," in *Philosophy and Democracy*, ed. Thomas Christiano (Oxford: Oxford University Press, 2003), 148.

44. Stuart Hampshire, *Justice Is Conflict* (Princeton: Princeton University Press, 2000), 23.

45. Oakeshott, "Voice of Poetry," 490.

46. Oakeshott, "Political Education," 58.

47. Chantal Mouffe, *On The Political* (London: Verso, 2005), 20. See also Chantal Mouffe, "For an Agonistic Public Sphere," in *Radical Democracy: Politics between Abundance and Lack*, ed. Lars Tønder and Lasse Thomassen (Manchester: Manchester University Press, 2005), 123–32, and Oakeshott, *On Human Conduct*, 158–82.

48. Mouffe, *The Return of the Political*, 68–69. One might suggest that, under the influence of Schmitt's ideas, Mouffe sacralizes conflict and decision in a way that Oakeshott does not.

49. Oakeshott's description of the politics of civil association cannot, for instance, accommodate public demonstrations or protests as legitimate forms of political action. Direct popular action appears as either the rage-filled cry of the

anti-individual or the public affirmation of enterprise association and its collective ends. E.g., Oakeshott, "The Masses in Representative Democracy."

50. Oakeshott, *On Human Conduct*, 188.

51. Ibid., 166.

52. Ibid., 180.

53. Michael Oakeshott, "Rationalism in Politics," in *Rationalism in Politics*, 5–42. For further development of these basic themes, see Oakeshott, *The Politics of Faith and the Politics of Scepticism* and *On Human Conduct*, 185–326. Thorough and informative discussions of rationalism can be found in the work of Debra Candreva, Paul Franco, and Stuart Isaacs.

54. For instance, Oakeshott criticizes Friedrich von Hayek's systematic advocacy of spontaneous rather than planned orders as partaking of "the same style of politics" ("Rationalism in Politics," 26). Oakeshott's criticism was aimed at *The Road to Serfdom*, and was perhaps well placed. Yet some of Hayek's later views of spontaneous social order likely bring him closer to the ideal of civil association, a framework of rules within which individual agency is left to generate institutional complexity. See Friedrich A. von Hayek, "Kinds of Order in Society," in *The Politicization of Society*, ed. Kenneth S. Templeton Jr. (Indianapolis: Liberty Fund, 1979), 501–23.

55. David Estlund, *Democratic Authority: A Philosophical Framework* (Princeton: Princeton University Press, 2008); Jürgen Habermas, *Between Facts and Norms*, trans. William Rehg (Cambridge: Polity Press, 1996), 287–328, 463–490; Benjamin Barber, *Strong Democracy*, 261–311.

56. Misak, *Truth, Politics, Morality*, 101.

57. Talisse, *Democracy and Moral Conflict*, 9.

58. Misak quoted in Talisse, *A Pragmatist Philosophy of Democracy*, 15.

59. Dryzek, *Deliberative Democracy and Beyond*, 1.

60. John S. Dryzek, "Rhetoric in Democracy: A Systemic Appreciation," *Political Theory* 38 (June 2010): 319–39. Dryzek claims that "when deliberative democrats think for very long about rhetoric they mostly come down on the side of allowing that it does have roles to play" (322). See also Bryan Garsten, *Saving Persuasion: A Defense of Rhetoric and Judgment* (Cambridge: Harvard University Press, 2006).

61. Simone Chambers, "Rhetoric and the Public Sphere: Has Deliberative Democracy Abandoned Mass Democracy?" *Political Theory* 37 (June 2009): 323–50.

62. Oakeshott expresses suspicion regarding the epistemic ideal of the "surer wisdom of the Many" which is essential to the deliberative democratic endeavor. See Oakeshott, "Vocabulary of a Modern European State," 248.

63. Oakeshott, "Voice of Poetry," 489.

64. Jean-François Lyotard and Jean-Loup Thébaud, *Just Gaming*, trans. Wlad Godzich (Minneapolis: University of Minnesota Press, 1985), 58. There is also some affinity to Bakhtin's concept of polyphony in which the voices remain independent despite coming to serve one another in their mutual articulation. Mikhail Bakhtin, *Problems of Dostoevsky's Poetics*, trans. R. W. Rotsel (Ann Arbor: Ardis, 1973), 17.

65. John Dryzek, for example, offers this criticism of Mouffe in "Deliberative Democracy in Divided Societies," *Political Theory* 33 (April 2005): 221.

66. Oakeshott's clearest discussions of these themes appear in "Political Education" and *On Human Conduct*, especially 158–84; and "Political Discourse," in *Rationalism in Politics*, 70–95.

67. Oakeshott, "The Voice of Conversation in the Education of Mankind,"188; 190; *On Human Conduct*, 256.

68. Michael Oakeshott, "Scientific Politics," in *Religion, Politics, and the Moral Life*, ed. Fuller, 109.

69. I thank Richard Flathman for his insistence upon this line of criticism, though I do not suppose that I have done it justice.

70. See Oakeshott, "The Voice of Conversation in the Education of Mankind," 187–89, where the concept and practice of conversation is introduced through analogies that call to mind stereotypes of Cambridge and Oxford intelligentsia.

71. This charge has been leveled at Oakeshott, for instance, by John White, "Wellbeing and Education: Issues of Culture and Authority," *Journal of Philosophy of Education* 41 (2007): 26.

72. Such lines of argument are frequently indebted to the work of Michel Foucault, *inter alia*, *Discipline and Punish: The Birth of the Prison*, trans. Alan Sheridan (New York: Vintage Books, 1977) and *The History of Sexuality, Vol. I: An Introduction*, trans. Robert Hurley (New York: Vintage Books, 1990). Related critical analyses of discursive power are central to much agonistic democratic theory. See, for instance, Mouffe, *The Democratic Paradox* and "For an Agonistic Public Sphere," as well as William E. Connolly, *Identity/Difference: Democratic Negotiations of Political Paradox* (Ithaca: Cornell University Press, 1991) and *The Ethos of Pluralization* (Minneapolis: University of Minnesota Press, 1995).

73. Michel Foucault, "Truth and Power," in *Power/Knowledge: Selected Interviews and Other Writings, 1972–1977*, ed. Colin Gordon, trans. Colin Gordon (New York: Pantheon, 1980), 132–33.

74. Michael Oakeshott, "The Political Economy of Freedom," in *Rationalism in Politics*, 388.

75. For instance, Foucault, "Truth and Power," 122–23.

76. Stephen Mulhall, *The Conversation of Humanity* (Charlottesville: University of Virginia Press, 2007); Stanley Cavell, *Conditions Handsome and Unhandsome: The Constitution of Emersonian Perfectionism* (Chicago: University of Chicago Press, 1990), esp. 101–26; Stanley Cavell, *Cities of Words: Pedagogical Letters on a Register of the Moral Life* (Cambridge: The Belknap Press of Harvard University Press, 2004), especially chapters 3 and 9; Cavell, *The Claim of Reason*, especially Part Four.

77. Cavell, *Cities of Words*, 173.

78. Ibid., 173–74. See also Sandra Laugier, "Wittgenstein and Cavell: Anthropology, Skepticism and Politics," in *The Claim to Community: Essays on Stanley Cavell and Political Philosophy*, ed. Andrew Norris (Stanford: Stanford University Press, 2006), 19–37.

79. Mulhall, *The Conversation of Mankind*, 63.

80. A similar critique of Oakeshott could be drawn from Lyotard's sketch, in *Just Gaming*, of democratic politics infused with a discursive, moral sensibility, uniting playfulness (as subversive and liberating) with the commitment that the gaming itself be just.

81. Mulhall's criticism of Oakeshott is based upon two passages, one from "The Study of Politics in a University" (*RP*, 187) and one from "The Voice of Poetry in the Conversation of Mankind" (*RP*, 490), and manifestly fails to account for or address the other conversation essay or any relevant part of *On Human Conduct*.

While this limitation of textual basis does not undermine Mulhall's position, it weakens that position substantially.

82. Cavell, *Cities of Words*, 173.

83. On this point Cavell's account of subjectivity and community resembles the views of Alasdair MacIntyre and Charles Taylor from which I distinguished Oakeshott's in Chapter Two.

84. Oakeshott, *On Human Conduct*, 41. Cavell similarly turns to conversation as a way to cope with questions about given or final senses of individual identity, and thus of the individual's place in community: "How can it be that one among the endless true descriptions of me represents *the* truth of me, tells me who or what I am? How can there be a key to my identity?" (Cavell, *The Claim of Reason*, 388).

85. Mouffe, *The Democratic Paradox*, 137.

CONCLUSION

1. Michael Oakeshott, "The Voice of Poetry in the Conversation of Mankind," 490.

2. Hannah Arendt, *The Human Condition*, 181–88.

3. Perhaps the most telling indication of his personal relationship to British Conservatism, as an ideological movement, was his choice to "declin[e] the Companion of Honor when offered it by Margaret Thatcher." Franco, *Michael Oakeshott*, 1.

BIBLIOGRAPHY

Abel, Corey, ed. *The Meanings of Michael Oakeshott's Conservatism*. Charlottesville, VA: Imprint Academic, 2010.

Ackerman, Bruce. "Why Dialogue?" *The Journal of Philosophy* 86 (January 1989): 5–22.

Adorno, Theodor, and Max Horkheimer. *The Dialectic of Enlightenment*. Translated by John Cumming. London: Verso, 1978.

Allan, George. *The Importances of the Past: A Meditation on the Authority of Tradition*. Albany: State University of New York Press, 1986.

Anderson, Benedict. *Imagined Communities*. 2nd Ed. London: Verso, 2006.

Arendt, Hannah. *Between Past and Future: Eight Exercises in Political Thought*. New York: Penguin Books, 1977.

———. *Crises of the Republic*. New York: Harcourt Brace, 1972.

———. *The Human Condition*. 2nd Ed. Chicago: University of Chicago Press, 1998.

———. *On Revolution*. New York: Viking Press, 1963.

Bakhtin, Mikhail. *Problems of Dostoevsky's Poetics*. Translated by R. W. Rotsel. Ann Arbor: Ardis, 1973.

Barber, Benjamin. *Strong Democracy: Participatory Politics for a New Age*. Berkeley: University of California Press, 1984.

Bellah, Robert, Richard Madsen, William M. Sullivan, Ann Swidler, and Steven M. Tipton. *The Good Society*. New York: Vintage Books, 1992.

———. *Habits of the Heart: Individualism and Commitment in American Life*. Berkeley: University of California Press, 1984.

Benhabib, Seyla. "Toward a Deliberative Model of Democratic Legitimacy." In *Democracy and Difference: Contesting the Boundaries of the Political*, edited by Seyla Benhabib. Princeton: Princeton University Press, 1996.

Berlin, Isaiah. *The Cooked Timber of Humanity: Chapters in the History of Ideas*. Edited by Henry Hardy. New York: Knopf, 1991.

———. *Four Essays on Liberty*. Oxford: Oxford University Press, 1969.

———. *Freedom and Its Betrayal: Six Enemies of Human Liberty*. Edited by Henry Hardy. Princeton: Princeton University Press, 2002.

———. *The Proper Study of Mankind*. Edited by Henry Hardy and Roger Hausheer. New York: Farrar, Straus, and Giroux, 1998.

———. *Vico and Herder: Two Studies in the History of Ideas*. New York: Vintage Books, 1977.

Bernstein, Richard J. *The Pragmatic Turn*. Cambridge: Polity, 2010.

Bloom, Alan. *The Closing of the American Mind: How Higher Education Has Failed Democracy and Impoverished the Souls of Today's Students*. New York: Simon and Schuster, 1987.

Bloor, David. *Wittgenstein: A Social Theory of Knowledge*. New York: Columbia University Press, 1983.

———. *Wittgenstein, Rules, and Institutions*. London: Routledge, 1997.

Botwinick, Aryeh. *Michael Oakeshott's Skepticism*. Princeton: Princeton University Press, 2011.

Boucher, David. "Oakeshott, Freedom, and Republicanism." *British Journal of Politics and International Relations* 7 (2005): 81–96.

———. "Politics in a Different Mode: An Appreciation of Michael Oakeshott 1901–1990." *History of Political Thought* XII (Winter 1991): 717–28.

———. "The Victim of Thought: The Idealist Inheritance." In *A Companion to Michael Oakeshott*, edited by Paul Franco and Leslie Marsh. University Park: Pennsylvania State University Press, 2012.

Bradley, Francis Herbert. *Ethical Studies*. 2nd Ed. Oxford: Oxford University Press, 1962.

Burke, Edmund. *Reflections on the Revolution in France*. Edited by J. G. A. Pocock. Indianapolis: Hackett, 1987.

Canovan, Margaret. *Hannah Arendt: a Reinterpretation of Her Political Thought*. Cambridge: Cambridge University Press, 1992.

Cavell, Stanley. *Cities of Words: Pedagogical Letters on a Register of the Moral Life*. Cambridge: Belknap Press of the Harvard University Press, 2004.

———. *The Claim of Reason: Wittgenstein, Skepticism, Morality, and Tragedy*. 2nd Ed. Oxford: Oxford University Press, 1999.

———. *Conditions Handsome and Unhandsome: The Constitution of Emersonian Perfectionism*. Chicago: University of Chicago Press, 1990.

———. *Must We Mean What We Say?* 2nd Ed. Cambridge: Cambridge University Press, 2002.

Cerbone, David. "The Limits of Conservatism: Wittgenstein on 'Our Life' and 'Our Concepts.'" In *The Grammar of Politics*, edited by Cressida Heyes. Ithaca: Cornell University Press, 2003.

Chambers, Simone. "Rhetoric and the Public Sphere: Has Deliberative Democracy Abandoned Mass Democracy?" *Political Theory* 37(June 2009): 323–50.

Coats, Wendell John Jr. *Oakeshott and His Contemporaries*. Selinsgrove, PA: Susquehanna University Press, 2000.

———. "Some Correspondences between Oakeshott's "Civil Condition" and the Republican Tradition." *Political Science Reviewer* 21 (Spring 1992): 99–115.

Cohen, Joshua. "Deliberation and Democratic Legitimacy." In *Deliberative Democracy: Essays on Reason and Politics*, edited by James Bohman and William Rehg. Cambridge: MIT Press, 1997.

Connolly, William E. *The Ethos of Pluralization*. Minneapolis: University of Minnesota Press, 1995.

———. *Identity/Difference: Democratic Negotiations of Political Paradox*. Ithaca: Cornell University Press, 1991.

———. *The Terms of Political Discourse*. 3rd Ed. Princeton: Princeton University Press, 1993.

Crary, Alice. "Wittgenstein's Philosophy in Relation to Political Thought." In *The New Wittgenstein*, edited by Alice Crary and Rupert Read. London: Routledge, 2000.

Dallmayr, Fred. *Dialogue Among Civilizations*. New York: Palgrave Macmillan, 2002.

Devigne, Robert. *Recasting Conservatism: Oakeshott, Strauss, and the Response to Postmodernism*. New Haven: Yale University Press, 1994.

Digeser, Paige, and Richard Flathman. "Oakeshott's *On Human Conduct*." In *The Cambridge Companion to Oakeshott*, edited by Efraim Podoksik. Cambridge: Cambridge University Press, 2012.

Disch, Lisa Jane. *Hannah Arendt and the Limits of Philosophy*. Ithaca: Cornell University Press, 1994.

———."Towards a Mobilization Conception of Democratic Representation." *American Political Science Review* 105 (February 2011): 100–14.

Downs, Anthony. *An Economic Theory of Democracy*. New York: Harper, 1957.

Dreyfus, Hubert J. *What Computers Still Can't Do: a Critique of Artificial Reason*. Cambridge: MIT Press, 1992.

———, and Paul Rabinow. *Michel Foucault: Beyond Structuralism and Hermeneutics*. 2nd Ed. Chicago: University of Chicago Press, 1983.

Dryzek, John S. *Deliberative Democracy and Beyond: Liberals, Critics, Contestations*. Oxford: Oxford University Press, 2000.

———. "Deliberative Democracy in Divided Societies." *Political Theory* 33 (April 2005): 218–42.

Elster, Jon. "The Market and the Forum: Three Varieties of Political Theory." In *Philosophy and Democracy*, edited by Thomas Christiano. Oxford: Oxford University Press, 2003.

Estlund, David. *Democratic Authority: A Philosophical Framework*. Princeton: Princeton University Press, 2008.

Feaver, George. "Regimes of Liberty: Michael Oakeshott on Representative Democracy." In *The Intellectual Legacy of Michael Oakeshott*, edited by Cory Abel and Timothy Fuller. Charlottesville, VA: Imprint Academic, 2005.

Fish, Stanley. "Mutual Respect as a Device of Exclusion." In *Deliberative Politics: Essays on Democracy and Disagreement*, edited by Stephen Macedo. Oxford: Oxford University Press, 1999.

Flathman, Richard E. *Freedom and Its Conditions*. London: Routledge, 2003.

———. *The Philosophy and Politics of Freedom*. Chicago: University of Chicago Press, 1987.

———. *Pluralism and Liberal Democracy*. Baltimore: Johns Hopkins University Press, 2005.

———. *The Practice of Political Authority*. Chicago: University of Chicago Press, 1980.

———. *Reflections of a Would-be Anarchist*. Minneapolis: University of Minnesota Press, 1998.

———. *Thomas Hobbes: Skepticism, Individuality, and Chastened Politics*. Newbury Park, CA: Sage, 1993.

———. *Towards a Liberalism*. Ithaca: Cornell University Press, 1989.

———. *Willful Liberalism: Voluntarism and Individuality in Political Theory and Practice*. Ithaca: Cornell University Press, 1992.

Fontana, Benedetto, Cary J. Nederman, and Gary Remer. "Introduction: Deliberative Democracy and the Rhetorical Turn." In *Talking Democracy: Historical*

Perspectives on Rhetoric and Democracy, edited by Benedetto Fontana, Cary J. Nederman, and Gary Remer. University Park: Pennsylvania State University Press, 2004.

Foucault, Michel. *The Birth of Biopolitics: Lectures at the Collège de France, 1978–1979*. Edited by Michel Senellart. Translated by Graham Burchell. New York: Palgrave Macmillan, 2008.

———. *Discipline and Punish: The Birth of the Prison*. Translated by Alan Sheridan. New York: Vintage Books, 1977.

———. *Foucault Live: Collected Interviews, 1961–1984*. Edited by Sylvère Lotringer. New York: Semiotext(e), 1996.

———. *The Foucault Reader*. Edited by Paul Rabinow. New York: Pantheon Books, 1984.

———. *The History of Sexuality, Vol. I: An Introduction*. Translated by Robert Hurley. New York: Vintage Books, 1990.

———. *Power/Knowledge: Selected Interviews and Other Writings, 1972–1977*. Edited by Colin Gordon. Translated by Colin Gordon, Leo Marshall, John Mepham, and Kate Soper New York: Pantheon Books, 1980.

———. *Security, Territory, Population: Lectures at the Collège de France, 1977–1978*. Edited by Michel Senellart. Translated by Graham Burchell. New York: Palgrave Macmillan, 2007.

———. *"Society Must Be Defended:" Lectures at the Collège de France:1975–1976*. Edited by Mauro Bertani and Alessandro Fontana. Translated by David Macey. New York: Picador, 2003.

Franco, Paul. *Michael Oakeshott: An Introduction*. New Haven: Yale University Press, 2004.

———. "Oakeshott as Liberal Theorist." *Political Theory* 18 (August 1990): 411–36.

———. "Oakeshott, Berlin, and Liberalism." *Political Theory* 31 (August 2003): 484–507.

———. *The Political Philosophy of Michael Oakeshott*. New Haven: Yale University Press, 1990.

Frankfurt, Harry G. *The Importance of What We Care About*. Cambridge: Cambridge University Press, 1988.

Friedkin, Noah E. "Choice Shift and Group Polarization." *American Sociological Review* 64 (1999): 856–75.

Friedman, Richard B. "Michael Oakeshott and the Elusive Identity of the Rule of Law." In *The Intellectual Legacy of Michael Oakeshott*, edited by Cory Abel and Timothy Fuller. Charlottesville, VA: Imprint Academic, 2005.

———. "What Is a Non-Instrumental Law?." *Political Science Reviewer* 21 (Spring 1992): 81–98.

Fuss, Peter. "Hannah Arendt's Conception of Political Community." In *Hannah Arendt: the Recovery of the Public World*, edited by Melvyn A. Hill. New York: St. Martin's Press, 1979.

Galston, William A. "Oakeshott's Political Theory: Recapitulation and Criticisms." In *The Cambridge Companion to Oakeshott*, edited by Efraim Podoksik. Cambridge: Cambridge University Press, 2012.

Gamble, Andrew. "Oakeshott's Ideological Politics: Conservative or Liberal?" In *The Cambridge Companion to Oakeshott*, edited by Efraim Podoksik. Cambridge: Cambridge University Press, 2012.

Garsten, Bryan. *Saving Persuasion: A Defense of Rhetoric and Judgment*. Cambridge: Harvard University Press, 2006.

Gerencser, Steven Anthony. "A Democratic Oakeshott?" *Political Research Quarterly* 52 (December 1999): 845–65.

———. *The Skeptic's Oakeshott*. New York: St. Martin's Press, 2000.

Gray, John. *Isaiah Berlin*. Princeton: Princeton University Press, 1996.

———. *Liberalisms*. London: Routledge, 1989.

———. *Two Faces of Liberalism*. New York: The New Press, 2000.

Gutmann, Amy, and Dennis Thompson. *Democracy and Disagreement*. Cambridge: Belknap Press of the Harvard University Press, 1996.

———. *Why Deliberative Democracy?* Princeton: Princeton University Press, 2004.

Habermas, Jürgen. *Between Facts and Norms*. Translated by William Rehg. Cambridge: Polity Press, 1996.

Hacking, Ian. *Historical Ontology*. Cambridge: Harvard University Press, 2002.

Hammer, Dean C. "Meaning and Tradition." *Polity* 24 (Summer 1992): 551–67.

Hampshire, Stuart. *Justice is Conflict*. Princeton: Princeton University Press, 2000.

Harris, Roy. *Language, Saussure and Wittgenstein: How to Play Games with Words*. London: Routledge, 1990.

von Hayek, Friedrich A. "Kinds of Order in Society." In *The Politicization of Society*, edited by Kenneth S. Templeton Jr. Indianapolis: Liberty Fund, 1979.

Hegel, G. W. F. *Phenomenology of Spirit*. Translated by A. V. Miller. Oxford: Oxford University Press, 1977.

Heyes, Cressida J. "Introduction." In *The Grammar of Politics: Wittgenstein and Political Philosophy*, edited by Cressida J. Heyes. Ithaca: Cornell University Press, 2003.

Himmelfarb, Gertrude. "The Conservative Imagination." *The American Scholar* 44 (Summer 1975): 405–20.

Hobbes, Thomas. *Leviathan*. Edited by Edwin Curley. Indianapolis: Hackett, 1994.

Isaacs, Stuart. *The Politics and Philosophy of Michael Oakeshott*. London: Routledge, 2006.

Janik, Allan. "Notes on the Natural History of Politics." In *The Grammar of Politics: Wittgenstein and Political Philosophy*, edited by Cressida J. Heyes. Ithaca: Cornell University Press, 2003.

Jones, K. "Is Wittgenstein a Conservative Philosopher?" *Philosophical Investigations* 9 (October 1986): 274–87.

Kaldis, Byron. "Worlds of Experience: Science." In *The Cambridge Companion to Oakeshott*, edited by Efraim Podoksik. Cambridge: Cambridge University Press, 2012.

Kateb, George. "Arendt and Individualism." *Social Research* 61 (Winter 1994): 765–94.

———. "Freedom and Worldliness in the Thought of Hannah Arendt." *Political Theory* 5 (May 1977): 141–82.

———. "Hannah Arendt: Alienation and America." *Raritan* 3 (Summer 1983): 4–34.

———. "The Idea of Individual Infinitude." *The Hedgehog Review* 7 (Summer 2005): 42–54.

———. *The Inner Ocean*. Ithaca: Cornell University Press, 1992.

———. *Patriotism and Other Mistakes*. New Haven: Yale University Press, 2006.

Kekes, John. "What is Conservatism?" *Philosophy* 72 (July 1997): 351–74.

Kripke, Saul. *Wittgenstein on Rules and Private Language*. Cambridge: Harvard University Press, 1982.

Laugier, Sandra. "Wittgenstein and Cavell: Anthropology, Skepticism, and Politics." In *The Claim to Community: Essays on Stanley Cavell and Political Philosophy*, edited by Andrew Norris. Stanford: Stanford University Press, 2006.

Lefort, Claude. *Democracy and Political Theory*. Translated by David Macey. Minneapolis: University of Minnesota Press, 1988.

Lyotard, Jean-François. *Just Gaming*. Translated by Wlad Godzich. Minneapolis: University of Minnesota Press, 1985.

MacIntyre, Alasdair. *After Virtue*. 2nd Ed. Notre Dame: University of Notre Dame Press, 1984.

———. *Three Rival Versions of Moral Enquiry: Encyclopaedia, Genealogy, and Tradition*. Notre Dame: University of Notre Dame Press, 1990.

———. *Whose Justice? Which Rationality?* Notre Dame: University of Notre Dame Press, 1988.

MacPherson, Crawford Brough. *The Life and Times of Liberal Democracy*. Oxford: Oxford University Press, 1977.

Mannheim, Karl. *Essays on Sociology and Social Psychology*. Edited by Paul Kecskemeti. London: Routledge and Kegan Paul, 1953.

Mansbridge, Jane. "Clarifying the Concept of Political Representation." *American Political Science Review* 105 (August 2011): 621–30.

Mapel, David. "Civil Association and the Idea of Contingency." *Political Theory* 18 (August 1990): 392–410.

———. "Purpose and Politics: Can There Be a Non-Instrumental Civil Association?" *Political Science Reviewer* 21 (Spring 1992): 63–80.

Marmor, Andrei. *Social Conventions: From Language to Law*. Princeton: Princeton University Press, 2009.

McGinn, Colin. *Wittgenstein on Meaning: An Interpretation and Evaluation*. Oxford: Basil Blackwell, 1984.

Minch, Michael. *The Democratic Theory of Michael Oakeshott*. Charlottesville, VA: Imprint Academic, 2009.

Minogue, Kenneth R. "The History of Political Thought Seminar." In *The Achievement of Michael Oakeshott*, edited by Jesse Norman. London: Duckworth, 1993.

———. *The Liberal Mind*. New York: Vintage Books, 1968.

Misak, Cheryl. *Truth, Politics, and Morality: Pragmatism and Deliberation*. London: Routledge, 2000.

Mouffe, Chantal. *The Democratic Paradox*. London: Verso, 2000.

———."For an Agonistic Public Sphere." In *Radical Democracy: Politics between Abundance and Lack*, edited by Lars Tønder and Lasse Thomassen. Manchester, UK: Manchester University Press, 2005.

———. *On the Political*. London: Verso, 2005.

———. *The Return of the Political*. London: Verso, 1993.

Mulhall, Stephen. *The Conversation of Humanity*. Charlottesville: University of Virginia Press, 2007.

Nagel, Thomas. *The View from Nowhere*. Oxford: Oxford University Press, 1986.

Nardin, Terry. *The Philosophy of Michael Oakeshott*. University Park: Pennsylvania State University Press, 2001.

Nietzsche, Friedrich. *The Will to Power*. Edited by Walter Kaufmann. Translated by Walter Kaufmann and R. J. Hollingdale. New York: Vintage Books, 1968.

Norris, Andrew. "'La chaîne des raisons a une fin.' Wittgenstein et Oakeshott sur le rationalisme et la pratique." *Cités: Philosophie, Politique, Histoire* 38 (2009): 95–108.

Nozick, Robert. *Anarchy, State, and Utopia*. New York: Basic Books, 1974.

Nyíri, J. C. "Wittgenstein's Later Work in relation to Conservatism." In *Wittgenstein and his Times*, edited by Brian McGuinness. Chicago: University of Chicago Press, 1982.

———. "Wittgenstein's New Traditionalism." *Acta Philosophica Fennica* 28 (1976): 501–12.

Oakeshott, Michael. *The Concept of a Philosophical Jurisprudence: Essays and Reviews 1926–1951*. Edited by Luke O'Sullivan. Charlottesville, VA: Imprint Academic, 2007.

———. "Contemporary British Politics." *Cambridge Journal* 1 (1947–1948): 474–90.

———. *Experience and Its Modes*. Cambridge: Cambridge University Press, 1933.

———. *Hobbes on Civil Association*. Berkeley: University of California Press, 1975.

———. *Lectures in the History of Political Thought*. Edited by Terry Nardin and Luke O'Sullivan. Charlottesville, VA: Imprint Academic, 2006.

———. *Morality and Politics in Modern Europe*. Edited by Shirley Robin Letwin. New Haven: Yale University Press, 1993.

———. *On History and Other Essays*. Indianapolis: Liberty Fund, 1999.

———. *On Human Conduct*. Oxford: Oxford University Press, 1975.

———. "On Misunderstanding Human Conduct." *Political Theory* 4 (August 1976): 353–67.

———. *The Politics of Faith and the Politics of Scepticism*. Edited by Timothy Fuller. New Haven: Yale University Press, 1996.

———. *Rationalism in Politics and Other Essays*. Revised Edition. Indianapolis: Liberty Fund, 1991.

———. *Religion, Politics, and the Moral Life*. Edited by Timothy Fuller. New Haven: Yale University Press, 1993.

———. *The Social and Political Doctrines of Contemporary Europe*. Cambridge: Cambridge University Press, 1939.

———. *The Vocabulary of a Modern European State*. Edited by Luke O'Sullivan. Charlottesville, VA: Imprint Academic, 2008.

———. *The Voice of Liberal Learning: Michael Oakeshott on Education*. Edited by Timothy Fuller. New Haven: Yale University Press, 1989.

———. *What Is History? and Other Essays*. Edited by Luke O'Sullivan. Charlottesville, VA: Imprint Academic, 2004.

O'Neill, John. "The Disciplinary Society: From Weber to Foucault." *The British Journal of Sociology* XXXVII (March 1986): 42–60.

Orwell, George. *Critical Essays*. Edited by George Packer. London: Harvill Secker, 2009.

Parekh, Bhikhu. *Hannah Arendt and the Search for a New Political Philosophy*. London: The MacMillan Press, 1981.

———. "Oakeshott's Theory of Civil Association." *Ethics* 106 (October 1995): 158–86.

Pascal, Blaise. *Pensées*. Edited by Anthony Levi. Translated by Honor Levi. Oxford: Oxford University Press, 1995.

Pettit, Philip. *On the People's Terms: A Republican Theory and Model of Democracy*. Cambridge: Cambridge University Press, 2012.

Pitkin, Hanna Fenichel. "Inhuman Conduct and Unpolitical Theory: Michael Oakeshott's *On Human Conduct*." *Political Theory* 4 (August 1976): 301–17.

———. "The Roots of Conservatism: Michael Oakeshott and the Denial of Politics." *Dissent* XX (1973): 496–525.

———. *Wittgenstein and Justice*. Berkeley: University of California Press, 1972.

Plotica, Luke Philip. "Michael Oakeshott's Democratic Voice." *Anamnesis* 2 (Fall 2013): 144–57.

———. "Public and Private: the Sense of the Political in Wittgenstein and Arendt." *Cadernos de Filosofia* 19/20 (2006): 305–19.

Pocock, J. G. A. *Politics, Language, and Time: Essays on Political Thought and History*. Revised Edition. Chicago: University of Chicago Press, 1989.

Podoksik, Efraim. *In Defense of Modernity: Vision and Philosophy in Michael Oakeshott*. Charlottesville, VA: Imprint Academic, 2003.

———. "Oakeshott's Theory of Freedom as Recognized Contingency." *European Journal of Political Theory* 2 (2003): 57–77.

Polhaus, Gaile, and John R. Wright. "Using Wittgenstein Critically: A Political Approach to Philosophy." *Political Theory* 30 (December 2002): 800–27.

Putnam, Hilary. *Reason, Truth and History*. Cambridge: Cambridge University Press, 1981.

———. "Rules, Attunement, and 'Applying Words to the World': The Struggle to Understand Wittgenstein's Vision of Language." In *The Legacy of Wittgenstein: Pragmatism or Deconstruction*, edited by Chantal Mouffe and Ludwig Nagl. Frankfurt am Main: Peter Lang, 2001.

Quinton, Anthony. *The Politics of Imperfection: The Religious and Secular Traditions of Conservative Thought in England from Hooker to Oakeshott*. London: Faber and Faber, 1978.

Rawls, John. *A Theory of Justice*. Revised edition. Cambridge: Belknap Press of the Harvard University Press, 1999.

Rehfeld, Andrew. "The Concepts of Representation." *American Political Science Review* 105 (August 2011): 631–41.

Riker, William H. *Liberalism against Populism: a Confrontation between the Theory of Democracy and the Theory of Social Choice*. San Francisco: W. H. Freeman, 1982.

Rorty, Richard. *Contingency, Irony, and Solidarity*. Cambridge: Cambridge University Press, 1989.

———, ed. *The Linguistic Turn: Recent Essays in Philosophical Method*. Chicago: The University of Chicago Press, 1967.

———. *Philosophy and the Mirror of Nature*. Princeton: Princeton University Press, 1979.

———. "Postmodernist Bourgeois Liberalism," *The Journal of Philosophy* 80 (October 1983): 583–89.

Rostbøll, Christian F. *Deliberative Freedom: Deliberative Democracy as Critical Theory*. Albany: State University of New York Press, 2008.

Rousseau, Jean-Jacques. "A Discourse on Political Economy." In *The Social Contract and Discourses*, translated by G. D. H. Cole. London: Everyman, 1994.

Sandel, Michael J. *Liberalism and the Limits of Justice*. 2nd Edition. Cambridge: Cambridge University Press, 1998.

———. "The Procedural Republic and the Unencumbered Self." *Political Theory* 12 (February 1984): 81–96.

Sanders, Lynn M. "Against Deliberation." *Political Theory* 25 (June 1997): 347–76.

Saussure, Ferdinand de. *Course in General Linguistics*. Edited by Charles Bally and Albert Sechehay. Translated by Wade Baskin. New York: Philosophical Library, 1959.

Schumpeter, Joseph A. *Capitalism, Socialism, and Democracy*. New York: Harper and Row, 1962.

Searle, John. *Speech Acts*. Cambridge: Cambridge University Press, 1969.

Sellars, Wilfrid. *Empiricism and the Philosophy of Mind*. Cambridge: Harvard University Press, 1997.

Shils, Edward. *Tradition*. Chicago: University of Chicago Press, 1981.

———. "Tradition and Liberty: Antinomy and Interdependence." *Ethics* 68 (April 1958): 153–65.

Skinner, Quentin. "The State." In *Political Innovation and Conceptual Change*, edited by Terrence Ball, James Farr, and Russell L. Hanson. Cambridge: Cambridge University Press, 1989.

Soininen, Suvi. *From a "Necessary Evil" to an Art of Contingency: Michael Oakeshott's Conception of Political Activity*. Charlottesville, VA: Imprint Academic, 2005.

Sunstein, Cass R. "The Law of Group Polarization." *The Journal of Political Philosophy* 10 (2002): 175–95.

Talisse, Robert B. *Democracy after Liberalism: Pragmatism and Deliberative Politics*. London: Routledge, 2005.

———. *Democracy and Moral Conflict*. Cambridge: Cambridge University Press, 2009.

———. *A Pragmatist Philosophy of Democracy*. London: Routledge, 2007.

Taylor, Charles. *Philosophical Papers, Vol. I: Human Agency and Language*. Cambridge: Cambridge University Press, 1985.

———. *Philosophical Papers, Vol. II: Philosophy and the Human Sciences*. Cambridge: Cambridge University Press, 1985.

———. *Sources of the Self*. Cambridge: Harvard University Press, 1989.

Tregenza, Ian. *Michael Oakeshott on Hobbes*. Charlottesville, VA: Imprint Academic, 2003.

Tsao, Roy T. "Arendt against Athens: Rereading *The Human Condition*." *Political Theory* 30 (February 2002): 97–123.

Villa, Dana. *Arendt and Heidegger: the Fate of the Political*. Princeton: Princeton University Press, 1996.

———. "Oakeshott and the Cold War Critique of Political Rationalism." In *The Cambridge Companion to Oakeshott*, edited by Efraim Podoksik. Cambridge: Cambridge University Press, 2012.

———. "The Philosopher versus the Citizen: Arendt, Strauss and Socrates." *Political Theory* 26 (April 1998): 147–72.

Warren, Mark. "What Should We Expect From More Democracy?: Radically Democratic Responses to Politics." *Political Theory* 24 (May 1996): 241–70.

Walzer, Michael. *Spheres of Justice: A Defense of Pluralism and Equality*. New York: Basic Books, 1983.

Weber, Max. *From Max Weber: Essays in Sociology*. Translated and Edited by H. H. Gerth and C. Wright Mills. Oxford: Oxford University Press, 1958.

Williams, Bernard. *In the Beginning Was the Deed*. Edited by Geoffrey Hawthorn. Princeton: Princeton University Press, 2005.

———. *Moral Luck*. Cambridge: Cambridge University Press, 1981.

Winch, Peter. *The Idea of a Social Science and Its Relation to Philosophy*. 2nd Ed. London: Routledge, 1990.

Wittgenstein, Ludwig. *Culture and Value*. Edited by G. H. von Wright. Translated by Peter Winch. Chicago: The University of Chicago Press, 1984.

———. *On Certainty*. Edited by G. E. M. Anscombe and G. H. von Wright. Translated by Denis Paul and G. E. M. Anscombe. New York: Harper and Row, 1972.

———. *Philosophical Investigations*. 3rd Ed. Translated by G. E. M. Anscombe. Upper Saddle River, NJ: Prentice-Hall, 1958.

———. *Remarks on the Foundations of Mathematics*. Edited by G. H von Wright, Rush Rhees, and G. E. M. Anscombe. Translated by G. E. M. Anscombe. Oxford: Basil Blackwell, 1956.

———. *Zettel*. Edited by G. E. M. Anscombe and G. H. von Wright. Translated by G. E. M. Anscombe. Berkeley: University of California Press, 1970.

White, John. "Wellbeing and Education: Issues of Culture and Authority." *Journal of Philosophy of Education* 41 (2007): 17–28.

Wolin, Sheldon. *Democracy Incorporated: Managed Democracy and the Specter of Inverted Totalitarianism*. Princeton: Princeton University Press, 2008.

Wright, Crispin. "The Moral Organism." In *The Philosophy of F. H Bradley*, edited by Anthony Manser and Guy Stock. Oxford: Oxford University Press, 1984.

Young, Iris Marion. "Difference as a Resource for Democratic Communication." In *Deliberative Democracy: Essays on Reason and Politics*, edited by James Bohman and William Rehg. Cambridge: MIT Press, 1997.

INDEX

Adorno, Theodor, 166n70
agency
in civil association, 74–75
conditionality of, 22–37, 44, 56, 59, 63–64, 93–94
conservative view of, 23–26
critical, 27–37
in enterprise association, 71–72
and freedom, 62–64
individual, 27–37
individualistic theories of, 18, 35
and language use, 27–32
and self-enactment, 30, 52–53, 64–66
social theories of, 18, 34–35
and teleology, 163n26
and tradition, 44–45, 47–50, 52–57
and understanding, 42–44, 58–59
Andreson, Benedict, 162n10
Arendt, Hannah, 96–98, 101–108

Bakhtin, Mikhail, 178n64
Barber, Benjamin, 126
Benhabib, Seyla, 116, 121
Berlin, Isaiah, 90–93, 95–96, 166n69
Bloor, David, 16, 24–26
Bosanquet, Bernard, 62
Botwinick, Aryeh, 165n45
Boucher, David, 148n22, 170n123
Bradley, Francis Herbert, 50–51, 92
Burke, Edmund, 50–51

Cavell, Stanley, 136–39, 151n18, 154n56
Chambers, Simone, 129
civility, 75–76
Coats, Wendell John, 9–10, 170n123
Cohen, Joshua, 116
Connolly, William, 28, 179n72
conservatism
attributed to Oakeshott and Wittgenstein, 22–26, 31–33
and rejection of critical agency, 24–26, 34–35
conversation
conditionality of, 119–20
and elitism, 133–34
as image of human conduct, 2–5, 118, 130–31, 143–45
as interpretive frame, 5–10, 12
as political ethos, 140–42
and power, 134–36
and responsibility, 136–40
contingency
and agency, 58–62
and freedom, 62
and understanding, 58–62
Crary, Alice, 152n31

democracy
aggregative, 114–15
agonistic, 120–24
as argument, 126–30
and civil association, 123–24
and consensus, 115–16, 121
as conversation, 119, 122–24, 128–32
deliberative, 114–17, 120–23, 126–27, 129–30, 133–40
and elitism, 133–34
epistemic, 116–17, 126–28
and legitimacy, 116–17

democracy *(continued)*
  malleability of the concept, 111–12
  and power, 134–36
  and rationalism, 125–26, 128
  and responsibility, 136–40
  and rhetoric, 127, 128–30
Dreyfus, Hubert J., 161n68, 166n59
Dryzek, John, 121, 127

Estlund, David, 116, 126

Fish, Stanley, 177n42
Flathman, Richard, 32, 90, 168n85m 169n110
Franco, Paul, 51–52, 90, 93, 95, 162n11, 165n45, 174n5
Frankfurt, Harry G., 163n18
freedom, 62–66, 101–103
French Revolution, 107–108
Foucault, Michel, 78–90, 134
Fuss, Peter, 171n129

Gamble, Andrew, 51–52
Gerencser, Steven Anthony, 113
Gray, John, 162n11, 164n33
Gutmann, Amy, 116, 121, 123

Hacking, Ian, 165n50
Hampshire, Stuart, 122
von Hayek, Friedrich A., 178n54
Hegel, Georg Wilhelm Friedrich, 50–51, 62
Herder, Johann Gottfried, 92
Heyes, Cressida, 153n38
Hobbes, Thomas, 67–68, 75
Horkheimer, Max, 166n70
individual
  as historical self, 15–16, 52–53
  manqué, 65
  as Oakeshott's methodological basis, 39–41
  as prior to society, 93–94
  as product of power relations, 87, 89
  Protean, 63–65, 75, 89
  as reflective consciousness, 42–44
  relation to community, 24–32, 35–36
  Wittgenstein on, 28–32
individuality
  and freedom, 65
  as infinitude, 65–66
  inherent in action, 40
  manifest in language use, 29–32
  and modern politics, 108
  and tradition, 44–45
Isaacs, Stuart, 148n22, 165n45

Janik, Allan, 153n46
Jones, K., 152n35

Kateb, George, 65, 101–102, 153n36, 173n151
Kant, Immanuel, 37

language
  as capital of practices, 28, 53–54
  attunement in use of, 35–36
  and community, 24–26, 29–32
  as intersubjective practice, 19–22
  conventionality of, 27–34
  individual acquisition and use of, 26–32
  Saussure's theory of. *See* de Saussure, Ferdinand
  Wittgenstein's theory of, 18–22
Laugier, Sandra, 157n20
Lyotard, Jean-François, 131

Machiavelli, Niccolò, 92, 166n67
MacIntyre, Alasdair, 47–50, 57
Mapel, David, 75, 165n45
Marmor, Andrei, 160n45
McGinn, Colin, 32
Minch, Michael, 113, 117–19
Minogue, Kenneth, 173n150
Misak, Cheryl, 116, 127
de Montaigne, Michel, 67
Mouffe, Chantal, 113, 118–24, 141
Mulhall, Stephen, 136–40

Nietzsche, Friedrich, 55

Norris, Andrew, 150n7
Nozick, Robert, 164n37
Nyíri, J.C., 16, 24–26, 51

O'Neill, John, 166n59
Orwell, George, 111

Parekh, Bhikhu, 6
Pascal, Blaise, 44
Pettit, Philip, 175n15
philosophy
  in conversation of humanity, 5, 36
  as critical practice, 36–37
Pitkin, Hanna Fenichel, 52, 162n11, 173n151, 174n5
pluralism. *See* plurality
plurality
  and enterprise association, 71–73
  and civil association, 74–76, 117–18
  as condition of democracy, 119–20, 123–24, 131–32
  and society, 93–96, 140
  of values, 91–92, 95–96
Pocock, John Greville Agard, 51
Podoksik, Efraim, 62, 95
politics
  as care for *respublica*, 98–100, 102, 104–105, 124, 131
  as care for the world, 101–102, 104–105
  as conversation, 119, 145
  displacement of, 105–108
practices
  attunement with respect to, 27–30, 35–36, 151n18
  conditionality of, 32–36
  and critical agency, 27–37
  as idioms of association, 73–74
  linguistic, 19–37
  and understanding, 59
Putnam, Hilary, 30, 57

Rabinow, Paul, 166n59
rationalism, 4, 52, 85, 125–26
Rawls, John, 56, 138
Rousseau, Jean-Jacques, 62, 164n41, 166n67
Rorty, Richard, 35, 60
Rostbøll, Christian, 116

Sandel, Michael, 160n53, 168n89
de Saussure, Ferdinand, 29, 153n48, 154n58
Schmitt, Carl, 123
Searle, John, 160n45
Segal, Jacob, 165n45
Sellars, Wilfrid, 58
Shils, Edward, 45, 54
Skinner, Quentin, 165n48
society
  individualistic conception of, 90–91, 93–96
  organic conception of, 92
Soininen, Suvi, 165n45
state
  and biopower, 85–86
  as civil association, 73–77, 96, 105, 109–10, 117–18, 123–24
  as enterprise association, 71–73, 76–77, 81–86, 106–108
  and governmentality, 85–86
  historical development of, 78–86
  Foucault's critique of liberal, 87
  and imagination, 68–69, 70
  juridical image of, 87–88
  Leviathan, 67–68
  medieval, 79–81
  and power, 88–89
  and rationalism, 85–86
  tension between conceptions of, 77

Talisse, Robert, 116, 127
Taylor, Charles, 47–50, 57
Thompson, Dennis, 116, 121, 123
tradition
  elements of, 44–45
  as inherited practices, 55–56
  interpretation of, 55–56
  intimations of, 53–54
  as language of self-enactment, 52–57

tradition (*continued*)
  moral horizon, 49–51
  as the present past, 45–46
  against rationalism, 52
  sacred, 54
  as vocation, 46–53
Tsao, Roy T., 172n142

Vico, Giambattista, 92
Villa, Dana, 159n34

Weber, Max, 166n59
Williams, Bernard, 27, 35, 154n50
Winch, Peter, 152n23
Wittgenstein, Ludwig, 16–37, 134